DESI KITCHEN

FROM JALANDHAR TO THE BLACK COUNTRY:
A CULINARY ROADMAP TO THE
SOUTH ASIAN DIASPORA IN MODERN BRITAIN

SARAH WOODS

PHOTOGRAPHY BY
LIZ & MAX HAARALA HAMILTON

MICHAEL JOSEPH
PENGUIN
Est. 1935

FOR PAPA-JI, BIBI-JI, MUM AND
DAD — THE ORIGINAL DESIS

My dad as a child with my granny, grandad and my aunty

CONTENTS

'**Desi**', a definition:

noun
a person of birth or descent from the Indian subcontinent, who lives abroad

adjective
local; indigenous

'Being the child of an immigrant has its own issues because your identity is so torn. You are part British, part not, not really accepted by Britain but not fitting in to the "Asian community". I wanted to pursue artistic things, but my parents wanted me to be a lawyer or a doctor or something. But having worked hard (for so long) . . . a few years ago my parents started to see the value in what I was doing. I've come to a point where this is me, I'm not going to be something for anyone, just be me.'

– Afreena Islam, performing artist

FOREWORD BY ATUL KOCHHAR

Sarah's passion for making authentic Indian home cooking accessible to all is commendable, and I am thrilled to hear of her achievements, including the publication of this mesmerizing cookbook filled with gorgeous recipes from desi kitchens all over modern Britain. Following on from her television debut on BBC One's *Britain's Best Home Cook*, which led to her leaving her day job to launch a successful desi food collection business during lockdown – not forgetting the fantastic supper clubs and pop-up restaurants in Cheshire – Sarah's story is truly inspirational.

Few cookbooks cover the diaspora of the Indian subcontinent in such depth and with such authority. Each of the book's stories and recipes are an absolute joy to read and cook through, and draw on tradition but also explore the desi cuisines that make up modern Britain with exacting attention to detail. All in all it's a great motivating step for the reader to take on board, growing the heritage with cooking and culture while spreading awareness of these diverse communities through their food traditions. With the publication of *Desi Kitchen,* I wish Sarah and her lovely family all the best of everything. May the cross-culture cooking continue to grow in the UK!

INTRODUCTION

Migration, the movement of people and food cultures, has created some of the best and most recognizable dishes in the world. What could be more British than the iconic fish and chips? Yet this originated from the Jewish immigrant community in London in the 1800s.

This book is a culinary roadmap of the South Asian diaspora in Britain today, for the lovers of masala baked beans, tandoori roast dinners, bacon naan rolls and the like. I've taken a look at the various communities from the Indian subcontinent, the dishes they brought with them to the UK and how these tastes have evolved, as well as how they have adapted to the regions in which they have settled. Each community is unique. Regional cooking varies hugely in technique, ingredients and produce – each has a different provenance and I'm excited to accentuate that.

In these pages I'll explore what it means to be second generation in Britain today, as far as our food culture is concerned. For me, Britain is my motherland, the country of my birth, and as such the food narrative starts with modern Britain as the source of origin. Our culture is unique, a hybrid of East meets West. Being second generation is a dichotomy of identity and food, it represents that delicious collision, the alchemy of bringing very different food cultures together. I'm setting out to tell that story and I've woven an immigrant vignette into each chapter to bring the communities to life; authentic voices from first-, second- and third-generation diaspora. We are united by a language of food, it breaks down the barriers: we are here, and this is what we contribute.

ABOUT ME

Becoming a finalist on the BBC One TV show *Britain's Best Home Cook* was a wonderful experience and set me on a path to follow my passion – food and feeding. The corporate world lost its lustre, as it was never my true calling. Retraining as a chef at Ashburton Chefs' Academy gave me the confidence to take the plunge and start a food business. The plan had always been to start off with supper clubs and then work towards having my own restaurant. Covid was a curveball to the best-laid plans – not to be deterred, my workaround was to launch a food collection business instead. I can't think of a better way to serve my community than through the sharing and breaking of bread, or roti as the case may be. Having now moved on to hosting restaurant pop-ups and takeovers, I hope that one day the restaurant dream will come true and I will have my very own.

Allow me to provide a little backstory. I was born into a food-obsessed family, and was always extremely greedy, so the passion to learn was very natural. I was taught at the elbow of two exceptional cooks: my mother and my paternal grandmother. My siblings and I were brought up by our grandparents, who came to Britain – the Black Country in the West Midlands – in the early 60s from Jalandhar in the Punjab, in India, when my dad was 12 years old. My grandad worked in the iron foundries, like many immigrants who were invited here to help support the industrial progression – be that in the cotton mills, steelworks, glass factories, the textile industry or wherever there were labour shortages. My dad was educated and grew up in Britain in the swinging 60s – he fancied himself as quite

the dandy, complete with handlebar moustache. He loved wrestling, *Monty Python* and The Kinks. He married my mum aged 21; he hadn't met her before – arranged marriages were common back then. The marriage, into a 'good family', had been brokered by a family friend. My mum, also from near Jalandhar, came to the UK in 1972, a beautiful, naïve young woman leaving her family for the first time and coming to a country she'd never been to before, to marry a man she hadn't met, and she didn't even speak the language fluently. My goodness, how petrifying that must have been, and how grateful I am that she was so brave. They had five children together: I am number four.

Growing up, since both our parents worked, we were raised by our grandparents. The way they did things had a huge influence on me: they grew their own fruit and vegetables, and what they didn't grow they'd get from friends; I distinctly remember as a little girl taking

delivery of a massive bunch of rhubarb from one such acquaintance. Waste was minimal, sacrilege in fact, and we always ate seasonal produce. I remember yoghurt being cultured near the fireplace, and they always cooked from scratch: we had traditions like chips and gravy every Friday, and 'desi' fruit crumbles and bread and butter pudding with lashings of Bird's custard were often on for pudding. Grandad even built a tandoor in the garden. We always had a house full of visitors and friends, a real sense of community and belonging defined by the sharing of food, and everybody was welcomed. We couldn't actually get rid of the visitors – it was a bit like living in Piccadilly Circus! Grandma actively encouraged it, so she could keep on top of the latest gossip, and she would hold court. The parties were legendary: lots of feasting food, the whisky and rum flowing – Punjabi men love whisky and a good argument – and the bhangra blaring. Of course the neighbours were invited too, so there were never any complaints. Movie nights would be Bollywood films – VHS videos rented from the local sari shop; my siblings never watched them but I always did, as I had a crush on the actor Amitabh Bachchan. My granny was partial to watching the *Carry On* films as well, and she'd often howl with laughter at the antics; she had a filthy sense of humour. Looking back, it was chaotic bliss.

My English friends always showed a fascination for our food, but it worked both ways. As much as I was puzzled by being questioned about making chapattis by the mums of my school friends, I was equally dazzled by pies and pasties, Yorkshire puddings, cakes and roast dinners; how intoxicating! I can count on one hand the Indian sweets that I actually like – I will happily pass on barfi, ladoos and gajrela, but give me crumble, shortbread, trifle, sponge cake, biscuits, tarts and custard! I've come across many a cookbook with its recipes rooted in a country on the other side of the world. I feel we need to focus on the here and now, the very exciting evolution of the British food scene based on the rich diversity that immigration has brought. As well as sharing recipes derived from my own Punjabi heritage, I look forward to lifting the veil on other communities, from the island of Sri Lanka all the way up to Kashmir, in the foothills of the Himalayas. Indian food is not one homogenous food type, but hyper-regional and nuanced. The second-generation desi layer removes the geographical borders, and this same cross-over forms part of our identity. The world has always had fusion inspired by travel, exploration and more recently an accelerated movement of people. Classical and traditional recipes will always have a place, but sometimes you have a craving or a 'chaska' that only desi flavours can satiate.

STORE CUPBOARD NOTES

All the spices and other ingredients that I use in my recipes are easily available either from your local Indian grocer or online, and I've suggested alternatives for any that I know are trickier to find; however, accessibility has never been better. This book includes a range of different recipes, some fast, others gloriously slow. My journey around the UK, into the households of different communities, was immersive. My mission is to share a level of authenticity, and that means learning about different processes and techniques; some of these are short, others are long. Food is so closely linked with culture, and I've been mindful to respect the context, as much as I can. As a Punjabi writing about food from different diaspora communities, I feel a sense of responsibility. Quite rightly, cultural appropriation is an important topic of debate, and I think it's essential not to strip recipes down to the point at which they are reductive and no longer representative of the dish or the culture you claim it to be from. I hope I've struck this tricky balance, because of course immigrant recipes can be 'inauthentic' by their very nature and I've flagged the cases where this applies. Some of the ingredient lists look long, but this is nothing to be daunted by; embrace the learning and I will be your step-by-step guide.

COOKING OIL

For the purposes of the book the cooking oil has been specified in tablespoons. This is to give you a guide, though I never actually measure it out. In most cases you want a thin layer of oil covering the base of your pan, so it can come down to the size of the pan you are using, the volume of onions, and of course the way oil spreads as it is heated. Use your judgement here.

CHICKEN AND EGGS

The eggs are always medium unless otherwise specified.

How to remove the skin from a whole chicken

A few recipes call for the use of a de-skinned chicken. I find the best way to do this is first to make a cut in the loose skin at the joint where the thigh and drumstick meet the breast. You will need a small sharp knife, and be careful not to cut the flesh. Use some kitchen paper for grip, take some of the loose skin where you have made the cut, and pull the skin away from the flesh. You may need the knife to help cut away points where the skin is more firmly attached, but it will pull off easily. You can either remove the wings or, again, make a cut in the loose skin around the joint, as before. Alternatively, you can ask your butcher to do this for you.

GINGER, GARLIC AND CHILLI PREP

There are a number of ways to prep ginger, garlic and chillies. The first is to batch-peel a load of each, then mince them separately in a mini-chopper with a scant amount of water, and freeze. Just destalk the chillies before mincing them. You can freeze the minced ginger, garlic and chillies flat in separate freezer bags, to make a 'bark', which is a space-saver, and snap off whatever you need to weigh out and defrost in the pan at the time of cooking. Some folks like to freeze their ginger and garlic in ice cube trays – do whatever works for you. If you do use an ice cube tray I would suggest that each cube should equate to 1½ teaspoons of minced ginger/garlic, which is roughly 3 garlic cloves or 15g of ginger. It keeps in the freezer pretty much indefinitely.

When it comes to green finger chillies, these can vary in level of heat; sometimes you can get a really tame batch, other times they're ferocious. You can generally tell by the smell. For consistency of heat I mince a combination of green finger chillies and Thai bird's-eye chillies. I like a bit of bang for my buck!

The second method is to blitz your ginger and garlic together in a processor (an equal volume of each) and make a paste. Store it in a Kilner jar or such like in the fridge. You just need a thin layer of oil on the top to help preserve it. It will keep for about a week. Same applies to chillies, which you mince separately. Note, minced fresh garlic can turn a shade of blue or green after a few days, but it's perfectly safe to eat – it's due to an enzyme reaction.

The third method is to weigh out the peeled ginger or garlic, and grate at point of need using a microplane grater.

I NEVER use shop-bought pastes and jars.

SALT

I use mostly fine sea salt in my recipes, but you can use flakes or whatever you wish. The important thing is to keep tasting your food at all stages of the cooking process and season to your liking.

BLACK COUNTRY & BIRMINGHAM

PUNJABI COMMUNITY

— · — · — · — · — · — · —

This region has the second largest Punjabi community in the UK, after Southall, West London. In the 1940s and 50s, citizens from the Commonwealth were invited to the UK in order to meet labour shortages, and many of those arriving in the Black Country from the Punjab found work in the iron foundries. The majority faith in India's Punjab is Sikhism, and other minority faith communities include Hindus, Muslims, Jains and Christians.

Soho Road, in Handsworth, Birmingham, is a cacophony of noise and vibrant colour, with the heady smells of delicious street food and the sometimes raucous hum of activity. Never more so than during Vaisakhi celebrations – the most revered festival in Sikhism. The main Vaisakhi parade and mela takes place in Handsworth Park. There is a smaller mela in nearby Smethwick, and a procession that leads to Handsworth. Brummies love any excuse for a party and it attracts people from all walks of life, bringing everybody together through the sharing of great food.

Punjabi cooking is renowned for its big and gutsy flavours, laden with butter and dairy. The Punjab is known as the breadbasket of India, as the region provides 20 per cent of India's wheat, despite only covering 1.5 per cent of its land area. It is also known as the birthplace of tandoori-style cooking. Tandoors were communal clay ovens used in villages. The food is generous to its core, and has adapted very well to the British palate. Birmingham is also synonymous with the Balti, of course.

No, these aren't the little molluscs. If you go into any chip shop north of London and ask for a scallop, what you will get is a sliced potato deep-fried in a golden, crisp batter. These have been given a Punjabi makeover, are very moreish, and are wonderful with an ice-cold beer or IPA.

CHIPPY SCALLOPS WITH A TWIST } WITH SALT, VINEGAR AND TOMATO KETCHUP

SERVES 4–6 (DEPENDING ON HOW GREEDY)

4 medium potatoes
vegetable oil, for deep-frying
3 heaped tablespoons unset yoghurt
1 heaped tablespoon cumin seeds

1 teaspoon garam masala
2 teaspoons sea salt flakes
2 teaspoons minced green finger chillies, or to taste

a pinch of Kasuri methi (dried fenugreek)
1 tablespoon chopped fresh coriander
1 egg
75g chickpea/gram flour (besan)

1. Peel the potatoes, then cut them into slices no thicker than a pound coin – either across or lengthways, whichever size you prefer. Place them in a bowl of cold water.
2. Heat some oil for deep-frying to about 170-175°C.
3. Put the yoghurt into a large mixing bowl and add the cumin seeds, garam masala, salt, chillies, methi and chopped coriander. Taste the mixture and adjust to taste. Now mix in the beaten egg and the chickpea flour to make a thick batter. If the batter gets too thick you can add a little cold water.
4. Drain the potatoes and pat dry on kitchen paper.
5. Coat the dried potato slices with the batter and deep-fry until cooked and golden.
6. Enjoy with salt, vinegar and tomato ketchup. Warning, these are addictive!

COOK'S NOTE You can replace the potatoes with cauliflower florets, and make cauliflower pakora nuggets, as it were. This is essentially a 'mother' batter, so you can interchange with any vegetable or even with leftover meat (this is a great way to use up turkey leftovers at Christmas). If you'd like an extra hit of flavour you can also lightly sprinkle them with chaat masala as soon as they come out of the fryer.

I had many Jamaican friends when I was growing up, and I LOVE a spicy patty! There is a large Afro-Caribbean community in the West Midlands, so I had to include a recipe that reflects that. Funnily enough, historically the patty is already a fusion of Cornish, African and Indian influences – I've just gone heavier with the Indian bit. Now I've called this a curry meat patty because it will work well with lamb, goat or mutton – so take your pick. The Scotch bonnet is fiery but the rich meat can stand its ground; these are utterly delicious!

CURRY MEAT PATTIES

MAKES 4 PATTIES

Filling

500g lamb, mutton or goat shoulder, cut into 2.5cm chunks

vegetable oil, for cooking

1 large brown onion, finely diced

3 spring onions, finely sliced

15g ginger, grated

15g garlic, grated

1 Scotch bonnet chilli, finely chopped or minced

2 teaspoons curry powder (your choice of mild or hot)

1 teaspoon allspice (pimento)

1 teaspoon mild Kashmiri chilli powder

200–250ml chicken or beef stock (I used ½ a jelly lozenge in 200ml water)

salt and pepper, to taste

chopped fresh coriander (optional)

Shortcrust pastry

250g plain flour

75g cold butter, cubed or grated

50g cold shortening/ lard, cubed or grated (note: you can use 125g butter if you prefer)

1 teaspoon ground turmeric

1 teaspoon garam masala

1 teaspoon sea salt

a pinch of caster sugar

approx. 100ml cold water (could be more or less depending on the flour absorption levels)

Egg wash

1 egg yolk (the egg whites are freezable, save for meringue)

1–2 tablespoons water

Garnish

nigella seeds

1. Begin by making the filling. Normally in a Jamaican curry the meat would be marinated in oil and spices overnight. We're not doing that, though. Start by browning the meat in batches in a medium to large saucepan (22–25cm) in a scant amount of oil. Remove and set aside.

2. In the same saucepan sauté both types of onion in 3 or 4 tablespoons of oil until softened – about 8–10 minutes on a medium heat – then add the ginger, garlic and chilli and cook out for a couple of minutes.

3. Add the powdered spices – curry powder, allspice and Kashmiri chilli powder – and give these a good mix through, then allow to toast for 30 seconds. If the pan is dry, add a splash of water to prevent the spices from burning.

→

4. Return the meat to the saucepan and gently stir everything together. Add the stock, bring to the boil, then reduce to a simmer. Cook, covered, for 1½ hours, until the meat is soft and tender. After 30 minutes, season with salt and pepper to taste. I don't add salt prior to this point as the stock will already be salty, so you need to gauge it.

5. Remove the rendered fat. You want to be left with soft and tender meat morsels in a dry and unctuous gravy. Add the optional coriander if you'd like, and allow to cool completely. Note: You could get organized and make the filling the night before.

6. Now make the pastry. Place all the pastry ingredients (except the water) in a food processor and pulse until you have a sand-like consistency. The fats should be kept as cold as possible – either coarsely grate or cut into small cubes. Add the cold water a little at a time, using the pulse setting again; the dough will begin to ball together and you may not need all the water (you want a play dough texture). Remove the dough from the food processor and shape into a thick disc, handling it as little as possible. Wrap in cling film or an alternative and rest in the fridge for 30 minutes.

7. Set your oven to 190°C. Roll out your pastry to the thickness of a pound coin on a lightly floured work surface. You want 17cm circles – I use a side plate to cut around. Place a pastry circle directly on an individual square of baking parchment. Place 2–3 tablespoons of filling in the centre of each pastry disc (don't be tempted to overfill them). Brush a little water around the edges, to act as a glue, then fold the pastry over the filling, so the top end meets the bottom and you create a half-moon/semicircle. Crimp the edges with a fork. Repeat, and re-roll the pastry as necessary – you may be able to eke out a fifth patty. (You can freeze them at this point if batch making.)

8. Brush the patties with egg wash and sprinkle with nigella seeds. Bake for about 20 minutes, or until cooked and golden. Devour!

The humble chapatti or roti is the staple of any Punjabi meal; most Punjabis are devout bread lovers. It's important to master this simple dough, as it's also the basis of parathas and puris, which we'll come to later. You can also make the plain-Jane chapatti a little funky by adding purées, such as beetroot, spinach and avocado, or kale. See paratha recipe overleaf.

CHAPATTI/ROTI

MAKES 8–10 CHAPATTIS

500g chapatti flour or atta (use a medium blend)

approx. 300–400ml cold water (this will vary according to the different absorption levels of your flour)

butter, for slathering once cooked

1. Place the flour in a large mixing bowl. Spread out your fingers, to use as mixers, and gradually add the water until the dough starts to ball. Knead for about 5–6 minutes, until the dough is smooth, elastic and fairly firm. Cover with a damp tea cloth and rest for about 30 minutes, or place in an airtight container and rest in the fridge until you want to use it.
2. When you are ready to make your chapattis, heat your tawa or non-stick frying pan (I use a 30cm frying pan) on a medium to high heat. It needs to be hot.
3. Dust your work surface with a little flour. Take a golfball-sized amount of dough, roll it between the palms of your hands until smooth, then flatten the dough ball into a disc.
4. Roll the disc into a thin circle with a rolling pin. I measured mine, and it was 22cm in diameter and 2mm thick. (It will vary according to the size of your dough ball but this is to give you a yardstick of what to aim for.) I like big chapattis, so I can tell people I only have one or two!
5. Lift the rolled chapatti and pat it from hand to hand to shake off any excess dry flour. This is an important step, as any excess dry flour will burn and spoil your chapatti.
6. Place the chapatti directly on to the dry frying pan or tawa. Using tongs, flip after 30 seconds. You will start to see little bubbles form. Take a clean dry tea towel and roll it into a ball, then gently pat the chapatti all over with it, this will encourage greater bubbles to form. After about 1½–2 minutes you'll be ready to flip the chapatti over (and it should be cooked through on one side). This is when the magic happens and your chapatti should puff up like a party balloon. It is said that how much your chapatti puffs up correlates to how hungry your diners are.
7. Remove the chapatti from the heat, and slather with butter. Repeat.

COOK'S NOTE You can finish the chapatti over an open flame once you've cooked one side (after the second flip), if you want to feel like a hero. Also the dough will keep in the fridge for 3–4 days in an airtight container.

A paratha is enriched with butter, and has layers. This is a really easy paratha introduction.

PLAIN PARATHA

· — · — · — · — · — · — · — · — · — · — · — · — · — · — · —

MAKES 8–10 PARATHAS

500g chapatti flour or atta (use a medium blend)

approx. 300–400ml cold water (this will vary according to the different absorption levels of your flour)

melted ghee/ vegetable oil

1. Follow the chapatti/roti recipe (see page 19) to step 4 of the method.
2. Once you have rolled out your chapatti to a thin, roughly 20cm circle, cover the whole surface with a thin layer of melted ghee or oil. Now fold in the edges to create a square shape. Start with the sides first, bringing the edges to the centre point and slightly overlapping, then fold the top and bottom edges to create the square.
3. Flatten the square out then gently roll into a thin square, 2–3mm thick, with your rolling pin, being careful that the ghee/oil does not ooze out, turning at 90° angles.
4. Place the paratha directly on the hot tawa/frying pan. Flip after a minute, using tongs. Then brush the up-facing side with melted ghee/ oil. Flip again, then brush the other side with ghee/oil too and flip again. Both sides should be cooked, crisp and golden brown.
5. Eat with glee! You can have the paratha with anything, from something as simple as pickles (achaar) and yoghurt, to any vegetarian dhals and sabjis or meat curries. You can also use these parathas in a roll – which we'll come to in later chapters.

COOK'S NOTE To make a flavoured chapatti dough, blitz your chosen vegetable (cooked as appropriate) into a purée flavoured with chillies, coriander leaves, lemon juice, cumin and salt, then mix it with the flour and 1–2 tablespoons of vegetable oil, then add water to combine into a dough.

This paratha is dope, there is no other phrase that more accurately describes it! It's a taste explosion. The layers are considerable, which is great, as it means there is more for sauce and gravy to cling to. What elevates this to the next level is the fresh mint worked into the dough and the dry masala rub. This would be a great pairing to everything from a plain and simple dhal to a decadent lamb curry – of course, lamb and mint are the perfect match.

LACHHA PARATHA

MAKES 8–10 PARATHAS

250g chapatti flour or atta
250g plain flour

8–10g fresh mint leaves, chopped
approx. 300–400ml cold water (this will vary according to different absorption levels of your flour)

Masala rub
4 teaspoons chaat masala
1 teaspoon ground cumin
½ teaspoon chilli flakes
½ teaspoon dried mint
½ teaspoon sea salt, or to taste
melted ghee or vegetable oil, for brushing

1. Put both flours into a large bowl, along with the chopped mint, and mix together. Using your fingers to mix, gradually add the water until the dough comes together. Knead for 5–6 minutes, until the dough is smooth, elastic and fairly firm. Cover with a damp cloth and rest for 30 minutes.
2. Mix together all the ingredients for the masala rub and set aside.
3. When you are ready to make your parathas, heat your tawa or large, non-stick frying pan on a medium to high heat. It needs to be hot.
4. Dust your work surface with a little dry flour. Take a golfball-size amount of dough, roll it between the palms of your hands until smooth, then flatten the dough ball into a disc.
5. Roll the disc into a thin circle with a rolling pin. Brush the up-facing side with ghee/oil all over, then sprinkle evenly with the dry masala rub.
6. Now, from the edge, start folding and creating 2–3cm creases, like a zigzag or concertina collapsing on itself, creating a single pleated strip. Ensure the oiled side is facing up.
7. Take one end of this pleated strip and roll it over to create a disc (imagine a cinnamon swirl shape) and tuck the end in. Lay the disc flat and roll into a thin circle.
8. Place the paratha on the hot tawa/frying pan. Flip after a minute, then brush with melted ghee/oil. Flip again, then brush the other side with ghee/oil and flip again. Both sides should be cooked, crisp and golden brown.
9. Scrunch up the paratha with your hands, by gently pushing in from the edges, to reveal the layers. Serve with your choice of dish and relish every mouthful.

When I was growing up, making this was a true labour of love, and a process spread across a couple of days (fear not, technology has moved us on to expedite this). It conjures certain memories for me: my grandparents would pick the mature spinach/saag grown in the garden, then the kitchen sink would be full of saag to be thoroughly cleaned as part of the preparation – you couldn't move for spinach! My sister and I would have a hand in chopping it occasionally, but my grandmother would take the lead, using a fearsome-looking device called a daat – imagine a foot scythe, a wooden block with a menacingly sharp curved blade at the front. She wouldn't use a blender as she felt it impaired the taste, so once all the greens were cooked they had to be pounded with a huge wooden pestle. It was a rigorous workout! The funniest thing about saag, or sarson ka saag, is that spinach is NOT the only ingredient; it's a whole medley of green vegetables and this version includes some great British veggies. Serve with parathas; trust me, it's worth all the prep.

GREEN GODDESS SAAG

MAKES ENOUGH FOR 8*

*The tarka is for half the amount of this saag and will serve 4. You can freeze the other half without the tarka. Simply defrost before use then make another tarka.

250g spinach
1 leek
½ a head of broccoli
500g Brussels sprouts
½ a savoy cabbage
100g kale, destalked
100g spring greens
50g fresh fenugreek leaves/methi (or 1 tablespoon dried fenugreek if you don't have this)

20g fresh coriander leaves, plus 1–2 tablespoons extra to garnish
approx. 1.5 litres water
30g ginger, grated
30g garlic, grated
2 teaspoons minced chillies
1 tablespoon sea salt
1–2 heaped tablespoons fine cornmeal

Tarka
30g butter, plus an extra knob
a little vegetable oil
1½ teaspoons cumin seeds
1 brown onion, finely sliced into half-moons
5–10g of garlic, grated
minced chillies, to taste
sea salt, to taste

1. Finely chop and slice your green veg. Make use of your food processor. You will need a large receptacle to put everything into.
2. Bring 1.5 litres of water to the boil in a large lidded saucepan – at least 28cm diameter and it should be deep too.
3. Chuck in the ginger, garlic, chillies and salt, then all the chopped greens, in stages. You may need to smush all this down into the boiling water, as there will be quite a volume. Don't be tempted to add more water at this point, as the salt will draw liquid out of the veg. Once all the greens are submerged, and at boiling point, reduce the heat to medium and simmer for 1½–2 hours; or until the largest pieces melt between finger and thumb.

4. You will need to tend it for a while. Don't allow the pan to run dry and catch – you can add more water. Likewise, if you've added too much water, you can remove some but don't discard it; you can replenish as it reduces during the cooking process.

5. Mix in the fine cornmeal. Take off the heat, and blend with a stick blender until smooth or to a consistency you are happy with. Test your seasoning – you'll then know what to compensate for in the tarka.

6. You can add a touch more water as necessary – you may not need to – then put the saucepan back on the hob and cook out for 10–15 minutes. Careful, it will spit, so replace the lid. Stir, then remove from the heat and set aside.

7. The finish is in sight: time for the tarka. This has to be made with butter. Melt the butter in a large frying pan (30cm) or saucepan and add a little splash of oil, which will prevent the butter from burning. Sauté the cumin, onions, garlic and chillies (in that order). Once the onions are softened, check the seasoning and adjust as necessary. The saag can take a fair bit of chilli. Add half the saag from the big saucepan to the tarka and mix through. (You can freeze the other half.) Then let it simmer for a couple of minutes and intertwine. Sprinkle liberally with chopped coriander and mix. See how vibrant the coriander looks. Now taste, and adjust the seasoning as necessary – it may need a touch more salt. Melt an extra knob of butter through the saag and serve with parathas.

> **COOK'S NOTE** You can split the prep for this: make the saag at the weekend and batch freeze. All you then have to do is defrost and make a fresh tarka for a mid-week meat-free indulgence.

I've tried to make this recipe as foolproof as possible, as I really want you to taste how delightful these samosas truly are. They have a special place in my heart – I have such fond memories from childhood, doing my bit in the samosa production line when mum and grandma used to make hundreds at once for various events, and it was all hands on deck to get them ready in time. I used to take these to school for my teachers too – no wonder I was so often teacher's pet!

PUNJABI SAMOSAS

MAKES 14 SAMOSAS

Dough
300g plain flour
½ teaspoon salt
38ml vegetable oil
approx. 100ml cold water
vegetable oil, for deep-frying

Filling
4–5 medium potatoes (approx. 700g peeled weight)
3–4 tablespoons vegetable oil
1½ teaspoons cumin seeds
1 level teaspoon fennel seeds
1 large brown onion, finely diced
1 teaspoon minced green finger chillies (these need to be hot – mix with Thai bird's-eye chillies if you need to pack more heat)
1–2 teaspoons sea salt
1 teaspoon garam masala
a pinch of Kasuri methi (dried fenugreek)
½ teaspoon Kashmiri chilli powder (optional)
30g butter
approx. 75g frozen peas
1 tablespoon chopped fresh coriander

'Glue'
1 teaspoon plain flour
7 teaspoons water

1. Let's make the dough first. Sift the flour and salt into a large mixing bowl, then add the oil. Mixing the oil with the flour is an important step, so take your time (3–5 minutes), rubbing between your fingers to ensure it is well incorporated with the flour.

2. Spread your fingers, to use as a mixer, and this will let you feel the dough too as it comes together. Add cold water gradually – you're not going to need much, only about 100ml. When the dough begins to ball together, start to knead. You will need a little more water – just dipping your hand into the water each time will be enough, don't overdo it. Knead your dough until it's smooth and fairly firm, but DON'T overwork it or your pastry will be tough. Cover with a damp cloth and leave to rest for 30 minutes.

3. On to the filling. Peel your spuds and chop them into equal pieces, then boil until cooked through. Allow to steam-dry.

4. Meanwhile heat the vegetable oil in a large frying pan on a medium to high heat. Toast the cumin and fennel seeds, then add the finely diced onion and chillies, reduce the heat to medium and allow the onion to soften and become translucent – this will take 7–8 minutes.

→

COOK'S NOTE This is a classic filling but you can riff on it. Chicken and potato is yummy (I add nigella seeds into the dough for those), or maybe even try an Indo-Korean mash-up with kimchee (confession – I'm slightly obsessed with kimchee). You can also use any leftover samosa filling to make a burrito – tightly wrap the spicy potatoes in a flour tortilla, brush with a little vegetable oil, top with a sprinkle of nigella seeds and bake. Serve with rajma (kidney bean masala, see page 96), rice, salad and yoghurt.

5. Then add the salt, garam masala, methi and Kashmiri chilli powder, if using, along with the butter. Toast the spices for 30 seconds. Taste for seasoning. I want you to feel HEAT from the chillies, so add more if it's not there. Do adjust as appropriate, then mix in the frozen peas.

6. Your potatoes will be ready by now. Crush them, don't completely mash. It's nice to have little nuggets of potatoes as well as a mashed texture. Mix them thoroughly with the spicy onions, along with the chopped coriander. Check the seasoning again now – remember, potatoes are bland old things, so you need plenty of chillies and more salt. This mixture should be all singing and all dancing. Allow to cool completely.

7. Make your glue paste by mixing the flour and water, and set aside.

8. Take your dough and divide it into seven equal balls – they'll weigh about 65g each.

9. You can either make your samosas in a production-line style – i.e. roll them all out and cut ready to be filled or do them one dough ball at a time. It's up to you. Each dough ball makes two samosas. Either way, roll each dough ball into a thin circle – no more than 20cm. You'll need a scant amount of dry flour on your work surface. Then cut the circle in half, giving you two semicircles. Reposition the top half to ensure both semicircles have the straight cut at the top.

10. Now fill the samosas. Don't over-fill. Each semicircle only needs about a tablespoon of filling, which you should place in the middle. Shape the top of the filling into a point – this will help when sealing. Dip your finger into the glue paste you made earlier – or use a small pastry brush – and apply a thin layer round the edge of the semicircle. Take the top left corner of the semi-circle, and bring to the bottom edge, half sealing the samosa and covering all the filling. Use your thumbs to gently press down the edges and remove any air pockets. Now repeat on the opposite side, creating the familiar triangular shape. Ensure the filling is packed in before doing so. Use your fingers to gently seal, and create a point at the top. Again use your thumbs at the bottom edge to ensure no air pockets have formed (your samosa will burst when deep-frying otherwise).

11. You're ready to deep-fry. You can freeze the samosas at this point if you're batch-making: place a little greaseproof paper between them to ensure they don't stick, then put them into freezer bags, or on a suitable tray, and cover with cling film. Defrost before frying.

12. I like to deep-fry in a wok, or a kadhai. Heat the oil – the temperature shouldn't be too hot, so maybe start at 160°C then increase to 180°C until the samosas are golden and cooked through. You can fry 2 or 3 at a time – don't overcrowd them. When cooked, place on kitchen paper to absorb any excess oil.

13. Serve with your favourite chutneys – or even tomato ketchup – and gobble up. You can present this as a samosa chaat by serving with chana masala, chutneys (tamarind and mint) and yoghurt, crispy sev and pomegranate seeds.

CHUTNEYS

Chutneys and pickles are a key component in Indian food: they can elevate a dish by a number of levels, and for flavour junkies – as most Indians are – they are culinary crack. My great-grandmother used to eat chapattis with pudina ki chutney (mint chutney) alone! Coriander and mint are really easy to grow in your garden, or window-box. Mooli (a large white radish) also grows very well in British gardens and allotments. Tamarind – which does not grow in Britain – is best used in its dried form in any case.

MINT OR CORIANDER CHUTNEY

Pair this with vegetarian dishes. It will keep for up to 5 days refrigerated.

1. Roughly chop the ingredients, blitz in a blender, along with a generous splash of water and it's ready!

40g fresh mint or coriander
1–2 green finger chillies, or to taste
5-6 spring onions (including the green part)
1 small tomato
salt, to taste

COOK'S NOTE To make coriander and lime raita, blitz 40g fresh coriander leaves, 1–2 green chillies, 4 spring onions (including the green part), the juice and zest of a lime, sea salt to taste and 250g Greek yoghurt in a blender.

MOOLI KI CHUTNEY

Pair this with vegetarian dishes. It will keep for up to 5 days refrigerated.

- -

125g mooli
½ a small red onion
1–2 green finger
   chillies, or to taste

1 small to medium
   tomato
salt, to taste

1. Roughly chop all the ingredients and blitz in a blender, along with a generous splash of water.

TAMARIND SAUCE

Pair this with kebabs and samosas. It will keep for 1–2 weeks refrigerated and freezes well.

- -

200g dried tamarind
   pulp
750ml–1 litre water
1 scant teaspoon sea
   salt
1 tablespoon finely
   chopped fresh
   coriander leaves
½ an onion, grated
1 large carrot, grated
minced green chillies,
   to taste

1 teaspoon ground
   dried bird's-eye
   chillies
½ teaspoon garam
   masala
1 tablespoon tomato
   ketchup
8 tablespoons caster
   sugar, or to taste
   (you can use jaggery
   instead)

1. Break the tamarind pulp into pieces and place in a medium saucepan, then cover with the water, starting with 750ml. Sprinkle in a scant teaspoon of sea salt. Bring to the boil, then lower the heat and simmer until the pulp has dissolved. Use a wooden spoon to help break it up. It should take no longer than 15–20 minutes. If you want a thinner chutney, add more water. Allow to cool.
2. Strain the liquid through a sieve using the end of a wooden spoon to press down; you want to ensure you extract all of the flavour from the remaining tamarind pulp before you discard it.
3. Mix in all the other ingredients, and taste. Adjust the seasoning as necessary: the flavour sequence you should get when tasting this is first sweet, then sour, then spicy. You will need to balance this.
4. Place in an airtight container and refrigerate; the flavour will develop. Warning: this is utterly addictive.

Punjabis don't really do dainty. Our food and portions are generous. So it got me thinking, what would a Punjabi canapé look like, if there could be such a thing? It would more than likely be indecently large – good news as far as I'm concerned – and come in puri form (deep-fried chapatti). I'm imagining a drinks reception, convivial chat, with build your own puri pick-and-mix condiments; any excuse to wheel out my hostess trolley and lazy Susan! Pair with gin cocktails.

LOADED PURIS } WITH TANDOORI KING PRAWNS AND CHANA MASALA

MAKES AT LEAST 16–18 PURIS (OR MORE DEPENDING ON THE SIZE!)

chapatti dough (see page 19)
tandoori marinade (see page 36)
vegetable oil, for deep-frying

Chana masala

vegetable oil, for cooking
1½ teaspoons cumin seeds
5cm cassia bark
2 black cardamom pods
1 dried Kashmiri chilli
1 large brown onion, finely diced
15g ginger, grated
15g garlic, grated
2–3 green finger chillies, slit in half lengthways
1 teaspoon ground turmeric
1½ teaspoons garam masala
1 teaspoon sea salt, or to taste
1 teaspoon tomato purée
200ml passata
2 x 400g tins of chickpeas, drained
chopped fresh coriander leaves

Tandoori king prawns

10 raw, peeled, de-veined king prawns (more if you prefer, but do ensure they're sustainably sourced)
vegetable oil, for cooking
1 teaspoon cumin seeds
1 teaspoon fennel seeds
½ a star anise
1 large banana shallot, finely diced
15g ginger, grated
15g garlic, grated
2–3 green finger chillies, slit in half lengthways
½ teaspoon ground turmeric
½ teaspoon garam masala
1 teaspoon sea salt, or to taste
400ml passata
knob of butter
chopped fresh coriander leaves

Accompaniments

mint chutney (see page 27 – add a hint of grated garlic to give it a gentle hum)
tamarind sauce (see page 28) or shop-bought tamarind ketchup
natural yoghurt (unset, so it will drizzle)
fine sev (crunchy deep-fried chickpea noodles – you can find these in any Indian grocer's and some supermarkets)
pomegranate seeds
1 small red onion, finely sliced
lemon/lime wedges
fresh coriander leaves
finely sliced chillies (for the heroes)

1. OK, so you need to be a bit organized with this one and you can prep many of these components ahead: like the chapatti/roti dough, the tandoori marinade and the condiments. The tamarind sauce freezes very well – I batch freeze – and the mint chutney keeps in the fridge for days.
2. Make the chapatti/roti dough and refrigerate.

3. Make up the tandoori marinade and refrigerate.
4. Prep the accompaniments and refrigerate as appropriate.
5. Start by making the chana/chickpea masala. Heat 3 or 4 tablespoons of vegetable oil in a medium saucepan on a medium to high heat and activate the whole spices: the cumin seeds, cassia bark, black cardamom and dried chilli. Once you can smell the aromas wafting up, tip in the onions, reduce the heat to medium, and sauté until the onions have become soft and translucent; this will take 7–8 minutes. Add the garlic, ginger and chillies and cook for a couple of minutes, then add the ground spices: turmeric and garam masala, and the salt. Toast the ground spices for 30 seconds – you may need to add a splash of water to prevent them catching. Add the tomato purée, give it a good mix, cook for 2–3 minutes, then pour in the passata. Bring to the boil, then reduce to a simmer for about 10 minutes. When you can see the oil separate on the surface of the masala, it is ready to taste – you can adjust the seasoning as appropriate.
6. Add the chickpeas to the masala and mix through, adding a splash of water. Bring to boiling point, then reduce to a simmer for a further 10–15 minutes. You want quite a dry consistency to place on top of the puris. Finish with chopped coriander. (Note: if you wanted to make a chana and spinach masala, you could stir through a couple of handfuls of young leaf spinach 3–5 minutes before the end of cooking.)
7. Repeat the above process for the tandoori king prawns. Prior to starting this masala, marinate the prawns in the tandoori marinade. The prawns only need 30 minutes to marinate (even though the marinade is not too acidic, you don't want these delicate prawns to be spoiled). See cook's note for what to do with leftover marinade.
8. Heat a couple of tablespoons of vegetable oil in a medium saucepan on a medium to high heat and activate the whole spices: cumin seeds, fennel seeds and star anise. Tip in the finely diced shallot, then reduce the heat to medium and sauté until softened and translucent. Add the ginger, garlic and chillies and cook for a minute or two, then add the ground spices and salt, followed by the passata. Simmer for about 10 minutes, taste and adjust the seasoning, then melt a knob of butter through this masala ready to receive the cooked prawns (see next step). Garnish the finished dish with the coriander.
9. Of course you can make all the above in advance, then you can reheat or keep warm as appropriate. It's the puris and prawns that should be cooked fresh or last of all. The prawns should be grilled on either side until cooked 'à la minute' – you can use skewers for dramatic effect. I use my oven grill set to a very high heat. It's nice to get a char for that tandoori vibe but without overcooking; you can use a chef's blowtorch to achieve this also.
10. When you're ready to make your puris, have your deep fryer/kadhai oil, whatever you're using, at 180°C.

→

11. Roll your puris out as you would a chapatti, but smaller. I use a chef's ring/cutter for puris, as I like them to be just so (11cm in diameter), but by all means freestyle. Make all the puris before you start cooking them, but just cook one at a time. Once rolled, shake off any excess dry flour and gently place one puri into the hot oil away from your body, so you don't get any splash back. Use a fish slice or slotted spoon to gently press the puri into the oil, which will force it to puff up, then flip it over. The puri should have a nice golden colour on both sides. Gently lift it out on to kitchen paper to absorb any excess oil. Repeat with the rest of the dough. You can wrap your puris in foil and keep them hot in the oven until you're ready to serve.

12. Serve 'family style', allowing your diners or guests to build their own.

> **COOK'S NOTE** There will be too much marinade for the amount of prawns you are using. So I would simultaneously make some tandoori chicken tikka using skinless and boneless chicken thigh pieces or lamb chops – you can steep these overnight in the fridge. Or simply freeze any marinade you don't use.

Vegetable dishes are often referred to as 'sabji' in Punjabi. When we were kids we'd use chapattis as a wrap. Stuff the sabji and a bit of salad in the middle, roll, and apply to face. It can be a bit messy, as it oozes if you squeeze too hard, but it's a great way to engage your kids with Indian food. Just omit the chillies for the less adventurous little ranis and rajas. I've started to cook the gobi (cauliflower) separately of late. It should be al dente for my taste, so it's easier to control this way. I also like to give it a little char.

ALOO AND CHARRED GOBI

SERVES 4–6

1 medium head of cauliflower, plus leaves
4–5 medium potatoes
vegetable oil, for cooking
2–3 teaspoons whole cumin seeds
1 whole star anise

1 large brown onion, finely chopped
2½ teaspoons sea salt, or to taste
20g garlic, grated
20g ginger, grated
1 teaspoon minced chillies, or to taste
1½ teaspoons garam masala

2 level teaspoons ground turmeric
40g butter, or more to taste
100–150ml water
150ml vegetable oil
1 tablespoon chopped fresh coriander leaves

1. Line a baking sheet with greaseproof paper and set aside.
2. Cut the cauliflower head into bite-sized florets and cut the leaves into 5cm pieces. Place in a bowl and set aside. Peel the potatoes and cut them into bite-sized pieces – these should be roughly the same size as the cauliflower. Rinse, place in a bowl of cold water, and set aside. Set your oven to 200°C.
3. First make the tarka. Heat 3 or 4 tablespoons of vegetable oil in a medium-large lidded saucepan over a medium to high heat. Then, let's flavour the oil with the whole spices: activate 1½ teaspoons of cumin seeds and the star anise. As soon as you can smell the aromas rise up, tip in the onions and 1½ teaspoons of salt. Cook out on a moderate heat until the onions become translucent and soft – about 8 minutes.
4. Add the garlic, ginger and minced chillies and cook out for a couple of minutes.
5. Now add the garam masala and 1 level teaspoon of turmeric, and toast for 30 seconds. If the pan is too dry, add a splash of water so the spices don't stick to the pan and burn. Add the butter.
6. Once the butter has melted, taste the mixture and check the seasoning. It should be salty, as you have a lot of bland vegetables to season.

Correct as necessary – you can certainly add more chillies if you like it hot.

7. Drain the potatoes but retain 100–150ml of the water they were sitting in. Toss them into the spicy onion mixture, along with the reserved water – this will help them to steam cook. Bring to the boil, then immediately reduce to a simmer and place a lid on the saucepan to trap the steam. Ensure the pan does not run dry – you may need to add a touch more water. It will take 15–20 minutes for the potatoes to cook through, depending on their size, and most of the liquid will evaporate.

8. Meanwhile, let's take care of the cauliflower. Mix 1 level teaspoon of turmeric into 150ml of vegetable oil. Place the cauliflower florets and leaves in a mixing bowl and cover evenly with the golden oil. Put these on your lined baking sheet, and season evenly with the remaining cumin seeds (add more if needed) and salt. Roast in the oven for 8–10 minutes to par cook (this will vary according to the size of your florets) and finish under a scorching-hot grill set to the highest temperature for a charred effect. Be sure to remove the greaseproof paper before doing so. You can also use a chef's blowtorch to create a char, whichever you prefer. Keep your cauliflower al dente. There is nothing worse than overcooked veggies!

9. Check your potatoes are cooked, then taste one and adjust the seasoning – they might need a smidge more salt. Put your potatoes on your serving dish, adorn with the charred cauliflower over the top and dress with a scattering of chopped coriander.

10. Serve with hot buttered chapattis, or parathas as a weekend treat. It's also lovely with a condiment, like a green chutney or a pickle, as well as the customary side salad kissed with lemon juice and sea salt, and a dollop of Greek yoghurt.

Roast dinners are a thing of glory! At Christmas we'd always have a very traditional roast turkey with all the trimmings – sage and onion stuffing, sprouts, pigs in blankets, the works. But come the next day, Mum would make pakoras from the leftover turkey meat, as we'd be craving a bit of heat and masala by then. This Punjabi spin on a weekly British institution is mind-blowing, and it comes loaded with mirch-masala. Familiar yet so far removed from traditional.

WHOLE ROAST TANDOORI CHICKEN DINNER } WITH SPICED ROASTIES, MAKHANI GRAVY AND CREAMED SAAG

SERVES 4

1 chicken (approx. 1.6kg), skin removed

Tandoori marinade

30g fresh coriander leaves, plus stalks

30g garlic, grated

30g ginger, grated

3–4 bird's-eye chillies

4 tablespoons vegetable oil

5 whole cloves

5 whole peppercorns, crushed

6 green cardamom pods (bruise to release the seeds, discard husks)

2 teaspoons sea salt

500g Greek set yoghurt

1 teaspoon ground turmeric

1¾ teaspoons garam masala

1 tablespoon Kashmiri chilli powder

1 tablespoon Kasuri methi (dried fenugreek)

a squeeze of lemon

Spiced roasties

1.5–2kg Rooster potatoes

4–6 tablespoons vegetable oil

cumin seeds

dried chilli flakes

sea salt

Kasuri methi (dried fenugreek)

minced green finger chillies (optional)

Makhani gravy

3–4 tablespoons vegetable oil

2 teaspoons cumin seeds

2 teaspoons coriander seeds, toasted and lightly crushed in a pestle and mortar

1 star anise

2.5cm cassia bark

3 whole cloves

3–4 green cardamom pods (bruise to release the seeds)

1 dried Kashmiri chilli

1 large banana shallot, finely diced

20g ginger, grated

20g garlic, grated

1 teaspoon minced green finger chillies, or to taste

½ teaspoon ground turmeric

½ teaspoon garam masala

1 teaspoon sea salt, or to taste

30g butter

1 teaspoon tomato purée

400ml passata

50ml double cream, or more to taste

Creamed saag

30g butter

a little vegetable oil

1½ teaspoons cumin seeds

3 green cardamom pods (bruise to release the seeds)

1 large brown onion, finely diced

20–30g ginger, grated

20–30g garlic, grated

1 teaspoon minced green finger chillies, or to taste

1 teaspoon ground turmeric

1½ teaspoons garam masala

1–2 teaspoons sea salt, or to taste

1kg spinach, washed and destalked

a good glug of double cream

1 tablespoon chopped fresh coriander leaves

1. First make the tandoori marinade. Blitz the coriander, garlic, ginger and chillies in a food processor with the vegetable oil to make a paste, then set aside. Pound the whole spices – cloves, peppercorns and cardamom seeds – to a powder in a pestle and mortar, using a little (extra) salt as the abrasive. Now combine all the tandoori marinade ingredients in a large bowl and set aside.

2. Make two or three slashes in the chicken legs and breast with a sharp knife – a couple of centimetres deep – to allow penetration of the marinade. Smother the chicken with the spiced yoghurt marinade, place in the bowl, cover and leave refrigerated overnight or for at least a few hours.

3. When you are ready to roast the bird, remove it from the fridge and allow to come to room temperature for 30 minutes. Preheat your oven to 180°C fan. Place the chicken in a large roasting tin, using a trivet so there is no direct contact. Loosely cover the chicken with foil so the spices do not burn, and roast for 1 hour. Remove the foil after an hour, then roast for a further 20–30 minutes, or until the chicken is cooked – remember to baste. You will need to increase the oven temperature to 200°C fan at this point so you get a nice char on the meat.

4. As soon as the chicken goes into the oven, prep the potatoes. Peel them, then cut them into equal sizes and parboil. Drain and allow to steam-dry, then coat with the vegetable oil and a sprinkle of cumin seeds, chilli flakes, sea salt, methi and the green chillies, if using; you can go as heavy or light with the spices as you like. Put the potatoes into the oven at the point when the foil is removed from the chicken. When the chicken is out of the oven and resting, the potatoes can cook through until crisp and golden.

5. Once the potatoes are prepped, start the makhani gravy. Heat the oil in a medium to large pan on a high heat and then add the whole spices: cumin, coriander seeds, star anise, cassia, cloves, cardamom and dried chilli. When they start to release their aromas, tip in the shallots, then reduce the heat to medium and allow them to soften. Add the ginger, garlic and chillies and cook out for a few minutes, then add the powdered spices – turmeric and garam masala, as well as salt – and toast for 30 seconds. Lob in the butter, as it will prevent the spices from catching (though if they do catch, add a splash of water). Add the tomato purée and cook out, then pour in the passata. Increase the heat and bring to the boil, then lower the heat to medium and simmer for 15 minutes, or until the oils separate on the surface of the sauce. Taste and adjust the seasoning. Add the cream, and some water if you'd like a thinner consistency, and simmer for a further 10 minutes. Remove from the heat. Strain and reheat before serving.

6. Make the creamed saag once the makhani gravy is done – that window when the foil is removed from the chicken and the spuds go into the oven is ideal. Heat the butter and a little vegetable oil in a large frying pan and then add the cumin seeds and cardamom. When they start to release their aromas, tip in the onions and cook until they have softened. Add the ginger, garlic and chillies, followed by the spices and salt, and cook out on a low to moderate heat.

→

7. Meanwhile, roll handfuls of spinach leaves into cigar shapes and chop them into 2.5cm pieces, quite thick. Wilt the chopped spinach in boiling water, no more than 30 seconds for young leaves, slightly longer for mature spinach. Drain the spinach thoroughly – you don't want waterlogged creamed saag – and stir into the onion mixture. Add a dollop of cream, stir in the chopped coriander, and adjust the seasoning as required. Remove from the heat and cover the pan.

8. When the chicken is cooked, remove from the oven, cover loosely with foil and rest as you bring the final elements together and reheat as necessary.

9. Serve the roast with a crunchy salad kissed with sea salt and lemon juice, and hot buttered chapattis, if you fancy it!

Dhal makhani is the Godfather of all dhals. This opulent dish is rich and decadent and bows to no other. Traditionally it's made with urid dhal, which is actually a bean and is also known as black dhal. It got me thinking how would this work with black beans – which I absolutely adore. The answer is jolly well indeed! This is a delicious twist on a Punjabi classic.

BLACK BEAN MAKHANI DHAL

SERVES 4–6

1 cup brown lentils
1 teaspoon whole coriander seeds
4 green cardamom pods (bruise to release the seeds)
vegetable oil, for cooking

2 teaspoons cumin seeds
5cm cassia bark
4 whole cloves
1 dried Kashmiri chilli (optional)
½ a star anise
1 large brown onion, finely diced
20g ginger, grated
20g garlic, grated

1–2 teaspoons minced green finger chillies, or to taste
2 teaspoons sea salt, or to taste
½ teaspoon garam masala
40g butter
1 tablespoon tomato purée
375ml water

150ml passata
3 x 400g tins of black beans, drained
a pinch of Kasuri methi (dried fenugreek)
1 tablespoon Greek yoghurt
2 tablespoons double cream
fresh coriander, to garnish (optional)

1. First cook the brown lentils – you'll need a large lidded saucepan. Brown lentils don't usually need a soak and will cook in under 30 minutes. Read the packet instructions, and cook until tender (please don't overcook them into a mush). You need three to four times the volume of water to lentils, so 3–4 cups of water. Bring to a rapid boil, then reduce to a simmer. Skim off any scum, and don't allow the pan to go dry. Remove from the heat, and set aside.

2. Toast the coriander seeds in a dry frying pan and transfer to a pestle and mortar. Lightly grind – they'll still have some texture – and set aside. Add your cardamom seeds to the mortar, with a pinch of salt to act as an abrasive, and grind to a powder.

3. Now make the tarka, the foundation of every curry. In a large (30cm) sauté pan or similar, activate your whole spices – cumin seeds, cassia bark, cloves, dried chilli, if using, and star anise – in 3 or 4 tablespoons of oil on a medium to high heat. When the fragrant aromas waft up, tip in the onions, crushed coriander and powdered cardamom, and reduce the heat to medium. Give these at least 10 minutes or so to allow the onions to soften and become translucent.

→

4. Next add the ginger, garlic and chillies, cook out for a couple of minutes, then add the salt and garam masala. Toast for 30 seconds, then drop in half of the butter (this will prevent the masala from catching). Once melted, add the tomato purée and give everything a good mix. You want a few minutes to cook the purée out. Add some water, about 125ml, to help it on its way.

5. Pour in the passata and bring to the boil, then simmer for a few minutes. When you see the tell-tale sign of the oil separating on the surface, it's time to taste and make your adjustments. Though it will taste salty at this point, you are likely to need more salt when the lentils and beans have been added.

6. Stir all your cooked lentils and beans through the tarka. You'll need extra water too, about 250ml. Ensure everything is mixed well, then bring to the boil and immediately reduce to a simmer. Taste again now – you'll probably need more salt. Add the methi, the rest of the butter, yoghurt and cream. You may want to hold some of the cream back for a decorative swirl just before serving. Allow to simmer for a little longer and for all of the flavours to develop – say another 10 minutes or so.

7. Enjoy, with glee! Pair with whichever bread takes your fancy, or with rice. I serve it with black cardamom rice, charred aloo gobi, yoghurt and a crunchy slaw. Though this dish could be a prized part of any celebration feasting table too!

COOK'S NOTE You can by all means go the classic route and use traditional whole urid dhal instead. Use 2 cups of urid dhal and soak overnight. Follow the packet instructions, though they will likely require an hour-long simmer. Some folks like to simmer them for much longer, until the dhal disintegrates to make it extra creamy and silky. Go with your personal preference.

There are lots of different lentils, and you can mix them for a more complex-tasting dhal. To confuse matters, you can cook with whole, hulled or split lentils too, which changes the taste further. Sometimes simplicity is best. The main dhal I had when I was growing up, and which I absolutely adore, is masoor ki dhal, which is split red lentils. When I fancy a healthy yet comforting lunch, I opt for this with buttered wholemeal toast!

MASOOR KI DHAL SOUP } WITH TOAST

SERVES 4–6

2 cups split red lentils
8 cups water
vegetable oil, for cooking

2 teaspoons cumin seeds
1 brown onion, finely chopped
15g garlic, grated
15g ginger, grated
1–2 teaspoons minced chillies, or to taste

1½ teaspoons garam masala
2–3 teaspoons sea salt, or to taste
1 teaspoon ground turmeric
200ml passata

20g butter
chopped fresh coriander leaves, to garnish
extra knob of butter, to serve

1. Rinse the lentils – they will need three or four washes but generally don't need soaking – and cook as per the packet instructions in a large lidded saucepan, partially covered. One cup of lentils will need four times the volume of water (as you want a thinner consistency here) and will cook in 25–30 minutes. Ensure the pan does not go dry, and remove any scum/foam that may form. Set aside.
2. Meanwhile let's make the tarka. Take a large frying pan, activate the cumin seeds in 3 or 4 tablespoons of vegetable oil on a medium to high heat. Tip in the onions, reduce the heat to medium and sauté until lightly golden.
3. Add the garlic, ginger and minced chillies, and cook out for a few minutes.
4. Now add the garam masala, salt and turmeric and toast for 30 seconds. If the pan is too dry, a splash of water will prevent the spices from burning. Pour in the passata, increase the hob heat, bring to the boil, then reduce to a simmer for 10 minutes or so.
5. When the oil has separated on the surface of the tomato mixture, that means it's cooked and ready to taste. Check the seasoning and adjust.
6. Ladle some of the cooked lentils into your frying pan – as much as you can – and mix with the tarka. Then transfer all the contents of the tarka pan into the lentil saucepan, and bring to a simmer. Check the seasoning again – you will need more salt; remember, lentils are bland and need to be brought to life! Add the butter and let it melt through the dhal.
7. Finally scatter with a flurry of chopped coriander leaves. Serve with buttered toast and an extra knob of butter melting into the dhal for that loving touch.

Chicken soup is synonymous with possessing mystical healing powers – we've all heard of the phrase 'Jewish penicillin'. Chicken 'thari' in our house was never a gravy but more of a broth. My mother would often whip up a vat full if any of us had the slightest sniffle. My little twist is the addition of roti 'noodles', which soak up the spicy broth and simply yield in your mouth. The option of the potatoes turns this into a hearty meal. Warning: if this is what medicine tastes like, your loved ones may pretend to be sick!

CHICKEN THARI SOUP } WITH ROTI NOODLES

SERVES 4

vegetable oil, for cooking

2 teaspoons cumin seeds

6 green cardamom pods (bruise to release the seeds)

5cm cassia bark

2 whole cloves

1 large brown onion, finely chopped

20g garlic, grated

20g ginger, grated

1 teaspoon chopped fresh coriander stalks

1–2 teaspoons minced finger chillies, or to taste

1 teaspoon ground turmeric

1½ teaspoons garam masala

2 teaspoons sea salt, or to taste

1 teaspoon tomato purée

150ml passata

4 skinless chicken thighs and 4 skinless chicken drumsticks (bone in)

1–1.5 litres water

2–3 medium potatoes, peeled and chopped into bite-sized pieces (optional)

a pinch of Kasuri methi (dried fenugreek)

1 tablespoon chopped fresh coriander leaves

4 chapattis (see page 19), rolled and finely sliced into noodles

finely sliced spring onion, for garnish

1. Heat 3 or 4 tablespoons of vegetable oil in a large lidded saucepan on a medium to high heat and activate the whole spices: cumin seeds, green cardamom, cassia bark and cloves. When the aromas waft up, add the onions and sauté on a medium heat until lightly golden.

2. Add the garlic, ginger, chopped coriander stalks and minced chillies. Cook out for a couple of minutes, then add the ground spices: turmeric and garam masala, and the salt. Toast for 30 seconds. You may need to add a splash of water to prevent the spices from burning.

3. Stir the tomato purée through the onion mixture and allow to cook for a minute or two, then pour in the passata. Increase the heat and bring to a simmer for 10 minutes or so. When you can see the oil separate on the surface that means it's ready to taste. Check your seasoning and adjust as necessary.

4. Add the chicken to the pan and mix using a wooden spoon, coating all the pieces on a high heat – this is a bhuna technique. You want to seal the meat but not let anything burn, so stir constantly.
5. Add the water and bring to the boil, then reduce to a simmer immediately, covering the saucepan with a lid, and allow the chicken to poach. (After 20 minutes add the potatoes if you are including them.)
6. When the chicken is cooked, soft and tender – after about 35–40 minutes – scoop out the chicken pieces with a slotted spoon. Allow to cool, then shred the meat from the bone – you can use two forks. Return the shredded meat to the pot and stir through, along with a pinch of methi and the chopped coriander. Make any final adjustments to the seasoning.
7. Place the roti noodles in each bowl just before serving – I always butter my chapattis – and ladle over the chicken and soup. Garnish with finely sliced spring onion.

KEEMA FOUR WAYS

Keema refers to minced meat. It's such a versatile dish I could dedicate a whole chapter to it! This comes down to good old-fashioned home economics though, doesn't it, presenting a cheap ingredient in a variety of different ways to keep folks interested. I generally use lamb mince, though you can use beef if you prefer – just ensure it's not too lean, as the fat is where the flavour is and I tend to use mince with a 15–20 per cent fat content. I'll share a base recipe, which I'll put in a filo pie, then I'm taking you to Mexico via India.

KEEMA FILO PIE

SERVES 4–6

vegetable oil, for cooking
2 teaspoons cumin seeds
1 whole star anise
1 large brown onion, finely chopped

25g garlic, grated
25g ginger, grated
2 teaspoons minced chillies, or to taste
1½ teaspoons garam masala
2 teaspoons sea salt, or to taste
1 teaspoon ground turmeric

200ml passata
1 teaspoon tomato purée (optional)
500g minced lamb/ beef (15–20 per cent fat)
225ml water
3–4 medium potatoes, peeled and cut into bite-sized pieces

125g frozen peas
1 tablespoon chopped fresh coriander
filo pastry (about 5–6 sheets)
approx. 125g melted butter or vegetable oil, for brushing
2 teaspoons nigella seeds

1. You will need a 23cm cake tin to make the pie.
2. We're going to start with the tarka as ever, the flavour foundation. Heat 3 or 4 tablespoons of vegetable oil in a medium to large lidded saucepan, on a medium to high heat, and activate the cumin seeds and star anise. Then tip in the onions, reduce the heat to medium and sauté until it becomes translucent and soft.
3. Add the garlic, ginger and chillies and cook out for a couple of minutes, then add the garam masala, salt and turmeric. If the pan is too dry add a splash of water so the spices don't burn. Allow the ground spices to toast for 30 seconds.
4. Pour in the passata and mix through. Increase the heat until the mixture is bubbling, then reduce to a simmer for 5–10 minutes. If you want a richer keema, with a greater tomato flavour, add the tomato purée prior to the passata and give it extra time to cook out. When you can see the

→

oil separate on the surface of the spiced tomato mixture it's cooked and ready to taste. Check the seasoning and adjust as necessary.

5. Add the mince, breaking it up with the end of a wooden spoon as you mix it through the tarka. Crank the hob heat to high, to seal the meat, then pour in the water and stir. Bring to a simmer, then cover with a lid. Allow to cook for 10 minutes, then add the potatoes. Put the lid on the saucepan, which will trap in the steam needed to cook the potatoes. The cooking time will vary according to how large your potato pieces are. This usually takes about 15–20 minutes.

6. Keep an eye on the pan, as you may need to add more water so the keema doesn't catch. If you go the opposite way and add too much water you can correct this by simmering the keema without a lid so the liquid can evaporate and the gravy can reduce. You want quite a dry keema.

7. Add the peas 5 minutes before the end of cooking, and finish with a flurry of chopped coriander leaves. Cool completely. You can get organized and make the keema the day before.

8. When you are ready to assemble your pie, set the oven to 180°C. Have your cake tin and melted butter/veg oil ready for brushing. Prepare a damp tea towel – filo pastry will dry out quickly so you will need this to cover the pastry sheets as you assemble. Brush the filo sheets – one at a time – with the butter/oil, and overlap these, oiled side down, in the cake tin (you'll need 4–5 sheets). Carefully fill the pie cavity evenly with the keema, and encase it with the overhanging pastry. Use the remaining sheet(s) to fill any gaps. If you are feeling artistic you can shape the filo to look like roses, but I prefer a rough and rustic scrunch. Brush the exposed pastry with more melted butter/oil and sprinkle with nigella seeds. Place the cake tin on a baking tray to catch any leakage. Bake for 30–40 minutes, or until cooked and golden.

9. Let the pie cool a little before dishing up, as this will also help to crisp up the pastry. Serve with a kachumber salad – cucumber, red onion and tomatoes topped with a squeeze of lemon juice and a few mint leaves – and a dollop of yoghurt.

KEEMA CON CARNE } WITH PILAU RICE AND SIDES

SERVES 4–6

Keema con carne
basic keema recipe, in filo pie (see page 46)
1 teaspoon tomato purée
1 x 400g tin of kidney beans, drained

Pilau rice (will serve 4)
1 cup basmati rice
vegetable oil, for cooking
1 black cardamom
5–6 black peppercorns
1 teaspoon cumin seeds
2 whole cloves

1 bay leaf
½ a small brown onion, finely diced
1 teaspoon sea salt, or to taste
a small handful of frozen peas
2 cups water

Cabbage slaw
¼ of a small red cabbage, finely shredded
¼ of a small white cabbage, finely shredded
½ a small red onion, finely sliced in half-moons

Slaw dressing
½ teaspoon black mustard seeds
½ teaspoon nigella seeds
½ teaspoon cumin seeds
½ teaspoon fennel seeds
120ml vegetable oil
2 tablespoons white wine vinegar
2 generous tablespoons honey
a pinch of salt

Tortilla chips
3–4 standard flour tortillas
vegetable/sunflower oil spray
nigella seeds
sea salt

Avocado crema
2 ripe avocados, peeled
1 small clove of garlic or less, to taste
1 tablespoon Greek yoghurt, or to taste
juice of 1 lime, plus a little zest
sea salt, to taste
minced finger chillies, to taste (optional)

1. First make the keema con carne, which can then be reheated prior to serving. See the basic keema recipe from the filo pie. In this case you will need the tomato purée for the richness I feel this dish needs. Replace the potatoes and peas with kidney beans, which should be added at step 5 instead of the potatoes. Like chilli con carne the flavour develops over time, so make it the night before, if you can.

2. The rice needs to be rinsed to remove any excess starch. Place in a bowl and cover with cold water, give it a swish to agitate, then rinse three or four times using a fine sieve. Cover with cold water again and set aside for at least 30 minutes.

3. To make the base for the pilau rice, sauté the whole spices – black cardamom, peppercorns, cumin seeds, cloves – in a couple of tablespoons of oil in a medium to large lidded saucepan. Once activated, add the bay leaf, then tip in the onions and salt. Allow the onions to soften and become translucent on a medium heat, then remove from the heat and set aside.

4. You can prep all your condiments while the rice is soaking. First the cabbage slaw. Toast the whole spices for the slaw dressing in a dry frying pan – mustard seeds, nigella seeds, cumin seeds and fennel seeds, and set aside. Whisk the dressing ingredients together – vegetable

→

oil, vinegar, honey and salt – then stir through the toasted spices. Dress the prepared slaw ingredients and refrigerate before serving.

5. Set your oven to 200°C. Cut the flour tortillas into quarters, then eighths, spray with veg/sunflower oil and sprinkle with nigella seeds and a little salt. Spread on a lined baking sheet and bake for 3–5 minutes, or until golden. Remove and allow to cool and crisp.

6. Make the avocado crema by blitzing all the ingredients in a blender until smooth. Refrigerate before serving.

7. Strain the rice through a sieve and stir through the onion mixture, coating it thoroughly. Stir in the peas. Now you'll need 2 cups of water. It's always a 1:2 ratio for the absorption method. I use boiling water from the kettle. Give everything a good stir and check for seasoning. Bring to boiling point, then put a tight-fitting lid on the pan (you can wrap the lid in a tea towel if need be) and immediately reduce the heat to medium, to a simmer. The rice needs 10–12 minutes to cook (you can check after 10 minutes – but not before), then remove from the heat. Allow to stand for another 10 minutes with the lid on; it will sit happily for quite some time. Fork the rice through before serving.

8. While the rice is standing, reheat the keema con carne.

9. Serve all the elements with charred lime halves, coriander leaves, dollops of Greek yoghurt and perhaps some finely sliced red chillies for the heroes. You could also make a chunky mint chutney with tomatoes to act as a salsa.

KEEMA BURRITOS

This is a great way to use up leftover keema con carne.

· ▬ · ▬ · ▬ · ▬ · ▬ · ▬ · ▬ · ▬ · ▬ · ▬ · ▬ · ▬ · ▬ ·

SERVES 4–6

1. Take a large flour tortilla, place 3 tablespoons of cold keema con carne in the middle, then wrap and roll tightly into a burrito. Repeat with the remaining tortillas. Place in an ovenproof dish, fold side down, top with grated cheese and bake in a 180°C oven for 25–30 minutes, or until piping hot and the cheese is melty and stretchy. Garnish with thinly sliced pickled chillies and coriander leaves. Serve with whatever sides or condiments you fancy.

KEEMA TACOS

Who doesn't love a taco Tuesday? And this is a lovely little twist.

· — · — · — · — · · — · — · — · — · — · · — · — · ·

MAKES 10 TACOS

basic keema recipe, in
filo pie (page 46)

Taco dough
300g Greek yoghurt
2 teaspoons cumin
seeds
1–2 teaspoons sea salt,
or to taste
2 teaspoons Kasuri
methi (dried
fenugreek)
300–400g plain flour
(dependent on flour
absorption)

White cabbage slaw
¼ of a small white
cabbage, finely
shredded

Green chutney
30g fresh mint leaves
4–5 spring onions
1–2 green finger chillies
1–2 tablespoons
vegetable oil
salt
a squeeze of lime
juice, and a little zest

Garnishes
sour cream or Greek
yoghurt
finely sliced spring
onion
chopped fresh
coriander
pickled chillies (for the
heroes out there)
finely chopped
red onion
lime wedges

1. Wo'll make the dough first. Mix the yoghurt, cumin seeds, salt and methi in a large bowl. Test the seasoning here, and if you're happy with it add enough plain flour to make a relatively firm dough. Place in an airtight container and rest in the fridge for 30 minutes.

2. Make the keema (see basic keema recipe on page 46), but leave out the potatoes and use peas only. Or you could dodge the vegetables entirely on this occasion.

3. Next the make the green chutney. Blitz all the ingredients in a blender until smooth. Taste and adjust the seasoning if necessary, then set aside.

4. Put your finely shredded cabbage into a bowl, and coat generously with the green chutney. You won't need all the chutney. Cover, then set aside at room temperature.

5. When you're ready to make the tacos, heat a frying pan or tawa on a medium to high heat. You want a taco that's about 10cm in diameter, so take an appropriate amount of dough – say ping-pong ball size – and roll into a thin round disc on a lightly floured work surface. Shake off any excess dry flour (as this will burn), place on the hot, dry frying pan/tawa and cook on each side for about 2 minutes. Batch-make all the tacos, or as many as you need, and wrap them in foil to keep them warm. You can then transfer to a low oven to keep warm until serving.

6. Serve family style, so people can build their own tacos.

> **COOK'S NOTE** The basic keema recipe lends itself to lots of different vegetables being added. For example, I often replace the peas and potatoes with fine green beans. Saag (spinach) is lovely too, as is chopped white cabbage. You could even have keema as a starter and put a couple of tablespoons in a lettuce leaf/cup.

I love the riot of colour in this salad! The black backdrop of the rice is a dramatic canvas for the vibrant green of the tikka and herbs, ruby pomegranate seeds, rouge peppers and golden sweetcorn. Just as well it tastes eye-poppingly good too! You'll be making this repeatedly.

GREEN CHICKEN TIKKA } WITH BLACK RICE SALAD

**SERVES 2
(WITH LEFTOVER
TIKKA FOR WRAPS)**

**Green/hariyali
marinade**

30g fresh coriander
  leaves

15g fresh mint leaves

50g young leaf
  spinach

10g ginger, grated

10g garlic, grated

1–2 teaspoons minced
  finger chillies, or
  to taste

juice of 1 lime

vegetable oil – a few
  generous glugs

250g Greek yoghurt

1½ teaspoons sea salt,
  or to taste

1½ teaspoons garam
  masala

1 teaspoon ground
  cumin

1 level teaspoon
  ground turmeric

6–7 skinless and
  boneless chicken
  thighs (this will feed
  the hungry, but left-
  overs are brilliant
  for sandwiches and
  wraps)

Rice salad

1 large red pepper

1 red onion

2–3 charred baby leeks
  (optional, lightly spray
  with oil and char on a
  griddle pan)

vegetable oil, for
  cooking

sea salt

a sprinkle of cumin
  seeds

1 sweetcorn cob

250g cooked black rice
  (you can buy pre-
  cooked pouches)

Dressing

3 tablespoons
  vegetable oil

juice and zest of 1 lime

1 small clove of garlic
  or ½ to taste, grated

1 teaspoon ground
  cumin

½ teaspoon ground
  coriander

a pinch or 2 of sea salt

½ teaspoon light
  brown sugar

½ teaspoon Kashmiri
  chilli powder

½ teaspoon chilli flakes

1 teaspoon chopped
  fresh coriander

½ teaspoon
  pomegranate
  molasses

Garnish

fresh coriander and
  mint leaves/micro
  herbs

finely sliced red chillies

65g pomegranate
  seeds

finely sliced spring
  onions

charred lime wedges
  (see page 196)

1. Start with the hariyali marinade. Blitz the coriander, mint, spinach, ginger, garlic, chillies and lime juice in a blender along with a few generous glugs of vegetable oil – enough to make a thick paste.

2. Put the yoghurt into a large mixing bowl and stir in the green paste, then mix in the salt, garam masala, ground cumin and turmeric thoroughly. Test the seasoning – you want to feel some chilli heat and it should be well seasoned. Adjust accordingly and set aside.

3. Cut your chicken into chunky bite-sized pieces, place in the marinade, cover and leave to marinate in the fridge, overnight ideally or for at least 2–3 hours. Preheat the oven to 200°C fan. Cut the pepper and

→

red onion into 2cm chunks, coat sparsely with oil, season with sea salt and a sprinkle of cumin seeds and roast until slightly charred at the edges – about 20–25 minutes.

4. Place the sweetcorn under a very hot grill, and grill until cooked and golden all over with a hint of a char. Hold the corn upright, and slice off the kernels. Discard the core and set aside.

5. Whisk all the dressing ingredients together in a small bowl and set aside.

6. When you are ready to bring the dish together, cook the chicken under a grill on the highest setting to recreate that fierce tandoori heat; you want a little char without burning.

7. Cook or heat your rice – I use a shop-bought microwaveable pouch for convenience, but follow the packet instructions if cooking your own. Toss the rice and vegetables (including the charred leeks, if using) with the dressing in a large bowl.

8. Serve your sizzling green chicken tikka on top of the rice salad, adorned with the various garnishes. Divine!

COOK'S NOTE You can make this dish vegetarian by replacing the chicken with paneer, halloumi or tofu.

A club sandwich is a classic combination of chicken, ham or bacon, lettuce, tomato and mayonnaise, often between toasted white bread, and fixed into place with a kitsch cocktail stick. I've reimagined what this combination would look like, influenced by multicultural Birmz – as Birmingham is affectionately referred to by locals. Prepare for your taste buds to be tickled!

BIRMINGHAM CLUB SANDWICH

SERVES 2

Pink pickled onions
½ a red onion, finely sliced into rings
lime juice
a pinch of salt
a good pinch of nigella seeds

Sandwich
100g cooked shredded ham hock (shop-bought)
vegetable oil, for cooking
a pinch of cumin seeds
1 heaped tablespoon mayonnaise
1 heaped tablespoon Greek yoghurt
1 heaped tablespoon premium mango chutney, plus extra for spreading
½ teaspoon mild curry powder, or to taste
1 teaspoon hot sauce, or to taste
a splash of white wine vinegar (optional)
300g leftover cooked chicken chunks (plain roast is fine – tandoori is better)
2 tablespoons sultanas
1 tablespoon flaked almonds
3 dried apricots, finely chopped
4 chunky slices of white farmhouse bread
mint chutney (see page 27)
gem lettuce leaves
fresh coriander leaves
1 tomato, finely sliced
cucumber, finely sliced

1. To pickle the red onions, cover them with a squeeze of lime juice and a pinch of salt and rub between your fingers. Then sprinkle with a pinch of nigella seeds and mix through. Set aside. They will start to pickle after 15–30 minutes, but the colour and flavour develop the longer you leave them. If you want a hot pink colour, pickle them overnight, covered.
2. Sauté the ham hock in a scant amount of vegetable oil with a sprinkle of cumin seeds, and cool. Set aside, covered.
3. Now make some coronation chicken: mix the mayo, yoghurt, mango chutney, curry powder, hot sauce and vinegar, if using, in a bowl. Check the seasoning, and once you're happy, fold through the chicken pieces, along with the sultanas, almonds and apricots. Set aside.
4. Next toast your bread. I like the char lines of a griddle pan, but toast it however suits you.
5. Now we're ready to assemble. Take a slice of toast and spread it with a thin layer of mint chutney, then layer with lettuce leaves, half the chicken, a sprinkle of coriander leaves, pickled onions, ham hock, tomatoes and cucumber. Top with the second slice of toast, smothered with extra mango chutney. Slice in half and spear with a cocktail stick for full effect.
6. Serve with French fries and brown sauce or tamarind ketchup.

To me there is nothing better than rounding off a meal with a British pud! I confess, Indian sweets – mithai – aren't really my thing. I grew up eating trifles, crumbles, bread and butter pudding, cake and custard, and tinned fruit with canned Tip Top cream; it was a 'thing' in our house and I always fought with my brother for the cherry (we did have lots of fresh fruit too, I must add). Puddings are so often the ultimate comfort food that frequently evoke nostalgia. Fond childhood memories for many of us include school dinner puddings – those lucky enough to experience the glorious ones, I must caveat – and this was one of my favourites: cornflake tart . . . mmmmm!

CRUNCHY CORNFLAKE TART

SERVES 6

Sweet pastry
60g icing sugar
60g cold unsalted butter, grated (use the coarsest side of your box grater; by grating you minimize handling)

140g plain flour
1 egg yolk, mixed with 1 tablespoon cold water
additional 1–2 tablespoons cold water
1 egg white, for glazing

Crunchy cornflakes
100g butter
100g soft light brown sugar
2 heaped tablespoons golden syrup (approx. 75–80g)
180g cornflakes
approx. 200g strawberry jam

1. You will need a 23cm deep-sided flan dish. I used a fluted carbon steel flan case with a removable base.
2. Make the pastry first – at chefs' school we call it a 'sweet paste'. At school we used our fingers, but I just use a food processor at home and I've adjusted the measurements for this recipe. Pulse the icing sugar, butter and flour together (if making by hand, work the butter with the sugar using your fingers, then sieve in the flour and use a spatula to bring the dough together rather than warm hands. Overworking will toughen the pastry and you want to keep it short, so work the gluten as little as possible). Mix the yolk with 1 tablespoon of water, then add that to the processor, and pulse again. The dough will start to ball. You want a soft but not sticky dough. You'll need a tiny amount more water but don't overdo it, a burst of continuous pulse will bring it all together.
3. Shape the dough into a flat disc with your hands, then wrap in cling film and refrigerate for 1 hour, or until firm.

4. Take the pastry out of the fridge and allow it to come to room temperature, which will make it easy to roll out. Meanwhile, grease and line your flan dish.

5. Roll out the pastry on a lightly floured surface. Keep rotating the pastry at 90 degrees to make it easier, you want a 3mm thickness. Gently ease the pastry into the flan case. Use a little excess pastry to form into a small dough ball, dip it in some dry flour (to prevent sticking) and use this to dab the pastry into the fluted sides. Let the pastry overhang at the edges, as it will shrink during baking and you can tidy it up at the end. Place on a baking sheet and pop it back into the fridge for another 30 minutes.

6. Heat your oven to 180°C. Place a cartouche (circle of greaseproof paper) inside the pastry case, fill with baking beans and blind bake for 10 minutes. After 10 minutes remove the beans and baking paper. Gently brush the base with the egg white to create a glaze and barrier to avoid a soggy bottom (you won't need all of it). Return to the oven and bake for another 10–12 minutes, or until the base is cooked through. Remove from the oven and allow to cool. Trim the overhanging pastry with a sharp knife.

7. Meanwhile, make the crunchy cornflake topping. Melt the butter, sugar and syrup in a large saucepan, then gently fold in the cornflakes, ensuring they are evenly coated. (I've allowed for extra, so you can make a couple of cornflake cupcakes for any little helpers. Just place the excess into fairy cake cases and allow to cool and set.)

8. Give the jam a little whisk so it spreads more easily, and spread it over the pastry base. Then adorn with a crunchy cornflake crown and spread this right across the tart. Return to the oven and bake for another 5 minutes.

9. Allow to cool, then slice and serve with custard or a drizzle of cream.

COOK'S NOTE I know the chilling of the pastry is a bit of a faff, but it really is worth it. It's the science bit, you see, and helps achieve a lovely short texture. Basically, resting and chilling help the glutens to relax and also ensure even hydration. We also handle this dough as little as possible – to keep the gluten strands short.

All our birthdays followed a set format: namely, big family gatherings including the extended family. Mum would make a fancy lamb curry, rice and naans, and we'd have samosas and pakoras. Granddad would get the rum or whisky out – any excuse. We'd maybe have tandoori chicken too if anybody had a 'chaska' – a craving – all pretty standard. But there were ALWAYS the following random items on the menu too: garlic bread, chicken liver pâté, quiche, cheese and pickles and a Sara Lee gâteau! My Italian friend Elisabetta – who I met on *Best Home Cook* – is a wonderful baker. She's taken inspiration from this humble frozen gâteau, and has given it a sophisticated makeover to celebrate my grown-up birthdays. Here's her delicious recipe.

ELISABETTA'S CHOCOLATE AND CHERRY BIRTHDAY CAKE

SERVES 12–15

Chocolate sponge
300g dark chocolate (70 per cent + cocoa)
200g unsalted butter, cubed
8 eggs
360g granulated sugar
500g self-raising flour
2 teaspoons baking powder

8 tablespoons boiling water
8 raspberries
10 cherries, halved and stoned (or jarred cherries in Kirsch)

Dark chocolate frosting
200g softened unsalted butter, cubed and at room temperature
370g icing sugar
110g cocoa powder

1½ teaspoons vanilla extract
130ml double cream
a pinch of salt
2–4 tablespoons milk (if needed)

Chantilly cream
100g icing sugar
600ml double cream
200g raspberries
20 cherries, quartered and stoned

Decorations
12 cherries
a punnet of redcurrants (optional)
chocolate shards, for around the edge of the cake (optional)
edible gold leaf flakes

1. Set the oven to 180°C fan. Line and grease two deep 20cm cake tins. For this cake you need two chocolate sponges, halved horizontally, making four tiers.
2. To make the sponge, first melt the chocolate and butter using a bain-marie. To do this, pour 5cm of boiling water from the kettle into a medium pan and bring to a simmer on the hob. Place a heatproof bowl on top of the pan – you want a snug fit without the bottom of the bowl touching the water. Break the chocolate into pieces, then place in the bowl with the cubed butter and stir until melted. Set aside.

→

3. Meanwhile, in a separate large bowl whisk the eggs and sugar together until they are pale and almost doubled in volume, then gently fold in the melted chocolate mixture, being careful not to knock the air out.

4. Sieve the flour and baking powder into the mixture, add the boiling water, then slowly fold everything together, making sure there are no floury lumps.

5. Divide the cake batter equally between the cake tins, and press an equal number of raspberries and cherries into each one. Use a palette knife to cover any exposed fruit and spread the mix evenly. Bake for 40–45 minutes, or until cooked. You can tell the cakes are cooked when the sponge bounces back to the touch, and is coming away from the edges of the tin. You can also insert a skewer into the centre of the cake; if it comes out clean the cake is cooked. Set aside to cool in the tins.

6. To make the buttercream, place the softened butter in a large mixing bowl and beat a little until it's fluffy. Add the icing sugar, cocoa powder, vanilla extract, double cream and a pinch of salt and beat until all incorporated. The consistency should be spreadable – add the milk if the mixture is too stiff, a tablespoon at a time.

7. For the Chantilly cream, sieve the icing sugar into the double cream and whisk until you have soft peaks, then fold in the raspberries. Set aside.

8. To decorate, remove the cakes from the tins and cut each one in half horizontally so you have 4 equal layers/tiers. Sandwich them together with the Chantilly cream, using a palette knife to ensure the cake is level, and adding a few quartered cherries to each layer. Cover the cake with the frosting, using a palette knife. First a crumb coating – a thin layer of frosting around the whole exterior – then pop the cake into the fridge for 30 minutes to chill and set, before adding a thicker, final coat of frosting. This will give you the best end result. Finally, get creative with a piping bag – use a nozzle of your choice – and decorate the cake as you wish. Attach the chocolate shards, if using. Bling the decorative fruit with edible gold leaf, using a fine artist's brush.

> **COOK'S NOTE** You can steep your cherries in Kirsch liqueur and spike your frosting with espresso (in lieu of the milk), should you wish.

I adored crumbles as a child. We ate a lot of them, as my grandparents had many fruit trees in their garden – apples, pears and plums. You can use spice – of course cinnamon and apples are a perfect match – however, I would like you to taste the jaggery in all its glory: fudgy, toffee-like, chewy in parts. You may not know what jaggery is – it's an unrefined Indian sugar made from sugarcane. So arguably this pudding is good for you, as unrefined sugar is better for your health!

APPLE AND JAGGERY CRUMBLE

SERVES 4

Filling
25g jaggery
55–60ml hot water
6 red Gala apples, peeled, cored and cubed

Crumble topping
200g plain flour
110g chilled butter, cubed
110g jaggery, chopped

a sprinkle of demerara sugar
a sprinkle of rolled oats

1. Set your oven to 180°C fan. Melt 25g of jaggery in the hot water. Stew the apples in this golden liquid over a medium heat for 10 minutes or so, until the apples have softened and the liquid has mostly evaporated. I keep the lid on the saucepan for the first 7–8 minutes to trap the steam, then take the lid off until the liquid has evaporated. Transfer to a shallow 1 litre pie dish.

2. To make the crumble, pulse the flour, butter and jaggery in a food processor until it resembles fine breadcrumbs. Note: if mixing by hand, the jaggery will soften on handling, so it's better to chill and grate it.

3. Evenly distribute the crumble mix over the apples, and finally sprinkle over a scant amount of demerara sugar, which will add some crunch, and a sprinkling of rolled oats.

4. Bake in the oven for 30–40 minutes, until crisp and golden. Allow to cool for 10 minutes or so, then serve with a little double cream, or Bird's custard for full retro kitsch (a nice crème anglaise is perfectly acceptable too!).

BRADFORD
& YORKSHIRE

KASHMIRI COMMUNITY

Kashmir was an independent princely state, sitting between modern-day India and Pakistan, situated above Shimla, the summer capital of the British Raj. Since partition in 1947 there has been much geopolitical tension in Kashmir, and territorial disputes between India and Pakistan have led to a number of Indo-Pakistani wars and ongoing troubles. China also has a minor role, administering the bordering land area. It's heartbreaking that a destination described by many as 'heaven on earth' should be blighted by barbed-wire checkpoints and the presence of armed troops.

There is a big Kashmiri community in Bradford, the majority of whom came from the Pakistani-administered Azad Kashmir region and practise the Muslim faith. A lot of migration took place from the 1950s and 60s to meet labour shortages in the textile industry in Yorkshire – Bradford is a mill city with a long history of wool and cotton production. Kashmiri food is heavily meat-oriented and rich from necessity, originating from the beautiful foothills of the Himalayas. Nose-to-tail eating is very much a feature, and no part of the animal is wasted – offal such as liver, kidney, tripe and trotters are very popular. Wazwan is an important ceremonial feast in Kashmiri culture, prepared for auspicious occasions such as weddings. It is considered to be an art form, and is presided over by a master chef called a wouste waz. A wazwan has a staggering 36 courses! Most of these courses are meat-based, with lamb being the meat of choice. In this chapter I will be looking at some typical wazwan dishes and cooking traditions. Kashmiri cuisine is very reflective of its diverse cultural history as a strategic stop along the Silk Route, rich with Persian, Turkish and Mughal influences.

ANIL NAWAZ (AGED 26)

Finance data scientist and youth football coach

Bradford, and Yorkshire in general, is home to a big Kashmiri and Pakistani population, and I wanted to shine a light on some of the fantastic work being done in the community. Bradford is one of the most deprived local authority districts in England: according to the English Indices of Deprivation published in 2019, Bradford was ranked 13th out of 317, with 1 being most deprived. The study reported that:

15 per cent of the district's households are in fuel poverty.

22 per cent of children are living below the poverty line.

13 per cent of working age people have no qualifications.

11 per cent of the working age population claim an out-of-work benefit.

Once known as an international wool capital, Yorkshire suffered terrible economic decline post deindustrialization. Anil's grandparents came to Bradford in the 1960s from Mirpur, a district in Azad Kashmir. Many people were displaced from its rural agricultural villages after the Pakistani government approved the construction of the Mangla Dam. The contract was awarded to a British engineering firm, Binnie & Partners, in 1961. Many displaced Mirpuris came to Britain and provided cheap unskilled labour for employers.

Anil currently manages and coaches a youth team at Allerton FC (Allerton is an area in Bradford) and has been heavily involved in grassroots football for a number of years. He tells me there are many children, particularly from the Kashmiri and Pakistani communities, who have given up on football mainly for social and economic reasons. He strives to make a difference for the community, and wanted to be involved at a club that helped to overcome these barriers, an affordable club with access to great facilities, open to children of all races, creeds and genders. The club has access to grounds at local schools and academies and has leased land from the council. Anil also runs free coaching programmes. The children he works with don't tend to get involved with school football, and feel more valued away from that setting. They aren't engaged with the education system, and football is their main outlet. It's a great way to learn life skills; they learn communication skills, team working, organization, timekeeping and such like: 'The ultimate goal is to get kids involved in football and also to find the next top talent in Bradford from the Asian community. At the moment this home-grown talent is lacking in the professional game . . .'

Understandably, football and sport in general are a low priority for parents compared to paying bills and putting food on the table. However, education and training, and having positive role models are important to truly succeed and break the link between social deprivation and academic underachievement, which then has consequences on opportunities in adult life. Having that parental and community support and the ability to integrate are key to success and progression.

Anil is a commendable ambassador for his community, and I hope he can find the next big talent in professional football because of what it represents. We need to give people hope and opportunity and we need people like Anil playing an active role, an active part in the wider community, to shape change and regeneration.

FASTING AND SPORT

Fasting is one of the five pillars of Islam. As a sportsperson, diet and performance are closely linked, and it can be very challenging to achieve peak levels when fasting. Some sportspeople opt to miss fasting and instead give 'fidya' (an obligation to make a charitable donation to those in need), or make up for missing a fast at another time. Others strictly observe fasting during the holy month of Ramadan. This can be managed through meal planning, to ensure they are taking on enough calories, hydration, protein and slow-release carbs to fuel training and recovery. Or training can be done a couple of hours after breaking the fast (iftar).

WRITTEN WITH DIETICIAN FAREEHA JAY

Fareeha has established herself as 'aap ki dietician' (your dietician) among Southeast Asian communities in the UK. She also has a huge following in Pakistan, her country of birth, where she is a published author, TV personality and prominent figure in the nutrition area. She came to the UK in 2004, is based in Plymouth, and campaigns tirelessly to promote better awareness around healthy eating and wellbeing for all age groups, from working with local schools, in community centres to delivering webinars to a global audience.

Fasting is a shared practice across all the communities and religions featured in this book, to varying degrees; in the Hindu faith the devout will often fast before puja (worship); Christian/Catholic Goans fast for Lent. Research has shown that there are significant health benefits to fasting, from managing blood pressure to cell regeneration to controlling blood sugar levels, cholesterol, heart disease.

From a desi perspective, Southeast Asian diets, particularly for the older generation, have often crossed over and have not really evolved to the new environment. You don't need to have that same diet on a daily basis when you are less active and have an office job that requires you to be sedentary for most of the day; which has led to health problems such as diabetes.

What so many of us do in the West is eat until we are full and we make ourselves feel ill. Then we take a short break from eating, and then do it all over again. But by breaking this cycle we are giving our bodies the time to recover. Fareeha is emphatic in stressing that as a dietician she would never suggest to her clients that they should fast all year round, but rather would promote healthy habits. Intermittent fasting as a short-term choice to cleanse and reset our bodies and overall health is one thing, but she does not advocate this long-term. A form of fasting she does support (outside of the holy month) is to keep a twelve-hour gap. So if your evening meal was at 7 p.m., the next time to eat again should be 7 a.m. and not before. 'This approach will stop bingeing at night, is a good habit and gives your digestive system a rest and time to rejuvenate.'

Fasting isn't suitable or sustainable for everybody, however, due to the adverse health effects. Fareeha tells me the important thing to note is that these groups (see below) are even exempted by the religion, and can give fidya instead.

Illness: *This can be mental or physical illness and for those who are dependent on medication.*

Children: *Children need nutrition, food and hydration for their growing bodies.*

Breastfeeding: *Women require a constant supply of hydration and nutrition when they are breastfeeding.*

Pregnant women: *The nutritional requirement increases during pregnancy, specifically in the second and third trimesters, therefore it is extremely important for pregnant women to keep themselves nourished.*

Elderly: *Fasting can put the weak and frail at risk of many health complications.*

To Fareeha, Ramadan and Eid are a time for celebration. It is that part of the year when families make time to be with each other and eat together, to connect, and enjoying indulgent food is an essential part of that. It's about sensible moderation, portion control and not eating such rich food habitually. 'The most important thing to remember is to enjoy what you eat and not feel guilty about it.'

British turnips are bang in season from October through to March. The humble turnip is often overlooked in favour of its racier root veg cousins – parsnips and carrots. However, the slow cooking yields a delicious sweetness and, paired with lamb, spice and heat – a bewitching combination. The slow-cooked meat on the bone adds a full-bodied depth of flavour, and teasing out the meltingly soft bone marrow is utterly irresistible! The Kashmiri basar masala really sets this dish apart.

SPICED LAMB SHANKS } WITH SHALGAM (TURNIP)

SERVES 4

4 lamb shanks (these will vary in size, so I haven't specified weight)

2 bay leaves

2 black cardamom pods

3 whole cloves

5 whole peppercorns

5cm cassia bark
vegetable oil, for cooking

2 brown onions, finely sliced into half-moons

30g ginger, grated

30g garlic, grated

1–2 bird's-eye chillies, split in half lengthways

1 teaspoon ground turmeric

1½ teaspoons basar masala (see page 81)

2 teaspoons sea salt, or to taste

2 x 400g tins of chopped tomatoes, blitzed to a purée

2 heaped tablespoons Greek yoghurt

2 small turnips, peeled and cut into chunky dice

a pinch of Kasuri methi (dried fenugreek)

1 tablespoon chopped fresh coriander

1. Put the shanks into a large saucepan and cover them with water. Add the whole spices: bay leaves, black cardamom, cloves, peppercorns and cassia. Bring to the boil, then simmer the meat for 30–45 minutes. Remove the lamb shanks and set aside. Don't discard the cooking liquid, as you may need it later.

2. Meanwhile, make the masala. In a separate pan, heat a few tablespoons of oil on a medium to high heat. Tip in the sliced onions, then reduce the heat to medium and cook for about 10 minutes until softened. Add the ginger, garlic and chillies.

3. After 10 minutes, add the turmeric, basar masala and salt. Toast these for 30 seconds, adding a splash of water if the pan becomes too dry, so the spices don't stick and burn, then pour in the tomatoes. Increase the heat and bring to a simmer. Allow to cook out for 5–10 minutes. When you can see the oil separate on the surface and it has taken on the tomato colour, that means it's cooked and ready to taste. Check your seasoning here. If it needs more chillies add them now, along with the yoghurt, mixing well. Remove from the heat until the lamb is ready.

→

4. Gently place the partly cooked lamb shanks in the masala and stir together, coating all the pieces. You may want to add a splash of water – you can use the cooking stock from the shanks – but beware of adding too much as the meat will shrink and will also release liquid during cooking. (If you do add too much water you can correct it at the end by simmering, uncovered, to reduce the sauce.)

5. Bring to the boil, then reduce the heat to a simmer, cover with a cartouche, and put a lid on the pan. Cook low and slow for 1½ hours. After this point, mix in the diced turnips and a pinch of methi (you may need to add more water – use the lamb cooking stock). Then return the pan to the hob and simmer for an additional 30 minutes, or until the meat is meltingly soft and unctuous and the turnips are cooked through.

6. Finally, scatter over a flurry of chopped coriander leaves and any other garnish you like. Serve with freshly cooked chapattis, or rice if you prefer.

COOK'S NOTE You can make a ginger/garlic paste as a time-saver. You just need to blitz an equal volume of each in a chopper or blender with a touch of water. You can keep this fresh in the fridge or store it in a freezer bag – flatten it like bark, and snap off whatever you need (see page 11).

This is a lovely and simple naan recipe that you can easily re-create at home, if you have a gas hob. You will need a tawa (a flat, round cast-iron pan) for this, though I have seen these cooked over coals or wood in a kadhai firebowl (like a wok), and you can use an upside-down dome-shaped cast-iron karahi: place it inside the firebowl to heat, then place the naan on the scorching hot karahi dome. Certainly a lot of theatre for your guests! You could make these in a non-stick frying pan, but you won't get the same effect – and skip the water step or you'll wreck your pan – though the naans will still be very tasty, especially when slathered with garlic and coriander butter!

LAVASA NAAN BREAD

MAKES 4 NAANS

5g easy-blend dried yeast (if doubling up you can use 7–8g dried yeast)

50ml warm water
5g caster sugar
230g plain flour
a pinch of salt

1. The first thing to do is 'bloom' the yeast. Place it in a small bowl with the warm water and sugar, and set aside for 10 minutes, by which time it will have bubbled up and activated.
2. Mix the flour and salt in a large bowl, then tip in the yeast mixture. Splay your fingers and start mixing. You will need some additional water to bring this into a dough – I used about 110ml, but this will vary.
3. Knead the dough for 7–8 minutes – you want a smooth dough that is neither too firm nor too soft, but somewhere in between. Place in a clean bowl and cover with cling film. Let it rest in a warm place for 1–2 hours, until it has doubled in size.
4. When you are ready to make the naan, heat your tawa on the maximum heat setting of your gas hob.
5. Knock the dough back, give it a light knead to bring it into a smooth dough again, and divide it into four equal portions. Take a portion and roll it into an 18–20cm circle on a lightly floured surface. Brush the side facing you with water – this will help it to stick to the tawa.
6. Place the wet side on the hot tawa, gently pressing it down. When you see the naan bubble up, carefully flip the tawa, holding it above the naked flame so the uncooked side can cook over direct heat. You are effectively recreating what happens in a tandoor oven.
7. Using tongs, remove the cooked naan from the tawa and repeat. You may wish to slather your naan with garlic and coriander butter (see cook's note).

COOK'S NOTE
You can whip up the garlic and coriander butter by mixing a couple of tablespoons of chopped fresh coriander, a grated garlic clove and a sprinkling of salt into 75–100g of softened butter.

Masala tchot (you don't pronounce the first 't') is a hugely popular street food, though unlike most grab-and-go fare it is incredibly healthy and low-fat, as well as being utterly delicious! It's made up of soft lavasa naan, smothered with a radish chutney, and topped with mashed white beans. The spicing is rather subtle, but the flavours and textures certainly amuse one's bouche! Having never tried this before, it was a wonderful new discovery.

MASALA TCHOT – MASHED PEA WRAP } WITH RADISH CHUTNEY

MAKES 4 WRAPS

lavasa naan bread (see opposite)
200g dried white peas (vatana) or dried chickpeas, soaked overnight in plenty of water with ½ teaspoon bicarbonate of soda

Radish chutney
½ a red onion
100g British red radishes, topped and tailed
1 green finger chilli, finely sliced
½ teaspoon toasted cumin seeds
¼ teaspoon mild Kashmiri chilli powder
¼ teaspoon sea salt, or to taste
100g thick Greek yoghurt or labneh
1 tablespoon chopped fresh mint or coriander

For poaching the peas
1 teaspoon sea salt
1 green finger chilli, split in half lengthways
½ teaspoon ground turmeric
2 whole cloves
4 black peppercorns

1. First prepare your lavasa naan (see page 70).
2. While the naan dough is proving, coarsely grate the onion and radishes, then squeeze out the liquid using a tea towel or muslin cloth. Place in a mixing bowl, then add the sliced chillies, toasted cumin seeds, chilli powder and salt. Add the yoghurt or labneh and give everything a good mix, followed by your choice of chopped herb. Have a taste, adjust if necessary and refrigerate.
3. The soaked peas will need to be thoroughly rinsed in four or five changes of water, to get rid of any remnants of bicarbonate of soda. Once washed, place the peas in a large saucepan and cover with water – be generous so the pan doesn't boil dry. Add the salt, chilli, turmeric, cloves and peppercorns and bring to the boil. Reduce to a simmer and cook for an hour, or until the peas are tender.
4. Drain the peas thoroughly – they should be quite dry. Lightly mash. Have a little taste – you will probably need a touch more salt. Keep warm while you finish making the lavasa naan.
5. Smother the hot naan first with a layer of radish chutney, then with a layer of mashed peas, then roll and apply to face.

Kashmiris love a kebab – beef, chicken or lamb – and there is a huge variety of kebabs ranging from boti kebabs, which are made from chunks of marinated meat, to finely ground galouti kebabs designed for toothless moghul nawabs. It is widely believed that it was Turkish traders who introduced the kebab to India, originating from 'shish kebab'. Shish is the Turkish word for 'sword', which Turkish soldiers used to skewer meat and grill on an open fire. Seekh kebabs are made from shaping spiced minced meat around a skewer, to form that iconic cylindrical shape. Mine are served with a Kashmiri lavasa naan and a yoghurt and walnut chutney, which is served with wazwan dishes.

SEEKH KEBAB NAANWICH } WITH YOGHURT AND WALNUT CHUTNEY

MAKES 4–6 KEBABS

1 large brown onion
1 teaspoon cumin seeds
½ teaspoon fennel seeds
2 teaspoons sea salt, or to taste

1½ teaspoons basar masala (see page 81)
2 teaspoons minced chillies, or to taste
15g garlic, grated
15g ginger, grated
2 tablespoons chopped fresh coriander leaves

500g lamb or beef mince (ideally 15–20 per cent)
vegetable oil
yoghurt and walnut chutney (see opposite)
lavasa naan (see page 70)

Garnish
pomegranate seeds
finely sliced red onion
finely sliced radishes
finely sliced cucumber
deep-fried green finger chillies, sprinkled with chaat masala

1. Grate the onion using a box grater, using long sweeps – you don't want a mush. Place the contents in the middle of a clean tea towel or muslin cloth, gather up the edges, twist the loose fabric, and squeeze out all the liquid. These grated onions need to be as dry as possible. Place them in a large mixing bowl.
2. Add the cumin, fennel, salt, basar masala, minced chillies, garlic, ginger and chopped coriander to the bowl. Mix together with a fork. Test a little and check the seasoning.
3. Now mix the minced meat into the onion mixture; use your hands – they're the best tool.
4. Cook a little test patty in a frying pan with a scant amount of oil in it. This is a foolproof way to check that the seasoning is spot on, and your last chance to make any adjustments.
5. Divide the seasoned mince into four or six equal parts, and shape each one around a metal or soaked bamboo skewer to form a cylindrical kebab. Have a bowl full of water handy – wet palms will stop the mixture sticking to your hands.
6. Grill until the kebabs are cooked through, turning so all sides get some heat. You could use your oven grill, in which case set it to the highest temperature and place the kebabs as close to the hot grill as possible,

or on a barbecue. They will take around 8–10 minutes. You can refrigerate the kebabs beforehand to allow them to firm up, and prep ahead.

7. Wrap your kebab in the lavasa naan to make a naanwich. You can either load up the naan before you roll or serve the garnishes and yoghurt dip separately. Would it be rude to have this with chips? I think not, go for it!

YOGHURT AND WALNUT CHUTNEY

The majority of India's walnut (akhrot) production comes from Kashmir. I remember my granny would always have a stash of walnuts at Christmas, which is what I associate them with – as well as lychees, apricots, almonds, pomegranates and much more. These are all grown in Kashmir, which neighbours Punjab, and she had a knack for sniffing out the best produce. This chutney is served with rich wazwan meat dishes and is a lovely accompaniment to the seekh kebab opposite.

½ a red onion, grated
1 green chilli, finely sliced

5g fresh mint leaves
¼ teaspoon salt, or to taste

200g thick Greek yoghurt or labneh
25g walnuts, roughly chopped

1. Use a muslin cloth or similar to squeeze out the water from the grated onion, otherwise the chutney will be sloppy. Put the onion into a mixing bowl and add the finely sliced chilli, then chop the mint and chuck that in too, along with the salt.
2. Finally mix through the yoghurt, followed by the walnuts, then taste and make any adjustments. Refrigerate until serving.

Every region has its own pakora recipes, which vary from village to village, home to home. They are one of the ultimate and most widely recognized Indian snacks. Pakoras can come in meat and fish varieties also. It's the use of typical Kashmiri spices like ginger and fennel that makes this particular recipe distinct. Whenever my mum would make them, we would have the leftovers in a Punjabi kadhi – a yoghurt-based curry. Not one of my favourites, but I very much enjoyed hot pakoras dunked in ketchup! As does my son now.

POTATO AND SPINACH PAKORAS

MAKES 15–18 PAKORAS DEPENDING ON THE SIZE*

* You will need an equal volume (not weight) of spinach, potato and onion. I suggest you start with the spinach (see step 1 below).

100g spinach
1 large brown onion, finely sliced into half-moons (approx. 190g prepped weight)
1 large potato (approx. 270g prepped weight)
3 heaped tablespoons yoghurt

1 heaped tablespoon cumin seeds
2 teaspoons sea salt
1 teaspoon basar masala (see page 81)
½ teaspoon fennel powder
½ teaspoon ground ginger

2–3 teaspoons chillies, finely sliced
30g fresh coriander, chopped
1 egg, beaten
approx. 100g chickpea flour (besan)
vegetable oil, for deep-frying
chaat masala (optional)

1. To chop the spinach, roll clumps of it into a cigar shape, and slice it 2cm thick. You want an equal volume of spinach, onion and potato. Next prep your onion, then peel the potato and slice 3–5mm thick, across not lengthways, and cut into 3mm matchsticks. Place the potato matchsticks in a bowl and cover with cold water. Drain thoroughly before you add them to the batter at step 5.
2. In a large bowl, mix together the yoghurt, cumin, salt, basar masala, fennel, ginger, finely sliced chillies, and chopped coriander. Have a taste, and if you are happy with the flavour, mix in the beaten egg.
3. Add the chickpea flour and stir to a paste. The consistency needs to be such that it will coat the veggies and bind, so it needs to be a thick batter.
4. Heat your oil for deep-frying to 170–180°C, or if using a wok or kadhai you can do the 'bread sizzle' test to check the oil is at the right temperature.
5. Now mix the prepped vegetables into the batter, using your hands to squish everything together. You can add a tiny splash of water if need be but not too much – the salt will draw out water from the veg.
6. Time to fry. You need 2 tablespoons, one to scoop out the mixture (ensure you have an equal amount of all the veggies in each scoop), the other to help gently place it in the hot oil. Be mindful not to overload the wok or fryer. Deep-fry the pakoras until cooked and golden, turning over as required.

7. Remove from the oil and drain on kitchen paper. You can hit the pakoras with a sprinkle of chaat masala for an extra flavour kiss should you wish to pucker up. Serve immediately, with tamarind sauce, minted yoghurt or tomato ketchup, a cold beer or a cup of chai. You decide, pick and mix!

COOK'S NOTE Pakoras are also known as bhajis in some regions of India. We like to make butties up north, and a bhaji butty is a desi classic. Butter 2 thick slices of white farmhouse bread, fill with hot pakoras and apply to face.

Rogan josh is a headline wazwan dish, and is normally made with lamb or mutton (note that many Indians refer to goat as mutton as well). This is a rich and spicy curry, with a deep red colour, owing to the use of red Kashmiri chilli paste and mawal – an extract from dried cockscomb flowers that imparts a red colouring. There are two versions of this dish, one with onions and garlic made by Kashmiri Muslims and one without, the Kashmiri Hindu version. I'm making a Muslim-style recipe – of course Hindus would not eat beef either – which is traditionally made with a shallot called praan. Naturally I am using Yorkshire beef, which will be cooked low and slow for 3–4 hours. Oxtail lends itself well to this curry, as would beef shin; I feel only bone-in meat will do.

OXTAIL ROGAN JOSH

SERVES 4

Chilli paste
8–10 dried red Kashmiri chillies, stalks removed
40ml hot water
sea salt

Rogan josh
1kg oxtail (you can use lamb shoulder – ask your butcher to cut it into small pieces; if using lamb, reduce cooking time accordingly and reduce the water to 300–500ml)
vegetable oil, for cooking
2 bay leaves
2–3 black cardamoms
4 green cardamoms (bruise to release the seeds)
5cm cassia bark or cinnamon
5 whole cloves
6 black peppercorns
1½ teaspoons cumin seeds
1 teaspoon fennel seeds
approx. 150g banana shallots, finely sliced lengthways
20g garlic, grated
20g ginger, grated
1 level teaspoon ground turmeric
1½ teaspoons garam masala
1–2 teaspoons mild Kashmiri chilli powder
2 teaspoons sea salt, or to taste
100–120g Greek yoghurt
1 litre water
a pinch of Kasuri methi (dried fenugreek)
chopped fresh coriander leaves
a squeeze of lime juice

1. Start by making the chilli paste. Soak the dried chillies in the hot water to start the rehydration process. After 15 minutes transfer the chillies and their liquid to a small pan, bring to the boil, then reduce the heat to medium and simmer for 5 minutes. The chillies will really swell up at this point and the liquid will reduce. Cool completely.
2. Grind the chillies and any remaining liquid to a paste in a small blender or using a pestle and mortar with a little sea salt as an abrasive. Set aside.
3. Pat the meat dry with kitchen paper. Heat a little vegetable oil in a large lidded saucepan, then add the meat and seal and brown it on all sides on a high heat. You will need to do this in batches, as you don't want to overcrowd the pan, and be careful as it will spit. Set the meat aside on a large plate.

4. Using the same pan on a medium heat, add a little extra oil and the whole spices: bay leaves, black and green cardamoms, cassia/cinnamon, cloves, peppercorns, cumin and fennel. When they start to release their aromas, tip in the sliced shallots and cook low and slow for 15 minutes, or until they are soft and lightly caramelized.
5. Add the garlic, ginger and chilli paste and cook out for a few minutes, then add the ground spices – turmeric, garam masala and chilli powder – and the salt and toast for 30 seconds. Stir in the yoghurt.
6. Return the seared meat to the pot and pour in the water – the meat should be submerged. Bring the masala to the boil, then reduce to a simmer and cover with the lid.
7. Simmer for 3–4 hours, or until the meat is tender. You can place a cartouche over the top and bake in the oven at 160°C fan if your saucepan is ovenproof or you use a cast-iron casserole.
8. Check and adjust the seasoning half an hour before it's cooked, then sprinkle with a little Kasuri methi and cook uncovered from this point to allow the gravy to reduce and become really unctuous. Garnish with freshly chopped coriander leaves and a kiss of lime juice to enliven. An authentic rogan josh should have a layer of rich red oil floating on the top, the oil having taken on the colour of the Kashmiri chillies.
9. Serve with rice, naan or chapattis.

Kashmir is renowned for its produce, from an abundance of fruit such as apples, pears, pomegranates and cherries, to spices such as precious saffron, to vegetables, rice, wheat, barley and corn, to highly coveted cashmere wool. I wanted to design a recipe that captures this as well as bringing in the Persian and Mughal influences, with sweet and savoury flavours and celebrating a plentiful region. The addition of the pakoras makes this a complete dish, and with the condiments – next level. See the cook's note for the meat version – it can't be Kashmiri without a meat option!

JEWELLED CAULIFLOWER RICE BOWL } WITH PAKORAS

SERVES 4

1 medium-sized cauliflower (approx. 400g of grated cauliflower florets – you can replace the cauliflower with freekeh or flattened poha rice, allow 60g of uncooked grain per person)
2 tablespoons vegetable oil

1 teaspoon cumin seeds
5g garlic, grated
5g ginger, grated
2 green cardamom pods (release the seeds and grind to a powder)
1 level teaspoon ground turmeric
1 teaspoon sea salt, or to taste
30–40g flaked almonds (or pistachios), toasted

4 dried apricots, chopped
2 tablespoons golden sultanas
1 tablespoon sour cherries, chopped (you could use barberries or cranberries)
1 tablespoon chopped fresh coriander
a handful of pomegranate seeds

potato and spinach pakoras (see page 74)

Condiments
a drizzle of pomegranate molasses
yoghurt and walnut chutney (see page 73)

1. Grate the cauliflower using the coarse side of a box grater or pulse in a food processor until the florets resemble rice. Set aside.
2. Heat the oil in a large frying pan, wok or kadhai over a medium to high heat. Add the cumin seeds and let them release their aromas, then add the garlic and ginger. Allow these to turn lightly golden, then reduce the heat to medium.
3. Add the ground cardamom, turmeric and salt and toast for a few seconds, then tip in the cauliflower 'rice'. Stir everything together and see the white cauliflower turn golden with turmeric.
4. Let the cauliflower heat through, then stir in the toasted almonds and dried fruit.
5. Garnish with chopped coriander and pomegranate seeds, drizzle with pomegranate molasses, and serve with potato and spinach pakoras and yoghurt and walnut chutney.

COOK'S NOTE This is a lovely side dish to grilled meats and various kebabs, and of course you can make it with freekeh, basmati rice or cooked poha (flattened rice). I often have it with tandoori lamb chops (see tandoori marinade, page 36). Marinate the meat overnight and grill the chops to your liking. Serve with naan breads and radish or yoghurt and walnut chutney on the side.

This is hands down the best way to eat chicken livers. Offal is very popular in Kashmiri cooking – it's rich in iron and nutrients. Chicken livers are my preference, quick to cook, soft and delicate; they're a much gentler introduction to offal than lamb liver. Kashmiris do not waste any part of the animal, and quite rightly; not so much nose-to-tail eating, more beak-to-toe in this case. Chicken kidneys are also a delicious delicacy, but they take a bit more cooking and preparation.

KALEJI KA SAALAN ON TOAST – CHICKEN LIVER MASALA ON TOAST

SERVES 4

vegetable oil, for cooking
1½ teaspoons cumin seeds
1 black cardamom
2 green cardamoms (bruised to release the seeds)

1 large brown onion, finely sliced into half-moons
15g ginger, grated
15g garlic, grated
2–3 green finger chillies, split in half lengthways
1½ teaspoons garam masala or

basar masala (see opposite)
1 teaspoon sea salt, or to taste
1 level teaspoon ground turmeric
100–150ml passata (you can use fresh tomatoes if you prefer)

500g chicken livers (remove any sinew; cut larger pieces in half)

Garnish
chopped fresh coriander
finely sliced red onion
lemon juice

1. Heat 4 tablespoons of vegetable oil in a large heavy-bottomed lidded saucepan or sauté pan on a medium to high heat. Add the cumin seeds and cardamoms, and once the aromas hit your nostrils, add the onions. Reduce the heat to medium and sauté until the onions have softened and are lightly golden – this will take 10–15 minutes.
2. Add the ginger, garlic and chillies, and allow these to cook out for a couple of minutes. I think the livers can take a good kick of chilli.
3. Add the garam masala or basar masala, salt and turmeric, and toast for 30 seconds.
4. Now pour in the passata. Stir and bring to a simmer for a few minutes. You may want to add a splash or two of water to make more 'gravy'. Taste the sauce, adjust the seasoning, and once you are happy, gently place the livers in the pan and coat with the masala.
5. Crank up the heat so the livers can come to temperature and seal, then reduce slightly and place the lid on to trap in the steam. The livers will be cooked in about 8–10 minutes.
6. Finally sprinkle over the chopped coriander, finely sliced red onion and a squeeze of lemon. Serve on fire-kissed toast of your choice, slathered in butter of course. Dig in with glee!

BASAR MASALA

You can buy this masala from an Indian grocer, but nothing beats making your own.

- -

1 tablespoon cumin
   seeds
1 tablespoon coriander
   seeds
1 tablespoon fennel
   seeds
5 whole cloves
8 green cardamoms
1 black cardamom
5cm cassia bark or
   cinnamon, broken
   into pieces

1 level teaspoon
   fenugreek seeds
1 teaspoon black
   pepper
1 mace blade
   (or ¼ teaspoon
   ground mace)
2 bay leaves
2 tablespoons mild
   Kashmiri chilli powder
a generous pinch of
   nutmeg

1. Toast all the spices – apart from the chilli powder and nutmeg – in a dry frying pan on a medium heat. Stir continuously and don't let any spices burn. The aromas will soon waft up. Remove from the heat and allow to cool.

2. Using a coffee or spice grinder, grind the spices to a powder, and mix with the chilli powder and nutmeg.

3. Store in a sterilized airtight container. If kept out of direct sunlight in a cool, dry place, it will keep for up to a year. (You can tell a masala should be discarded when it has lost its fragrant aroma.)

A wazwan starter dish, these are traditionally made with mutton ribs, but lamb ribs are just as good. They're cooked twice: first poached until tender in an aromatic broth, then oven roasted with a honey and vinegar glaze and spice rub. These are very rich, and I like to serve rich grilled and tandoori meats with sharp pickles, such as watermelon (see page 84). Whipped feta is also a delightful counterpoint, and herbs such as dill and mint.

TABAKH MAAZ – LAMB RIBS

SERVES 4

1kg lamb riblets, cut into pieces (ask your butcher to do it)

Poaching broth
2 litres hot water
20g ginger, grated
20g garlic, grated
3 bay leaves
1 whole mace blade

5cm cassia bark or cinnamon
2 black cardamom pods
4 green cardamom pods (bruise to release the seeds)
8 black peppercorns
6 whole cloves
2 teaspoons ground turmeric
2 teaspoons sea salt

1 tablespoon fennel powder
½ tablespoon ground ginger
250ml milk

Dry spice rub
1 teaspoon basar masala (see page 81)
½ teaspoon garlic granules
½ teaspoon onion granules
½ teaspoon sea salt

Rib glaze
65g runny honey
13ml red wine vinegar

Garnish
finely sliced red onion
dill fronds and torn mint leaves
pickled watermelon (see page 84)
whipped feta
flatbreads

1. Fill a large saucepan with 2 litres of hot water (use a kettle for speed), and bring to the boil on a high heat. Just as it's coming to the boil, add all the poaching broth ingredients, apart from the milk.
2. Place the ribs in the boiling broth. You can drop the heat to an equivalent of about 8 out of 10 but you need to maintain a rolling boil.
3. After 30 minutes remove the ribs. Add the milk to the pan and bring back to the boil. Replace the ribs and continue to poach for another 20 minutes, or until tender.
4. Remove the ribs from the broth and set aside. (If you are cooking in two stages, refrigerate or freeze the ribs in the broth so they don't dry out.)
5. Heat your oven to 200°C fan and line two large baking trays with greaseproof paper. Mix together the ingredients for the dry spice rub. Make up the glaze by mixing the honey and vinegar together in a small bowl and brush this on to the ribs, then place these in a large mixing bowl. Sprinkle evenly all over with the dry spice rub, then place the coated ribs on the prepared trays – half on each. Roast for 20-30 minutes, turning them at the halfway point, until sticky and caramelized.
6. Serve with finely sliced red onion, dill fronds and mint leaves, pickled watermelon, whipped feta and flatbreads.

I first tried compressed watermelon at chefs' school, where it was made using a vac-pack machine. The watermelon pieces were placed in a gastrique pickling liquor. The compression really changed the texture – not to mention the pop of colour – and they were then cut into small cubes and served as a canapé, topped with a whipped feta quenelle and a deep-fried basil leaf. Utterly divine! Here's a home-style recipe that you don't need a vac-pack machine for. This pickle is delicious with grilled meat, kebabs, tandoori meats and paneer, grilled halloumi, or indeed whipped feta. Thank you, Chef Ross – aka Ashburton's answer to Poldark – for the inspiration.

PICKLED WATERMELON

SERVES 4–6

½ a large watermelon

Pickling liquor
125ml white wine vinegar
100g caster sugar
a pinch of salt

2 teaspoons coriander seeds, toasted, then lightly crushed in a pestle and mortar

1. You can prep the elements ahead prior to serving. Cut the watermelon into bite-sized cubes, discarding the rind, white flesh and any visible pips. Place in an airtight container and refrigerate.
2. Mix the ingredients for the pickling liquor together in a large mixing bowl, making sure the sugar is completely dissolved. Decant into an airtight container and refrigerate.
3. Place the watermelon on your presentation dish and drizzle all over with the pickling liquor prior to serving. You can steep for longer if you prefer lip-puckering pickles.
4. Serve with barbecued, grilled and tandoori meats, paneer, halloumi, feta . . . it's very versatile! Some finely sliced red onion in addition to the above is lovely too.

I don't want my vegetarian friends to feel excluded, so here's a non-meat alternative to the lamb ribs. I've given these corn ribs a Kashmiri accent by smothering them in a basar masala butter. They are super-easy to make, and the hardest part is actually cutting the corn cobs into quarters – you will need a large sharp knife and some good knife skills. If you don't possess both of these, I would suggest you grill your corn cobs whole or snap them in half. Meat eaters will be VERY jealous!

MASALA CORN RIBS

SERVES 2

2 whole corn on the cob

Masala butter
70g softened butter, at room temperature
1 teaspoon basar masala (see page 81)

½ teaspoon garlic granules
½ teaspoon onion granules
½ teaspoon sea salt

To serve
charred lime halves (see page 196)
chopped fresh coriander
yoghurt and walnut chutney (see page 73)

1. Set your oven to 180°C fan.
2. Mix together all the ingredients for the masala butter and set aside at room temperature.
3. Please take the utmost care when cutting the sweetcorn – I can't stress this enough. I find that the easiest way to do it is to lay each cob flat and use the knife to score a line along the centre from top to bottom. Insert the tip of the knife in the centre – where you have already scored – and apply pressure downwards to cut straight through, then repeat on the other side. Once you have cut the cob in half, quarter it – it doesn't matter if any of the pieces break. Use whatever method works best for you.
4. Brush each piece generously with the masala butter, then place on a baking sheet lined with greaseproof paper.
5. Bake for about 25 minutes (I love the way these curl up). You could also air-fry them in half the time. Brush with extra masala butter as soon as you take them out of the oven.
6. Serve with charred lime halves, a garnish of chopped coriander and yoghurt and walnut chutney. Though I do like to have these with my spicy firecracker mayo too (see page 206)!

Kashmiris love meat so much, you will find they also put it in their vegetarian dishes! Ruangan chaman is a paneer dish cooked with tomatoes, and is often included as a non-meat dish in the multi-course wazwan. I'm opting for achari paneer instead, which is very popular throughout the northern regions of India, including Kashmir. It is rich, tangy and spicy, because of the pickling spices used in the masala and the mustard oil; this is paneer with a lot of attitude! I find the sweetness in the corn offers a delightful counterpoint.

ACHARI PANEER } WITH SWEETCORN

SERVES 4

2–3 tablespoons mustard oil

2 whole dried Kashmiri chillies

½ teaspoon nigella seeds

¼ teaspoon fenugreek seeds

½ teaspoon fennel seeds

1 teaspoon cumin seeds

½ teaspoon black mustard seeds

1½ red onions, cut into 3cm dice

1–2 green finger chillies, split in half lengthways

10g ginger, grated

10g garlic, grated

1 level teaspoon ground turmeric

1 teaspoon mild Kashmiri chilli powder

1 teaspoon garam masala or basar masala (see page 81)

1 teaspoon sea salt, or to taste

100g tinned sweetcorn (drained weight)

½ x 400g tin of tomatoes, blitzed to a purée

400g paneer, cubed into bite-sized pieces (freshly made is best. If using shop-bought, plunge it into a bowl of just-boiled water for 5 minutes, then drain and pat dry with kitchen paper to give it that soft home-made feel)

approx. 100ml water

1. Heat the mustard oil in a large saucepan on a medium to high heat, then add your whole spices: dried chillies, nigella seeds, fenugreek seeds, fennel seeds, cumin seeds and mustard seeds. When they start to release their aromas, add the diced onions and split chillies. Reduce the heat to medium and allow the onions to soften for a few minutes.

2. Add the ginger and garlic, cook out for a few minutes, then add the ground spices – turmeric, chilli powder and garam masala – and the salt, and let them toast in the pan for 30 seconds. Add the sweetcorn and stir, ensuring the kernels are coated in the mixture. You may need a splash of water to prevent the spices from sticking and burning.

3. Tip in the tomatoes, then give everything another stir and simmer for 10 minutes. When you see the oil separate on the surface of the masala, have a taste. Adjust if necessary.

4. Add the cubed paneer along with the water and gently mix together. You can add a touch more water if you'd like more of a gravy. Bring to a simmer and cook for a further 10 minutes or so to develop the flavours.

5. Serve with rice or hot buttered chapattis.

Folks from Yorkshire are very specific about their tea, and it's home to some of the UK's most famous tea rooms. The only trouble is deciding which delectable cake recipe to put in this chapter; I am spoilt for choice. The very first proper afternoon tea I attended was at an after-school Latin club; these took place towards the end of the summer term and my teacher, Madame Walker (she was my French teacher too), had commissioned some of my mum's samosas as part of the spread. The crustless sandwiches I wasn't too bothered about, but I made a beeline for the quiche and the cakes . . . flapjacks, tarts, millionaire's shortbread, sponge cakes. Lemon drizzle is one of my all-time favourites, and this is my mother-in-law's famous WI-stamped recipe – except I've added poppy seeds, which I adore in baking, as do Kashmiris.

LEMON AND POPPY SEED DRIZZLE CAKE

SERVES 6

115g Stork margarine or softened unsalted butter, at room temperature
finely grated zest of 1 lemon

170g caster sugar
2 eggs
170g self-raising flour
4 tablespoons milk
1 tablespoon poppy seeds

Drizzle
75g icing sugar
juice of 1 lemon

1. You will need a 900g (2lb) loaf tin and a non-stick loaf tin liner.
2. Cream together the margarine or butter, lemon zest and sugar in a large mixing bowl.
3. Whisk in the eggs – don't worry if the mixture looks like it has split.
4. Sift in the flour, and mix with the eggs, sugar and margarine. Loosen the mixture with the milk, and stir in the poppy seeds.
5. Put the batter into your lined non-stick loaf tin, then transfer it to the middle of a cold oven and immediately set the temperature to 160°C fan. Bake for an hour; you can check after 45 minutes, as ovens vary. (If your loaf cake cracks it's because the oven was too hot. It will still taste yummy, mind you.)
6. Make up the drizzle just before the cake is due out of the oven. If you'd like a hard crust to form, don't make the drizzle too runny, just a pourable consistency – go steady with the lemon juice. If you'd like a very moist cake, you can make the drizzle more runny but you won't get a crust. It all depends on the size of your lemon!
7. Remove the cake from the oven, but leave it in its tin. Pierce the loaf all over with a skewer, then pour over the drizzle while it's still hot. This will ensure the syrup is absorbed much better – spoon over any syrup that pools at the edges.
8. Allow to cool completely before serving. That's the only difficult part. This cake also freezes very well if you choose to batch-make.

GLASGOW

PAKISTANI COMMUNITY

Glasgow is the largest city in Scotland by population, and the most
ethnically diverse. This cultural melting pot offers us a very exciting food
scene, and the coming together of the region's fantastic natural produce
and larder, coupled with cooking techniques from different cultures, lends
itself to a delicious culinary evolution. The city's Pakistani community makes
up the largest ethnic minority. Migration grew steadily from the 1950s, from
a number of different communities. Many early Pakistani settlers came to
the Gorbals area and worked as 'pedlars', selling goods door-to-door, and
in the public transport system. A large number came from the Pakistani
side of Punjab, notably Faisalabad and Lahore. By the 1970s, people from
the community had established themselves as entrepreneurs, business
and restaurant owners, in the professions and local government, all of
which is archived and catalogued through Glasgow Museums together
with Colourful Heritage. Since 1990 the Glasgow Mela has celebrated the
contribution its multicultural communities make – a festival of music, dance
and arts hosted by the City Council.

SABRINA BUTT (AGED 35)

Presently a full-time mum, formerly a buyer for a fast-fashion brand

Sabrina is a third-generation Scot who proudly identifies herself as a Scottish Pakistani. She lives in south Glasgow and is a full-time mum to two children under five. Her story starts with her paternal grandfather, who came to Glasgow in 1949. Following Independence and partition in 1947, he moved from Jalandhar in East Punjab – which remained part of India – to Faisalabad (formerly Lyallpur), in the newly formed state of Pakistan on the west side of Punjab. The partition of India was complicated: put in the simplest terms it was driven by religious division between Muslims and Hindus, resulting in the creation of a principally Muslim state of Pakistan, and a Hindu-dominated state of India. The provinces of Punjab and Bengal were split along religious lines, resulting in the displacement of millions of people, creating refugees on both sides in the most large-scale and brutal movement of people.

Sabrina's grandad would often tell his children and grandchildren the story of how he came to Scotland with only £5 in his pocket. Like many immigrants at that time, he came to the Gorbals area. He only intended to stay for a short while en route to Canada, but ended up staying and setting down roots in a city and a country he came to love too much to ever want to leave. He was able to speak a good amount of English, and started off selling door-to-door: tights (stockings) and clothes. After a short while, once he was settled, he called for his wife to join him. Sabrina's grandmother was able to sew and work a sewing machine, so the two of them worked in unison – she would make the dresses and various other garments for her husband to sell. The business grew organically and soon they were able to move into large-scale manufacturing and open a factory that went on to employ hundreds of people: '[That generation] had a different level of focus, they had to, to survive. He grafted, sheer blood, sweat and tears into making his life what it ultimately became. He faced cultural barriers and challenges, suffered setbacks, but the mentality was to just get on with things and not complain. He didn't really know anybody in the city apart from my grandmother and it was a real struggle to make ends meet. But he quickly found the gaps in the market and applied himself to filling those. He set up a very successful clothes manufacturing business (kilts and duffel coats), went on to open a factory employing so many local people and he contributed a huge amount to the community. Charity is culturally very important . . . he helped to fund the building of the Glasgow central mosque. Everybody knew him and he was very well respected.'

Sabrina tells me how focused her grandad was on making sure he adapted and fitted in to Scottish culture. He wanted to make a contribution to the wider community, not just his own, as an expression of gratitude for the opportunities afforded to him and the people who welcomed him. This is an important narrative to share, and a powerful sentiment that echoes down through the generations of his family.

We talk about the importance of charity, which is one of the five pillars of Islam. During the first lockdown Sabrina cooked meals for frontline workers during the holy month of Ramadan. The '1 million meals' initiative was set up to feed NHS staff, to keep them going through extended shifts while the virus was at its crippling peak. She was keen to contribute to the scheme and donated 250 meals in total: 'I very much acknowledge all my blessings and all that I have. So I believe it is important to give back. Donating money is one thing, but physically putting love into meals is more meaningful to me because I love to cook and feeding people is such a joy.'

I ask Sabrina why she's so passionate about fusion food: 'Being Pakistani and Scottish at the same time I've grown up here born and raised – as were my parents – so lived very much Scottish. But at the same time I can't ever forget my roots. I've grown up in a Pakistani household, very Westernized, and I grew up eating all the Western food that everybody else eats here, but then I also had lots of curries and proper traditional Pakistani and Indian food. My mum has always liked to blend flavours and has been a fusion cook all her life and because of that I've been exposed to the different tastes and textures. I just love spicy, flavourful food. When I say spicy, I don't necessarily mean heat but different layers of flavour. I like to blend them with pasta or spiced mashed potatoes to add an extra oomph to that. It speaks to all my taste buds.'

I daresay this is a sentiment shared by most second and third generation diaspora. Our identity is unique and that is transferred on to our food; we are not one or the other. Sabrina tells me about a memory that has stuck with her: she went to Pakistan when she was eighteen, and stayed for an extended period of time to visit her grandmother as a break before starting university. She went to a beauty parlour with her cousin to have her hair done: 'I'm not fluent in Urdu or Punjabi, but I got the gist of what she [the hairdresser] was saying to me, which was along the lines of: "You're not from here, are you? You look like a foreigner." And I hadn't said a single word to her; I hadn't even spoken from the time that I arrived. But it's always stuck with me, that memory . . . Maybe I am a foreigner in Pakistan.'

I joke that I'm surprised more of us don't have split personalities: balancing these very different identities isn't necessarily easy, and you find yourself having to justify yourself to each of them.

What could be more quintessentially Scottish than 'neeps and tatties', the traditional accompaniment to haggis – along with a wee dram of whisky – on chilly Burns Night! Swede is a delicious and underused vegetable, and a perfect partner to much-loved keema. The trick is to roast the swede separately, I find. It has a completely different texture to potatoes, and I much prefer it roasted, as the texture of the topping will be firmer than just boiling and mashing it. Of course you can also use 50/50 haggis to lamb mince in the keema for full effect. To me this desi twist on a British classic is sheer poetry.

NEEPS AND TATTIES KEEMA PIE – TWISTED SHEPHERD'S PIE

SERVES 4–6

Keema
vegetable oil, for cooking
1–2 teaspoons cumin seeds
1 black cardamom pod
5cm cassia bark or cinnamon
3 whole cloves
1 large brown onion, finely diced

15g ginger, grated
15g garlic, grated
1–2 teaspoons minced bird's-eye chillies, or to taste
1½ teaspoons garam masala
1 teaspoon ground turmeric
2 teaspoons sea salt (reduce if cooking with haggis, as it is already salty)

1 tablespoon tomato purée
100ml passata
500g lamb mince (10–15 per cent fat), or 250g lamb mince and 250g crumbled haggis
200ml water
a pinch of Kasuri methi (dried fenugreek)
80–100g frozen peas

Mash topping
1 swede, peeled and cut into 2.5cm dice (approx. 475g prepped weight)
sea salt and black pepper, to taste
vegetable oil, for cooking
4 Rooster potatoes, peeled and cut into 2.5cm dice (approx. 650g prepped weight)
50g butter
50–70g sharp Scottish Cheddar, grated
1 egg yolk

1. Set your oven to 180°C fan. Toss the diced swede in a little vegetable oil, season with sea salt and pepper, and roast on a lined baking tray for about 40 minutes, until soft and golden.
2. Meanwhile make the masala for the keema. Heat 3 or 4 tablespoons of vegetable oil in a medium to large lidded saucepan, then add the whole spices: cumin seeds, cardamom, cassia/cinnamon and cloves. When they start to release their aromas, add the diced onion and sauté for 5–10 minutes on a medium heat, until the onions become translucent and soft.

→

3. Get the spuds on for the mash too. Boil them in water until cooked through, then drain and allow to steam-dry; don't rush this step, as you don't want sloppy mash. Note: You can boil both the swede and potato but do this separately, as the swede takes longer to cook. Steam-dry both thoroughly, to avoid the dreaded waterlogged mash.

4. Back to the masala while the potatoes are boiling. Add the ginger, garlic and minced chillies to the onions, cook out for a couple of minutes, then tip in the ground spices: garam masala and turmeric, and the salt. If the pan is too dry, add a splash of water so the spices don't stick to the pan and burn.

5. Add the tomato purée and passata and mix, then increase the heat and bring to a simmer. After 5–10 minutes you will see that the oil on the surface of the spiced tomato mixture has taken on the tomato colour, which means it's ready to taste. Check your seasoning here and adjust; you want a bit of a kick.

6. Add the mince (and the crumbled haggis if using) and mix together thoroughly, then crank the heat to maximum, breaking up the meat with the end of your wooden spoon as you do so. You want to seal and separate the mince. Add the water, along with a pinch of methi, and stir. Bring to a simmer, cover with a lid and cook for 25–30 minutes.

7. Keep an eye on it – don't let the pan get too dry and catch. Add the frozen peas 5 minutes before it's cooked. You want the keema to be quite dry, so cook uncovered for a little longer if need be, to reduce and evaporate any liquid.

8. Your potatoes will be ready by now – if they aren't already. Remember, don't rush the steam-drying step, and don't let them go cold either. Mash the potatoes with butter and salt (say ½ teaspoon). You may find it easier to mash the swede separately then combine it with the mashed potato – it requires more elbow grease, as it's quite fibrous. Mix in the grated cheese, taste and adjust the seasoning. Then mix in the beaten egg yolk – this will give the mash a golden and crispy topping when baked.

9. Reheat the oven to 180°C fan. Assemble the pie in an ovenproof dish (I use a 28cm oval ceramic dish), with a base layer of keema (you can fish out the cassia and black cardamom) topped with mash. Bake in the oven for 35–45 minutes, or until bubbling and golden. Rest for 10 minutes or so before serving.

> **COOK'S NOTE** Leftover keema and cheese toasties are knockout. Add a little diced red onion, a few fresh coriander leaves and extra diced chillies for the heroes – oh do come hither!

Saalan lends itself really well to a slow cooker, as all it really involves is putting all the ingredients into a pot and cooking slowly until the meat is tender. No tempering, frying, nothing – just put everything in the pool. There follows a process called 'bhun', meaning to cook down and reduce over a more intense heat; which is what a lamb bhuna is. Unlike a bhuna, which is dry or 'suka', saalan has a nice gravy. Shorba is the Urdu word for broth, so you add even more water after the 'bhun' stage to make a shorba, and you can add diced potatoes at this point too. (The Punjabi word for broth is thari, it's the same thing.) This is a traditional recipe that hits the spot every time!

LAMB SHOULDER AND CHOP SAALAN

SERVES 4–6

1½ brown onions (finely sliced if caramelizing, finely diced if not)

750g boneless lamb shoulder or leg, cut into 2.5cm dice

4–6 lamb cutlets

2 whole dried Kashmiri chillies

2–3 black cardamom pods

5cm cassia bark

8–10 whole black peppercorns

5 whole cloves

1 teaspoon ground turmeric

2 tablespoons yoghurt

1 teaspoon cumin seeds

1 heaped teaspoon ground coriander

20g ginger, grated

20g garlic, grated

1½ teaspoons sea salt, or to taste

1 teaspoon mild Kashmiri chilli powder

300ml passata

approx. 300ml water

3 tablespoons vegetable oil or ghee

3–4 green chillies, split in half lengthways

½ teaspoon Kasuri methi (dried fenugreek)

1½ teaspoons garam masala

Garnish

chopped fresh coriander

ginger matchsticks (dunk these into boiling water, then rinse under cold water two or three times; this will take the fiery edge off)

COOK'S NOTE To make this saalan extra special, you can replace the water with 300g of yoghurt and the passata with 300g of chopped fresh tomatoes. As ever with yoghurt, gently heat it on a low to medium heat to bring it to a simmer so it doesn't split. Very rich and decadent!

1. Place all the ingredients – apart from the oil or ghee, green chillies, methi and garam masala – in a large saucepan and mix well. Add enough water to just cover the meat. Bring to the boil, then reduce to a simmer and cook, covered, until the meat is tender. It will take around 1½–1¾ hours. (If you choose to use caramelized onions, they will provide a greater depth of flavour. Cook them on a medium to low heat in a little ghee or oil beforehand.)

2. Once the meat is tender, have a little taste. It probably needs a little more salt – about ½ teaspoon. Time to 'bhun' now, which is done uncovered. Add the oil or ghee, green chillies and methi. Increase the heat to an equivalent of 7 out of 10. Gently stir as the gravy reduces – being careful not to break up the meat – to prevent the meat from sticking. It will take about 5–7 minutes to get a good thick gravy consistency.

3. Finally sprinkle over the garam masala and stir through. Garnish with chopped coriander and ginger matchsticks for a fancy touch. Tuck in with hot chapattis or rice, salad and a dollop of yoghurt. Sheer joy!

A large number of British Pakistanis originate from West Punjab. After partition in 1947, the province was split, with East Punjab remaining as part of India. My grandparents came from Jalandhar in East Punjab. Rajma chawal is often described as Punjabi soul food and it's a dish that unites East and West. I dare say every household has their own little nuanced way of making this – and I definitely prefer the shortcut of using tinned beans – but we are all united by this delicious combination of rice and beans! A golden oldie right here and I've kept it traditional.

RAJMA CHAWAL – KIDNEY BEAN MASALA AND RICE

SERVES 4

Rajma masala
vegetable oil, for cooking
1–2 teaspoons cumin seeds
1 large brown onion, finely diced
1–2 green finger chillies, or to taste, split in half lengthways
10g ginger, grated
10g garlic, grated
1 teaspoon ground turmeric
1 teaspoon garam masala
1½ teaspoons sea salt, or to taste
200ml passata
2 x 400g tins of kidney beans, drained
250ml water
chopped fresh coriander, to garnish

Chawal/rice
1 cup basmati rice
2.5cm cassia bark
3 whole cloves
2 green cardamom pods (bruise to release the seeds)
1 teaspoon dried red chilli flakes (to taste, you may want to reduce to ½ teaspoon)
¼ teaspoon tomato powder (optional)
½ teaspoon sea salt, or to taste
2 cups hot water

To serve
plain yoghurt
mint chutney (page 27)

1. Place the rice in a large bowl and cover with cold water. Give it a swish to agitate, then rinse three or four times using a fine sieve. Cover with cold water again and set aside for at least 30 minutes.
2. Heat 3 or 4 tablespoons of vegetable oil in a large lidded saucepan on a medium to high heat, then add the cumin seeds. When they start to release their aromas, tip in the onions and chillies. Reduce the heat to medium and cook the onions for about 10 minutes until softened.
3. Add the ginger and garlic, and cook out for a few minutes, then add the ground spices: turmeric and garam masala, and the salt. Toast these for about 30 seconds, then pour in the passata. Increase the heat to maximum and bring to the boil, then reduce the heat to medium and simmer for about 10 minutes. When you can see the oil separate on the surface of the mixture, stir in the kidney beans, followed by the water. Bring back to the boil, then reduce to a simmer.

4. Simmer, partly covered, for 15 minutes or so, then remove from the heat and check the seasoning – you might want a touch more salt. Garnish with a little chopped coriander.

5. Meanwhile get on with the rice. You could make a traditional black cardamom-spiked pilau rice – see page 49 – but I've amplified the flavour of the rice here. Drain the rice in a sieve, then set aside. Heat a couple of tablespoons of vegetable oil in a medium-sized lidded saucepan, then add the whole spices: cassia, cloves, cardamom. When they start to release their aromas, reduce the heat and add the dried chillies, tomato powder and salt, then after a few seconds stir in the drained rice, ensuring all the grains are evenly coated.

6. Now add 2 cups of just-boiled water. Give everything a stir and have a taste of the liquid – you may need a touch more salt. Increase the heat to maximum, and as soon as the water reaches boiling point again, place a tight-fitting lid on the pan (you can wrap the lid in a tea towel if need be) and reduce the heat to medium.

7. You can check the rice after 10 minutes but not before – it may need another 2 minutes, but if not, remove from the heat.

8. Allow to stand for another 10 minutes with the lid on. Before serving, fork the rice through – a spoon will break the long grains.

9. Serve the rajma chawal with a dollop of thick and creamy yoghurt; a touch of mint chutney also adds a certain frisson! The rajma is great with buttered chapattis too, and a few thin slivers of red onion . . . yum!

Now this is one of those dishes that doesn't look the prettiest but the flavour does all the talking! This is my attempt to turn this ugly duckling into a beautiful swan, and to try to make it look as good as it tastes. I've reimagined the bhurtha here, serving it as a dip rather than a sabzi, on a layer of labneh flecked with curry oil and a drizzle of pomegranate molasses. This dish is for sharing, and to be dunked into with torn bread. I like to find the nuggets of diced roasted aubergine. You need a gas hob for this dish – if you don't have one, you can use the activated charcoal method to infuse the smoke: put a white hot piece of charcoal into a small dish, drizzle a tablespoon of ghee on to the charcoal, which will cause it to smoke, then place this smoking dish in the cooked bhurtha saucepan and pop the lid on the pan to trap the smoke. You can smoke meat dishes this way too. It's delicious!

LOADED BAINGAN BHURTHA – SMOKED AUBERGINE

· ▬ · ▬ · ▬ · ▬ · ▬ · ▬ · ▬ · ▬ · ▬ · ▬ · ▬ · ▬ · ▬ · ▬ · ▬ ·

SERVES 4–6 AS A STARTER

3 large black aubergines
vegetable oil, for roasting and cooking
sea salt

1 teaspoon cumin seeds, plus extra for roasting
1 star anise
1 large brown onion (or 2 small ones), finely sliced into half-moons
2 green chillies, split in half lengthways

7g ginger, grated
7g garlic, grated
½ teaspoon ground turmeric
1 teaspoon garam masala
1 teaspoon salt, plus extra for roasting
150ml passata
1 teaspoon tomato purée

Garnish
labneh (or thick Greek yoghurt)
curry oil (see page 289)
finely diced red onion
dill fronds
pomegranate seeds
pomegranate molasses

1. Set your oven to 200°C fan.
2. Start by prepping the aubergines. Use the largest aubergine for presentation – put that to one side for now. Fire up the two largest rings on your gas hob, on full and maximum flames. Place the other 2 aubergines directly on the flames.
3. Back to the presentation aubergine: cut this in half from top to bottom. Dice one half into chunky 2.5cm pieces. Lightly score the other half around the entire perimeter, about 0.5cm from the edge, then score the middle in a criss-cross; don't pierce the outer skin. This step will make it easy to scoop out the flesh once roasted.
4. Keep an eye on the flaming aubergines. You want them to burn and char. Use tongs to turn them and ensure each side is charred.

→

5. Place the diced aubergine in a large mixing bowl, toss with a couple of tablespoons of vegetable oil, and season with sea salt and a sprinkle of cumin seeds. Gently massage the scored aubergine half all over with a scant amount of oil. Place it cut side up on a lined baking sheet and season with a little sea salt. Place the diced aubergine alongside it.

6. Your charred aubergines will be ready by now too. Lift these on to a separate lined baking sheet. Roast all the aubergines for 20 minutes, or until they are very soft when squeezed. The aubergine half and dice may need an extra 5 minutes. Remove from the oven and allow to cool.

7. Meanwhile make the masala. Heat 3 or 4 tablespoons of vegetable oil in a medium to large saucepan on a medium to high heat. Add the whole spices – cumin and star anise – and when they start to release their aromas, tip in the onions and chillies and reduce the heat. Cook the onions low and slow for 15–20 minutes, to lightly caramelize them; the volume will reduce by half. Add the ginger and garlic and let them cook out for a couple of minutes.

8. The aubergines should be ready to scoop out by now. First the presentation half: using a spoon, gently scoop out the flesh, being careful not to break the skin, and set aside. Next cut the charred aubergines in half from top to bottom, and gently spoon that flesh out too, discarding the charred exterior. Roughly dice the flesh, then place in a bowl and set aside.

9. Once the onions have caramelized, add the ground spices: turmeric and garam masala, and the salt. Toast these for 30 seconds, then add the passata and tomato purée. Increase the heat and bring to the boil, then reduce the heat and simmer for 7–8 minutes. When you see that the oil has separated on the surface, have a taste and adjust the seasoning accordingly.

10. Stir in the aubergine flesh (this is often referred to as caviar) and the diced pieces. Mix thoroughly and simmer for 5–10 minutes or so. This is a baingan bhurtha, which you can eat with chapattis.

11. Smother your serving plate with a thin layer of labneh or Greek yoghurt. Place the empty presentation aubergine half on top – we're using this as a serving vessel – and load it up with the hot bhurtha. Garnish with finely diced red onion, dill fronds and pomegranate seeds. Drizzle with curry oil and pomegranate molasses, and tuck in with toasted charcoal sourdough, naan or crispy seeded lavash flatbread.

Most of the Scottish langoustine catch, aka scampi, is exported whole to Europe. The tail meat, which we know in the UK as scampi, is a sustainable alternative to declining cod and haddock stocks. There was a time when monkfish tail was sold as scampi in the UK, before food labelling legislation took effect, and before its stocks fluctuated too.

You can use any fish in this recipe really; hake and tilapia are good options too. If you buy supermarket fish, be sure it carries the blue MSC (Marine Stewardship Council) label, and is certified sustainable, or ask your fishmonger about traceability.

LAHORI 'SCAMPI' PAKORA

SERVES 4 AS A STARTER

400g scampi, or hake, or tilapia (cut the fish fillets into 5cm pieces)
juice of 1 lemon
½ teaspoon ground turmeric
¼ teaspoon salt
2–3 tablespoons cornflour

Batter
1½ teaspoons toasted cumin seeds
1½ teaspoons toasted and crushed coriander seeds
¾ teaspoon garam masala
½ teaspoon dried red chilli flakes
1 teaspoon mild Kashmiri chilli powder
½ teaspoon garlic granules
½ teaspoon Kasuri methi (dried fenugreek)
½ teaspoon salt
125g chickpea/gram flour (besan)
150–160ml water
oil, for deep-frying

Note
Carom (ajwain) seeds are typically added to the batter mix, but I detest this spice vehemently. You can add ½ teaspoon if you really want to.

1. Get your wok, deep fryer or kadhai ready for deep-frying. The temperature of the oil should be 180°C.
2. Pat the scampi or fish dry with kitchen paper. Put it into a bowl and add the lemon juice, turmeric and salt, then leave to marinate for a few minutes, ensuring each piece is evenly coated. (Use gloves if you don't want your fingers to stain.)
3. Meanwhile, prepare the batter. Put the cumin seeds, crushed coriander seeds, garam masala, chilli flakes, chilli powder, garlic granules, methi, salt and chickpea flour into a large bowl and use a whisk to mix together. Then stir in the water to form a fairly thick batter. Set aside.
4. Put the cornflour on a flat plate. Place each piece of scampi or fish in the cornflour, shaking off any excess – you want it to be lightly coated – then dip in the batter to lightly coat and fry until cooked and golden. Do this in batches – the scampi or fish pieces won't take long, around 2–4 minutes total cooking time, depending on their thickness. Turn as necessary.
5. Drain on kitchen paper.
6. Scampi is traditionally served with chips and beans, but you can have it with a green mint chutney as a starter, or in a taco with other accompaniments (see the fish taco recipe, page 146).

COOK'S NOTE
You can cook a whole fillet this way and make a full-blown desi fish and chips. A side of hero peas (see page 286) with shallots, chillies and coriander is obligatory.

I could hardly come to Scotland without deep-frying something! I'll forgo the deep-fried Mars bars, but I am quite partial to a little retro fried chicken in a basket, as a treat. This one has been given a Pakistani twist, with love from Glasgow. A cold can of Irn-Bru to wash it down is a must!

FRIED CHICKEN IN A BASKET

SERVES 4

4 boneless chicken breasts

Marinade
100ml vegetable oil

1 teaspoon garlic granules
1 teaspoon onion granules
1 teaspoon ground ginger

1 teaspoon Kashmiri chilli powder
½ teaspoon paprika
½ teaspoon cayenne
½ teaspoon garam masala
1 teaspoon sea salt

Seasoned flour
approx. 250g plain flour
sea salt and black pepper
oil, for deep-frying

1. First we're making an oil-based marinade. In a large mixing bowl, whisk all the spices into the oil.
2. Flatten out the chicken breasts – you want these to be the same thickness the whole way across, for even cooking. Place each one on a chopping board, cover with a layer of cling film and bash with a heavy-bottomed saucepan is the way I do it. Put the chicken into the marinade. Leave to marinate overnight ideally, but you can get away with a minimum of an hour.
3. Place the flour in a large mixing bowl, season generously with salt and pepper – around ½ teaspoon of each – and mix. Half fill a separate bowl with water. Take a chicken breast and shake off any excess oil, then dredge in the seasoned flour, ensuring you coat every nook and cranny. Shake off the excess flour, then plunge the chicken into the water for a second; this ensures the flour sticks to the breast. Shake off any excess water, then coat the breast in the seasoned dredge again, and set aside on a tray ready for deep-frying. Repeat with the other 3 breasts. You could use seasoned panko breadcrumbs for the second dredge if you prefer.
4. Deep- or shallow-fry at about 180°C to seal the chicken – if the temperature is too low it will just soak up the oil – then reduce to around 150–160°C and cook through until crisp and golden. It will take 12–15 minutes, depending on how thick the fillets are (if shallow-frying, turn at the halfway point). Drain on kitchen paper, let them rest for a minute, then cut each one into three or four strips.
5. Serve in a basket with fries, your choice of sauce, and maybe even a slaw for full kitsch. I like two sauces: a mango chutney and straight-up ketchup, but in separate pots!

COOK'S NOTE Mild curry powder mixed into mayonnaise is very reminiscent of chip shop curry sauce. Try dunking your chips into that. Give it a whirl!

For some people a biryani has a mystical property where pleasure meets an almost spiritual experience. Traditionally it would be cooked in a handi, a clay or copper pot, but you can use a casserole dish. My version follows the dum pukht method – the biryani will be sealed in puff pastry. I'm using chicken thighs in this recipe, but you can use any meat – or indeed vegetables and whole eggs. Wonderful Scottish game such as grouse, pheasant, duck and venison would also work a treat. The theatre of opening the pastry lid at the table, and the mesmerizing aromas that waft up, will leave your diners enthralled.

DUM BIRYANI

SERVES 4–6

640g skinless, boneless chicken thighs, cut into large chunks

1 x 375g sheet of ready-rolled puff pastry

egg wash (1 small beaten egg + 1 tablespoon water)

sea salt

a sprinkle of nigella seeds

cucumber and pomegranate raita, to serve (see page 106)

Marinade

10g ginger, roughly chopped

10g garlic, roughly chopped

3–4 green finger chillies, snapped in half

15g fresh coriander

1 teaspoon dried mint

1 level teaspoon sea salt

1 teaspoon garam masala

2 tablespoons vegetable oil

200g Greek yoghurt

Masala sauce

3–4 tablespoons ghee or vegetable oil

1 teaspoon cumin seeds

2.5cm cassia bark

3 whole cloves

6 green cardamom pods (release the seeds and grind to a powder)

1 brown onion, finely diced

5g ginger, grated

5g garlic, grated

½ teaspoon ground turmeric

½ teaspoon dried red chilli flakes

½ teaspoon sea salt

300ml passata

100ml water

Rice

2 cups basmati rice

½ teaspoon ground turmeric (optional)

a generous pinch of saffron strands

2 tablespoons milk

1 tablespoon melted ghee

chopped fresh coriander

caramelized onions (optional)

1. The marinating step is really important, to tenderize your meat. Blitz the ginger, garlic, chillies, coriander, dried mint, salt, garam masala and oil in a blender or similar. Then tip in the yoghurt and blend that through too. Decant into a large mixing bowl (have a taste, it's so good!), then drop in the chicken pieces, making sure they are all evenly coated. Refrigerate and leave to marinate for 1–2 hours.

2. Meanwhile make the masala sauce. Heat the ghee in a large saucepan on a medium to high heat, then add the whole spices: cumin, cassia, cloves and cardamom. Once they start to release their aromas, add the onions and sauté on a medium heat until softened, followed by the grated ginger and garlic. Cook these out, then add the ground spices – turmeric and dried chilli flakes – and the salt, and let them toast for 30 seconds. Now pour in the passata and water, bring to the boil, then reduce the heat to medium and simmer for 5–7 minutes.

→

COOK'S NOTE Scottish game would be wonderful in a biryani and is in season from around September to December – the time will vary depending on the meat you choose. You can use meat on the bone, and get your game bird jointed and cut into pieces at the butcher. Just adjust the cooking times – a biryani should have beautifully tender meat. Tandoori game is also utterly delicious – the marination is the key!

3. Add the chicken to the pan along with its marinade, and stir together. Heat gently to bring to a simmer, then simmer for 25 minutes. Taste and make any adjustments. Remove from the heat.

4. While the chicken is simmering, you can prepare the rice. Rinse it thoroughly; you'll need a few changes of water – the rice water should be clear. Cook using the free boil method until 70 per cent cooked: fill a large saucepan generously with water, season with salt and bring to the boil. Tip in the rice, stir and cook for 7–8 minutes (rather than the usual 10–12) on a medium heat. If you want your rice to have a vibrant colour all over, add the turmeric to the cooking water.

5. Heat your oven to 180°C fan. Remove the pastry from the fridge so it can come to room temperature and will be easier to handle. Soak the saffron in the milk. Grease the inside of your handi or casserole dish with a scant amount of ghee. Also melt a tablespoon of extra ghee to drizzle over the biryani before it's sealed.

6. It doesn't really matter how you layer your biryani. I place half the curry on the bottom, then top with half the rice. The next layer is the rest of the curry, topped off with the remaining rice (curry-rice-curry-rice) – as long as the top layer is rice it's all good.

7. Drizzle the soaked saffron in milk over the top rice layer, plus a drizzle of melted ghee, some chopped coriander and caramelized onions, if you are using these.

8. To seal, roughly measure and cut the pastry required for the lid, and use the scraps to form a strip of pastry around the rim of the dish, which the pastry lid will rest on; you need to ensure it's airtight. Crimp the edges and cut away any excess pastry. Egg wash, then sprinkle over a little sea salt and nigella seeds. (Note: You can skip the pastry and use a casserole lid instead. Seal it with a strip of chapatti dough around the rim before securing the lid tightly into position.)

9. Bake for 20 minutes in the preheated oven.

10. Serve with raita below.

CUCUMBER AND POMEGRANATE RAITA

This is a simple raita to serve with the biryani. I've kept the flavours quite neutral so you can give centre stage to the main event!

1. Grate the cucumber, using the coarse side of a box grater. Then place the grated cucumber in a clean tea towel or muslin cloth and squeeze out all the liquid.

2. Mix the cucumber with the yoghurt in a bowl, and season with sea salt, dried mint and toasted cumin seeds, if using.

3. Adorn with pomegranate seeds. Refrigerate until serving.

125g cucumber
100–150g yoghurt
a pinch of salt
a pinch of dried mint

½ teaspoon toasted cumin seeds (optional)
a handful of pomegranate seeds

Glaswegian restaurant Shish Mahal has an ongoing legal campaign to be recognized as the original creators of one of Britain's favourite dishes, chicken tikka masala, which they assert was created in the early 1970s by the owner, when a customer complained about dry tandoori chicken! Whether they achieve D.O.P. status or not, the popularity and appetite for this dish grows ever greater. Here's a popular desi twist!

SPAGHETTI ALLA CHICKEN TIKKA MASALA

SERVES 4

600g boneless chicken breasts, cut into 2.5cm dice

tandoori marinade (see page 36 – you'll only need half, so use the other half to make something else: tandoori Portobello mushrooms, lamb chops, paneer, salmon fillets, etc.)

vegetable oil, for cooking

1 large brown onion, finely diced

5g ginger, grated

5g garlic, grated

1 teaspoon garam masala

½ teaspoon ground turmeric

1 teaspoon chilli powder

½ teaspoon sea salt

½ teaspoon finely ground black peppercorns

1 x 400g tin of chopped tomatoes, blended to a purée

1 teaspoon Kasuri methi (dried fenugreek)

50–100ml double cream, or to taste

300–400g spaghetti (75–100g dried pasta per person)

fresh coriander leaves, to garnish

1. Put the chicken pieces into a bowl with the tandoori marinade and leave to marinate overnight ideally, refrigerated.
2. Before cooking, allow the chicken to come to room temperature for 30 minutes.
3. Heat 3 or 4 tablespoons of oil in a large saucepan, and fry the onions on a medium heat until lightly golden. Add the ginger and garlic and cook out for a couple of minutes, then tip in the ground spices: garam masala, turmeric, chilli powder and the salt and pepper. Toast these for 30 seconds, then pour in the blended tomatoes. Give everything a good stir, bring to the boil, then reduce the heat and simmer for 15 minutes.
4. Meanwhile sauté the chicken pieces in a separate large saucepan in a little oil, shaking off any excess marinade. Once you've sealed the meat, cook it covered for 5–6 minutes, then set aside. Be careful not to overcook, as chicken breast can easily dry out and doesn't need long to cook through. The sauce/marinade may split as the yoghurt cooks, but that's OK.
5. Back to the masala: crush the methi into the sauce and stir in, along with the cream. Fold the chicken tikka pieces through the sauce and simmer for 10 minutes, then remove from the heat. Taste and adjust the seasoning.
6. While the chicken is simmering, cook your pasta, seasoning the water with plenty of salt. Once cooked, drain and toss through the tikka masala. Garnish with a little coriander before serving.

COOK'S NOTE Make a korma by adding a cashew paste. Soak 100g cashew nuts in just-boiled water for 20 minutes then blend with some of the soaking water. Stir this through your masala at step 5, same time as the cream.

Salmon is certainly up there as one of Scotland's most luxurious ingredients. At Christmas we always treat ourselves to a smoked side of salmon in our house. But it can be a wonderful midweek ingredient too, and fish is the ultimate fast food. We are going to cook this 'Cajun' style but use a dry Lahori-style spice blend instead. It really couldn't be easier to whip this dish up! A little local Scottish honey brings the sweet to match the spice.

MASALA SPICED SIDE OF SALMON

SERVES 4

1 side of salmon (about 600g)
1 tablespoon vegetable oil
1 tablespoon runny honey

Spice seasoning
1½ teaspoons toasted cumin seeds
1½ teaspoons toasted and crushed coriander seeds
¾ teaspoon garam masala

½ teaspoon dried red chilli flakes
1 teaspoon mild Kashmiri chilli powder
1 level teaspoon salt, or to taste
½ teaspoon methi (dried fenugreek)

½ teaspoon garlic granules
½ teaspoon onion granules

1. Set your oven to 200°C fan.
2. Massage the salmon with the vegetable oil. Place it on a lined flat baking tray, skin side down, and brush the side facing you all over with honey.
3. Mix all the seasoning ingredients together: cumin, coriander, garam masala, chilli flakes, chilli powder, salt, methi, garlic and onion granules.
4. Scatter the seasoning all over the salmon and allow to sit for 10 minutes.
5. Oven bake for about 15 minutes, or until cooked.
6. Serve with cucumber and pomegranate raita (see page 106) and rice or spiced roasties (see page 36). Pink pickled onions (see page 55) will provide a delightful sharpness.

COOK'S NOTE Don't serve the skin, but retain this and make crispy salmon skin scratchings. Place the skin on a baking tray with a rack – it should be placed directly on the rack so that air can circulate around it. Bake at 180°C fan until crispy – it will take 7–9 minutes, and the skin will get crispier as it cools. Season and munch.

Peshawari naan from Peshwar, in north-west Pakistan, is a popular sweet bread, filled with sultanas, coconut and almonds. So it got me thinking, what it would be like to transfer these flavours on to a very British pudding? I designed this dish with Eid in mind; a rich, sweet and decadent treat to look forward to after breaking a fast, which comes from a humble slice of stale bread. The rose water really lifts this pud to another level and brings in the Mughal influences, but be careful, as it can easily overpower. Adorn with dried rose petals for an extra special touch as part of the feast.

PESHAWARI BREAD AND BUTTER PUDDING

SERVES 6–8

spreadable butter or margarine
8 slices of stale white bread
50g sultanas
50g coconut flakes

50g almond flakes
200ml whole milk (semi is fine)
300ml double cream
60g caster sugar
3 eggs

zest of ½ an orange
2 teaspoons rose water
1–2 tablespoons demerara sugar
grated nutmeg (optional)

COOK'S NOTE
You can brush the top of the pudding with an apricot glaze if you want to be extra fancy. You will need to wait for the pudding to cool to room temperature. Melt a couple of tablespoons of jam with a splash or two of water in a small saucepan, and brush over the pudding before serving.

1. Set your oven to 160°C fan.
2. Grease a 1 litre ceramic pie dish or similar with butter. Butter the sliced bread on both sides and cut diagonally into quarters, so you have little triangles.
3. Arrange these in your dish, overlapping and ensuring you have lots of pointy bits sticking up, as these will go lovely and crispy during baking. I don't ever remove the crusts, as these go EXTRA crispy.
4. Scatter the sultanas, coconut flakes and almond flakes all over, tucking them into the crevices to prevent them burning during baking – though I do like a few gnarly sultanas and toasted nuts in my pudding, I confess.
5. Make the custard by whisking the milk, cream, caster sugar, eggs, orange zest and rose water together. Pour over the bread. Allow to soak for 30 minutes (ideally you should do this, but you can bake straight away if you're in a hurry).
6. Sprinkle all over with demerara sugar and a little grated nutmeg, if using. Bake in the middle of the oven for 30–40 minutes, or until crisp and golden on the top and the custard has set.
7. Serve with honey drizzled figs, and cream or custard.

KENT & SOUTH-EAST ENGLAND

NEPALI COMMUNITY

There is a special relationship between Britain and Nepal, as exemplified by the British army's famous links with the Gurkhas, which span over two centuries. Immigration from Nepal grew rapidly from the early 2000s, partly due to changes in legislation regarding the right of settlement in the UK for ex-Gurkhas. According to the Centre for Nepal Studies UK, Nepalis are predominantly based in the South-East: Kent, Berkshire and Hampshire, which are close to army bases, and London. The fusion elements of Nepali food are most exciting, as the nation is flanked by India and China; this is prominent in the regions closest to these borders, not to mention the traces back to the Silk Road. Indo-Chinese food is hugely popular, and I'd like to pay some attention to that as well as to some more authentic Nepali dishes. Kathmandu, the capital of Nepal, is centrally based and heavily influenced by Newari culture; Newars are considered to be the original settlers in the Kathmandu valley. This cuisine is quite unique – key features include tempering spices, the use of mustard oil, and a spice called timur pepper. Timur is a cousin of the lip-numbing and tongue-tingling Szechuan pepper, and has the same delightful citrus notes. It's an important ingredient in Nepali cooking.

RAJIV KC (AGED 34)

Head chef at Rajiv's Kitchen

I talk to Rajiv just before he starts the prep for a packed-out Saturday night service; he has a residency at a London restaurant at this time, a stepping-stone on the path to finding and acquiring a permanent space of his own. He's a busy chap, and sleep-deprived – father to a teething 18-month-old son, first child with wife Charlotte – yet radiating enthusiasm for doing what he loves to do. It was perhaps always Rajiv's destiny to become a chef proprietor – he was born in a kitchen: 'Apparently Mum went into labour after lunch and I popped out right there.'

Rajiv came to the UK 14 years ago, to study for his degree. His family are originally from Gulmi, a mountainous region that is located in central Nepal close to the Chinese border; Kathmandu is a two-night bus ride or car drive away. Because it's very mountainous, it's not so easy to travel from one part to another. The family moved to Kathmandu in 1998, after his grandfather passed away, but they still retain the ancestral home in Gulmi. After completing college in India, he chose to come to the UK to go to university. The family gave him a few options – USA, Canada, UK or Australia: 'I chose the UK because I was fascinated by the history of this country. I always wondered how this tiny island could come to dominate the whole world. I had an idea in my mind about how it would be, but of course the reality was different from my fantasy.' He giggles.

As a 'side-hustle' while studying, Rajiv tutored children with learning difficulties in maths – which he still does. After graduation the plan was to go back to Nepal, but he got a job at a bank. Doctor, engineer and banker were acceptable professions to his family. He worked at the bank for two years, but developed a health condition that prevented him from working for a year. It was during this period of recovery and convalescence that he started to run supper clubs from his flat to keep himself occupied and to earn money. The supper club scene in London was starting to take off at the time, and it was his ex-flatmate who suggested the idea and that they should use their front room as the venue, having tasted his delicious and authentic Nepali food, and with the absence of any other Nepalese options. At the first supper club there were only three guests; however, as word spread, Rajiv soon found himself cooking for 40 people. 'I remember when I did my first 40 I struggled. For that number you have to hire a venue, and you're not familiar with the kitchen, the equipment, how the layout should be . . . or when you start to run out of food during service. It can be very stressful.'

It is a chef's worst nightmare, the prospect of running out of food, I can certainly attest to that. And the stress of running a kitchen is made worthwhile only when you see the response on the faces of the people who are eating your food: 'The reaction was overwhelming, so then all the stress ebbs away.'

The cooking had a healing effect while Rajiv was unwell, a connection to the home comforts that the food of childhood brings, providing an anchor. It was difficult and lonely being in a different country, a young man away from the support structure of family and friends and adapting to a very different culture. Unsurprisingly he didn't go back to the bank, and decided to resign and become a chef full-time.

One of the biggest challenges Rajiv felt he faced when he first arrived was not having proper Nepalese food. It was a real hunt to find a good restaurant, and whenever he went to one what they served was actually Indian food. 'That really upset and disappointed me. It's not Nepalese if you simply call something a Kathmandu curry and put momos on the menu.'

He travelled to Hoxton, Reading, Aldershot, only to be presented with generic fodder. There are more authentic offerings to be found in Gurkha-focused communities near army garrisons – Kent and Hampshire – but it takes some searching. He seems surprised when I tell him that eight out of ten Indian restaurants are actually Bangladeshi, so they're not strictly speaking Indian either. We talk about misconceptions about Nepali food, which is so often lumped in with Indian or Chinese food without being given a billboard of its own. It's so important to put a spotlight on authentic regional cooking, the various diaspora countries and communities, the nuances, rather than on one homogenous lump. We touch on cultural appropriation. Using certain spices, in a particular combination and technique, defines that region. If you strip this back you end up with something generic and no longer reflective of the cuisine of that culture – it's clumsily taken out of the cultural context without providing an explanation of what it should be, the deviation. 'People who follow recipes aren't always the most confident cooks, they like to simplify things. But then the complexity of the flavours is lost.'

These skills and context can easily be learned, and when people come to understand the difference between home food and restaurant food there will be enlightenment. The public will be able to find the authentic regional food. Rajiv likes to pick dishes from different regions of Nepal on his menus to demonstrate this diversity: 'There's more to Nepalese food. There are 143 different tribes in Nepal, so that's goat curry cooked in 143 different ways. If you give the same ingredients to different people they will all cook differently. The same dish changes from region to region, village to village. I try to give that experience to people that haven't been to Nepal, so they'll want to visit Nepal.'

I ask Rajiv where the calling came from to be a chef – it's a big change from working in a bank, after all. He had been cooking since he was 12 years old, and was always interested in watching his mother or grandmother in the kitchen. In Nepali culture – which is similar to Parsi culture – when women have their monthly cycle they are not allowed in the kitchen for those days. 'My mum and my sister used to have their cycle at the same time, which meant I ended up cooking for four days.'

So what was the food like on Rajiv cooking days, I tease. I ask what feedback he received: 'Sometimes Mum would love it, but at other times she would scold me! There was some praise but most often scolding . . . She always gave me instructions but I didn't always follow them. I'd add ingredients or take some away.'

It sounds as though it was a baptism of fire, but that can often be the best possible training, being thrown in at the deep end and getting searingly honest reviews! My own mother believes she has 'magic hands' based on how delicious her food is – a veritable alchemist – and she is still not prepared to relinquish that title; my status remains that of apprentice, to much mirth. Sadly Rajiv's mother is not entirely supportive of his career choice: 'My family is not happy that I'm cooking. My mum is embarrassed; she has begged me to do something other than cooking.'

Unfortunately elements of the archaic systems of caste still remain in place in Nepal, and indeed in India. Rajiv is from the Brahmin and Chhetri or ruling warrior class, with greater expectations placed on him. I hope his family will come round to the idea when he establishes a successful restaurant. Life is too short to be doing something that you do not enjoy for an infinite period of time, and his chosen career path brings so much joy to other people. Not everybody has that ability. There are few professions and industries where you can elicit these strong emotional responses. Rajiv's dream is to move to Cornwall or Devon and open a field-to-fork farm restaurant, making the best use of seasonal produce. He jests that he may have to rely on winning the lottery to make his dream come true, but he's already on the right trajectory. Supper clubs to pop-ups or residency to restaurant is an acknowledged path. Luck is nothing more than when readiness and preparation meet opportunity. I look forward to dining at his restaurant.

As the name would suggest, sekuwa would normally come on a skewer. Sekuwa is a delicious kebab, and a very popular street food that's cooked over an open wood or coal grill. I decided to make a pork chop version here and accompany it with a delightful potato dish that Rajiv introduced me to from his home region of Gulmi. Of course you can also dice your meat, thread it on to a metal or soaked bamboo skewer and make this the authentic way.

PORK CHOP SEKUWA

SERVES 4

480–500g pork loin steaks (see cook's note)

Marinade

1 brown onion, peeled and roughly chopped

15g ginger, roughly chopped

15g garlic, roughly chopped

1 teaspoon ground cumin

1 teaspoon ground coriander

1 teaspoon garam masala

½ teaspoon ground turmeric

1½ teaspoons sea salt

1½ teaspoons chilli flakes

1½ teaspoons chilli powder

1 tablespoon honey

3 tablespoons vegetable oil

juice of 1 lime

1. Blitz the onion, ginger and garlic into a paste using a mini chopper or similar, and transfer to a large mixing bowl.
2. Add the rest of the marinade ingredients and mix everything together. Have a taste, and adjust if need be.
3. Put the pork loin steaks into the marinade, ensuring each one is smothered. Marinate for at least 2 hours, or ideally overnight.
4. Grill on a wood- or coal-fired barbecue until cooked. The steaks will take about 5–6 minutes on each side. Alternatively you can grill them using your oven grill set to the maximum heat, getting the steaks as close to the hot grill as possible.
5. Serve with chukauni potato salad (see page 118), a green leaf salad, Nepali slaw (see page 118) and flatbread (see page 146).

> **COOK'S NOTE** This quantity of marinade could easily take more meat. You can also use different cuts of pork, such as shoulder steak, pork belly or bone-in pork cutlets. I've used loin steaks because they cook quite quickly and are lean, but just adjust the cooking time according to the cut you choose to use. You could also use lamb or mutton, or chicken, as an alternative.

CHUKAUNI POTATO SALAD

Chukauni is a potato and yoghurt dish that very much reminds me of the potato salads served at barbecues, except that this one has a little kick.

1. Boil the potatoes in a pan of water until cooked, then drain and allow to steam-dry.
2. In a large mixing bowl, combine the yoghurt with the red onion, spring onions, chilli powder, salt, garlic, green chillies and lime juice. Give everything a good stir.
3. Add the cooked potatoes, ensuring they are evenly coated and thoroughly mixed.
4. For the tempering, heat the oil in a small to medium frying pan over a medium to high heat. Once hot, add the fenugreek seeds, and as soon as they start to sizzle and toast, remove from the heat and add the turmeric. Swirl the pan and after a couple of seconds carefully pour over the potatoes. Stir and mix this through.
5. Garnish with coriander leaves and crushed red chillies.

SERVES 4–6

700g new or baby potatoes, sliced in half (roughly the same size)
215g Greek set yoghurt
1 small red onion, finely diced
3 spring onions, including the green part, finely sliced
1 teaspoon chilli powder
1 teaspoon sea salt
½ a clove of garlic, grated
2 green finger chillies, finely sliced
juice of 1 lime

Tempering
3–4 tablespoons vegetable oil
½ teaspoon fenugreek seeds
½–1 teaspoon ground turmeric

Garnish
fresh coriander leaves
a sprinkle of crushed red chillies

NEPALI SLAW

This has a lovely dressing, which keeps well. Just whip up as much or as little as you require, and keep any leftover dressing in an airtight jar in the fridge. I always make a batch. By all means use a different combination of shredded vegetables.

1. Whisk all the dressing ingredients together in a clean jar until emulsified. Transfer to the fridge – it will keep for a week.
2. Put your prepped cabbage, carrot and red onion into a big bowl and pour over the dressing. Scatter over some fresh coriander leaves.

SERVES 8–12

Dressing
3 tablespoons vegetable oil
1 tablespoon sesame oil
4 tablespoons white/ rice wine vinegar
3 tablespoons honey
1 tablespoon soy sauce
1 clove of garlic, grated
25g ginger, grated
½ teaspoon sea salt
½ teaspoon ground Szechuan pepper (or timur, if you can get it)

Veggies
100g white cabbage, finely shredded
200g red cabbage, finely shredded
200g carrots, grated
100g red onion, finely sliced into half-moons
fresh coriander leaves

If you've never had a momo before, you are in for a treat! Momos are delightful small dumplings, often filled with either finely chopped vegetables or minced meat. They are synonymous with Nepali snack culture, though hugely popular throughout India. These will seriously have you drooling. Momos come in a number of varieties: they are most often steamed, can come in a soup (jhol momos), can be deep-fried or, my personal favourites, 'pot stickers' called kothey momos, which are pan-fried and steamed. I do confess, I'm not the best at pleating momos, but it is great fun, and I promise you, you will get better with practice. It's a great activity for a dinner party, I've found, and gets your guests involved with some live prep! There are dumpling presses for those who love a gadget.

VEGETABLE AND PANEER MOMOS

MAKES 20 MOMOS

Dough/wrappers
200g plain flour
a pinch of sea salt, ground in a pestle and mortar
approx. 100ml body-temperature water (36–37°C)
cornflour, for dusting

Note
You can use gyoza wrappers as a shortcut, and purchase these frozen in supermarkets – defrost before use.

Filling
125g Savoy cabbage, roughly chopped
70g carrots, peeled and roughly chopped
40g spring onions, including the green part, roughly chopped
50g green bell pepper, roughly chopped
15g garlic, grated
15g ginger, grated
1 green finger chilli, finely sliced
½ teaspoon sea salt
1 tablespoon chopped fresh coriander
½ teaspoon crushed Szechuan pepper (or timur, if you can get it)
1 tablespoon vegetable oil
100g paneer, crumbled (replace with tofu or chopped mushrooms for a vegan version)

Note
You will need a steamer and greaseproof or baking parchment. At Chinese wholesalers you can get perforated parchment in round discs, which would be ideal. If using a roll of greaseproof paper or parchment, cut it into individual small squares (8cm x 8cm). You can also use cabbage leaves.

1. First the dough. Mix the flour and salt together, then add the water a little at a time – splay your fingers to mix it all together. You don't want a dough that's too sticky and wet – you'll need about 100ml of water. If the dough is too soft, shaping the momos could be tricky. Knead the dough for 5–7 minutes, really working the glutens, until you have a smooth, fairly firm and elastic dough. Cover with a damp tea towel and leave it to rest for 30 minutes.

2. Now make the filling. Put the cabbage, carrot, spring onion, pepper, ginger, garlic and chilli into a food processor and pulse to a fine chop – you don't want a mush.

→

3. Transfer to a mixing bowl. If you have an excess of water – you may not do, I don't often need this step – squeeze this out. But we do want juicy momos so it mustn't be drained dry. Mix in the salt, chopped coriander, Szechuan pepper, vegetable oil and crumbled paneer. Give everything a good mix and taste. If you want to pack an extra punch you can add a level teaspoon of dark soy and white wine vinegar – but I don't think it necessarily needs it for paneer (though tofu or mushrooms definitely would).

4. You're going to make half-moon shapes. Take a section of the dough and roll it out as thinly as you can – you can use cornflour to lightly dust your work surface to prevent it from sticking. Then use a 9–10cm chef's ring or cutter and cut out about four discs – depending on how quickly you can work before the dough dries, you may be able to do more at a time. Return any scraps of dough to your bowl and cover with a damp cloth so they don't dry out – we will reuse this.

5. Place a dough disc in the palm of your hand, then put a tablespoon of filling in the centre – the dough is quite robust and can take a decent amount. Bring the lower edge or corner of the dough up to meet the top and start to seal the momo, creating a pleat or fold as you do so, pinching to seal at the top. Repeat this the whole way along – it will start to look similar to a pasty – until completely sealed. Place on a lightly oiled baking tray while you prepare the rest of the dumplings.

6. When you are ready to cook your momos, have your steamer ready – either a bamboo steamer over a saucepan or a stainless steel steamer, which I actually prefer – and wrap a tea towel around the lid. The bottom pan will need 10–13cm of boiling water and a steady medium to high heat (an equivalent heat of 7 out of 10). Have your greaseproof paper or baking parchment ready too – see the note in the ingredient list.

7. If using perforated parchment, insert this into the steamer basket, or place the momos on individual pieces of parchment paper or cabbage leaf. Steam cook for 7–8 minutes – they won't feel sticky when done. You will need to do this in batches.

8. Serve with a spicy tomato momo chutney (see opposite) or simply with a little soy sauce or chiu chow chilli oil.

MOMO KO ACHAR – SPICY TOMATO MOMO CHUTNEY

Momos are commonly served with this chutney to dip into.

- -

ENOUGH FOR
20–30 MOMOS

vegetable oil, for cooking

1 red onion, roughly chopped

15g garlic

approx. 7g ginger (half the volume of the garlic)

½ teaspoon crushed Szechuan pepper (or timur, if you can get it)

400g fresh tomatoes, de-skinned and roughly chopped (see cook's note below)

2 tablespoons tomato ketchup

1 teaspoon white wine vinegar

½–1 level teaspoons dark soy sauce

Optional (for more heat)

½ teaspoon chiu chow chilli oil

a touch more vinegar (½ teaspoon)

a dash of toasted sesame oil

1. Heat a few glugs of oil in a wok, kadhai or large frying pan on a fairly high heat. Add the onions, garlic and ginger and stir-fry until softened.

2. Add the Szechuan pepper and toast for 30 seconds, then tip in the chopped tomatoes. You want these to soften and start to break down. Stir in the ketchup and vinegar, and enough water to get to your desired sauce consistency. Simmer for a couple of minutes, then remove from the heat. Taste, then leave to cool.

3. Once cool, transfer to a blender and blitz until smooth, unless you prefer a chunky sauce. Season with soy sauce. If you want more heat, add the chilli oil, a touch more vinegar and a dash of toasted sesame oil (be careful and sparing with this, as it can overpower). Make this fresh on the day, ideally, or you can refrigerate it for up to 3 days.

COOK'S NOTE To de-skin tomatoes, make two cuts at the bottom of each tomato (to look like a cross). Place in a large mixing bowl and cover with boiling water. Leave for a minute or two, then plunge them into cold water. You will be able to easily peel away the skin from the site of the cuts, and remove the eye at the top.

Non-vegetarian momos can come in any variety. In the Himalayan region, yak and buffalo meat are favoured – not that readily available in most supermarkets, so we can stick to chicken, pork, prawn or even turkey. This dish involves deep-frying the momos before stir-frying them through a spicy and tangy sauce; it's more of a restaurant-style offering. You can make this with veggie momos too, or change the meat to your preference. Try whatever you fancy. I think it's best to keep the fillings quite simple and spice the sauce. A little hack with the meat momos is to add a bit of water to the mixture to make them extra juicy. These meat momos can also be steamed and served with the spicy tomato momo chutney (see page 123).

C: MOMOS AKA CHILLI MOMOS

SERVES 4 AS A STARTER (MAKES 16–20 MOMOS)

momo dough (see page 120)
vegetable oil, for deep-frying

Filling

250g minced chicken (7 per cent fat, preferably thigh or leg) (see note)
5g garlic, grated
5g ginger, grated
½ a green finger chilli, finely chopped
25g spring onions, including the green part, finely sliced
1 tablespoon chopped fresh coriander

½ teaspoon crushed Szechuan pepper (or timur, if you can get it)
¼ teaspoon sea salt
1–2 tablespoons water
1 teaspoon dark soy sauce

C: momo chilli sauce

vegetable oil, for cooking
10g garlic, finely chopped
1 green finger chilli (or bird's-eye if you want it hot), split in half lengthways
1 red onion, cut into 3cm dice
½ teaspoon ground cumin
½ teaspoon ground coriander

¼ teaspoon sea salt
½ teaspoon crushed Szechuan pepper (or timur, if you can get it)
2 medium-sized tomatoes, de-skinned and roughly chopped (see cook's note, page 123)
1 red or green pepper, cut into 2.5cm dice
2–3 tablespoons tomato ketchup
1 teaspoon dark soy sauce
1 teaspoon white wine vinegar
1 tablespoon sriracha (optional)
50–75ml water

Slurry

½ tablespoon cornflour, mixed with 25–50ml water

Garnish

spring onion greens or chives, finely sliced
fresh coriander leaves
deep-fried vermicelli noodles (optional)

Note

You can replace the minced chicken in the filling with minced pork or prawns, and add a little finely shredded cabbage or mangetout if so inclined.

1. Make your momo dough and let it rest.
2. Hand-mix all the filling ingredients – don't be tempted to whack it all into a food processor – if you overmix, the meat will be rubbery when cooked.
3. When you are ready to assemble the momos, make the 'money bag' shape. Take a section of the dough and roll out as thinly as you can – you can use cornflour to lightly dust your work surface to prevent it sticking. Then use an 8cm chef's ring or cutter and cut out about four discs – it depends on how quickly you can work before the dough dries, and you may be able to do more at a time. Return any scraps of dough to your bowl and cover with a damp cloth so they don't dry out – we will reuse these.
4. Place a dough disc in the palm of your hand, and put a heaped teaspoon of filling in the centre. You want to bring up all the edges to encase the filling, creating a fold or pleat each time and pinching as you do so, all the way along. You'll end up with that money bag shape. Twist the top to properly seal – we do not want these bursting open, especially as we're deep-frying them. Place them on a lightly oiled baking tray while you prepare the rest of the dumplings.
5. To deep-fry the momos, heat oil to 165°C in your wok, kadhai or deep-fryer. Carefully fry the momos until cooked and lightly golden – it will take 6–8 minutes. You will need to fry them in batches and drain on kitchen paper. Set aside. You could even air-fry them.
6. As soon as the momos are ready, start the sauce. Heat 2 or 3 tablespoons of oil in a separate wok, kadhai or similar on a fairly high heat. Add the garlic, green chilli and diced onion and stir-fry for a few minutes until softened, then add the ground cumin, coriander, salt and Szechuan pepper. Toast for 30 seconds, then tip in the chopped tomatoes. Allow the tomatoes to start to break down a little, then add the diced pepper. Give these a couple of minutes, stirring continuously so nothing catches. Have a little taste.
7. Season with the ketchup, soy sauce, vinegar and sriracha, if using, and give everything a good mix. Add some extra water – 50–75ml – to get to your desired sauce consistency, along with the cornflour slurry.
8. Place the momos in the sauce and ensure they are all coated; you'll see the sauce thicken and coat the momos. Have a final taste of the sauce and make any last-minute adjustments.
9. Garnish with finely sliced spring onion or chives and coriander leaves. You could also crown the momos with a little nest of deep-fried rice vermicelli noodles for a wow factor.

Choyela is a hugely popular Newari dish. To many it's considered to be a comfort food, and it ranges from being a feasting dish during festivals to a snack that is taken with a few shots of the local firewater. There tend to be two types of choyela: 'haku', which is grilled and blackened, and 'mana', which is boiled. Lamb and chicken are most popular, and in some regions of Nepal, buffalo meat. We are making it haku style.

LAMB CHOYELA (CHOILA) SALAD } WITH FINE GREEN BEANS

SERVES 4

700–750g lamb neck fillet

Marinade
30g garlic, roughly chopped
30g ginger, roughly chopped
4–5 green finger chillies, roughly chopped
30g fresh coriander
1 teaspoon white wine vinegar
3 tablespoons vegetable oil

Dry masala
1 teaspoon ground coriander
1 teaspoon ground cumin
1 teaspoon chilli powder
1 teaspoon crushed Szechuan pepper (or timur, if you can get it)
1 teaspoon sea salt, or to taste

Tempering
4 tablespoons vegetable oil
½ teaspoon fenugreek seeds
¼ teaspoon cumin seeds
1–2 dried red chillies, broken into pieces
½ teaspoon ground turmeric

Salad and garnishes
200g fine or extra fine green beans, trimmed and cut in half
1 red onion, finely sliced into half-moons
4–6 spring onions, finely sliced
fresh coriander leaves
fresh mint leaves
finely sliced radishes
lime juice
deep-fried rice vermicelli noodles (optional)

1. Slice your lamb as you would for a carpaccio, except you want thicker medallions, say 1cm thick. Remove any excess fat and sinew, and flatten using the blade of your knife.
2. To make your marinade, blitz all the ingredients to a paste in a mini chopper or blender – garlic, ginger, chillies, coriander, vinegar and oil. Transfer to a mixing bowl, then add the lamb and coat all the pieces. Cover, then leave to marinate overnight ideally, refrigerated.
3. Mix together all the ingredients for the dry masala and set aside.
4. Before grilling the meat, allow it to come to room temperature so it can relax. Ideally you would grill on a wood or coal-fired barbecue, but you can use your oven grill – just heat it to the maximum temperature and place the meat as close to the hot grill as possible so you can get a nice char. It will take a couple of minutes on each side. Once cooked, transfer

it to a large bowl and coat with the dry masala. Allow to rest while you cook the beans.

5. Boil the green beans for 2–3 minutes, then drain and place in a bowl of cold water to prevent any further cooking – we want to keep these 'al dente'. Once cooled, drain again, dry on kitchen paper and mix with the lamb.

6. Next we'll temper the spices. Heat the oil in a small to medium frying pan over a medium to high heat. Once hot, add the fenugreek and cumin seeds, and the broken dried chillies, and as soon as they start to sizzle and toast, remove the pan from the heat and add the turmeric. Swirl the pan and after a couple of seconds carefully pour the contents over the lamb and green beans. Stir and mix this through. Season with a touch of lime juice.

7. Present your lamb and beans on a large serving plate, studded with the various garnishes.

8. Serve with roti, or in a lettuce cup as Rajiv likes to have his, or with jewelled cauliflower rice (see page 78). I find that deep-fried crispy vermicelli rice noodles add a delightful crunch.

DHAL BHAT TARKARI — LENTILS, RICE AND VEGETABLE CURRY

This is my version of this Nepalese staple. This iconic combination has a number of variations, from region to region and based on what's seasonal. I wanted to give this an unmistakable Nepali stamp. The whole ensemble is usually served on a steel thali (or on tapari – a leaf plate) and comprises a dhal, steamed rice, vegetable curry, greens and a pickle. You can use any dhal, but washed split mung or yellow dhal is very popular. My vegetable curry is 'aloo ko achar', a pickled potato dish. Mustard oil is used in a lot of Nepali cooking, and for pickling; generally any achari dish. Sadly mustard oil doesn't really agree with my palate, so I avoid it or at least use it sparingly. Tempering is also a key feature of Nepali cooking. The greens are not Nepali, simply stir-fried Swiss chard. You could use spinach, fresh methi (fenugreek leaves) or mustard greens if you prefer.

YELLOW DHAL

1. Rinse the dhal thoroughly, and drain. Heat a couple of tablespoons of vegetable oil in a large lidded saucepan on a medium to high heat, and sauté the garlic, ginger and green chillies.

2. Add the ground spices – turmeric and garam masala – and the salt, and toast, then tip in the finely chopped tomatoes. You may need a splash of water to help this on its way. Have a quick taste at this point, and if you are happy stir in the dhal, followed by the cold water. Bring to the boil, then immediately reduce the heat to medium and simmer, covered, for 15–20 minutes, or until cooked.

3. Add more water if need be – you want a loose consistency. You will also need more salt, probably about another ½ teaspoon, but to your own taste. Remove from the heat and set aside.

→

SERVES 4–6

1 cup yellow dhal (washed split mung dhal)

vegetable oil, for cooking

7g garlic, grated

7g ginger, grated

1–2 green finger chillies, split in half lengthways

½ teaspoon ground turmeric

1 teaspoon garam masala

1 teaspoon sea salt, or to taste

2 medium tomatoes, de-skinned and finely chopped (see cook's note, page 123)

4 cups cold water

Tempering

1–2 tablespoons vegetable oil

½ teaspoon mustard seeds

2 dried red chillies, broken into pieces

½ teaspoon onion seeds (kalonji) (see cook's note, page 130)

4. Next the tempering. Heat a couple of tablespoons of vegetable oil in a small frying pan on a medium to high heat. Once the oil is hot, pop in the mustard seeds, then, after about 30 seconds, the chilli pieces. When the mustard seeds start to crackle, add the onion seeds and remove from the heat. After a few seconds, carefully drop the sizzling spices on to the dhal. Love that hiss!

5. Give the dhal a good stir – it's now ready to serve, with steamed rice, aloo ko achar (see opposite), stir-fried Swiss chard (see below) and a pickle of your choice. I won't judge if you'd like a buttered roti too.

> **COOK'S NOTE** I am using the onion seeds as a replacement for a Nepalese ingredient called jimbu. Jimbu is a herb belonging to the onion family, and is commonly used in its dried form.

STIR-FRIED SWISS CHARD

Swiss chard is a delightful ingredient, easy to grow and best cooked very simply. You can add a little julienne of ginger if you want, in equal volume to the garlic.

1. Rinse the chard thoroughly and dry. The stalks take longer to cook than the leaves, so cut them off where the leaf meets the stalk. Bunch the stalks together and slice them fairly fine, discarding any woody parts. Then roll the leaves into a big cigar and slice them into 1cm strips. Keep the leaves and stalks separate.

2. Heat a couple of tablespoons of vegetable oil in a sauté pan or frying pan on a medium to high heat. Add the finely sliced garlic, followed by the chilli. When the garlic starts to turn a light golden colour, chuck in the chopped stalks. Cook these for a couple of minutes, then add the leaves. Stir everything together and season with a little salt and pepper. Add a splash of water to help things along. The chard will be ready in minutes.

3. Serve with your Nepali dhal bhat tarkari (page 128).

SERVES 4

200g Swiss chard
vegetable oil, for cooking
5g garlic, finely sliced
½ a red chilli, finely sliced
sea salt and pepper, to taste

ALOO KO ACHAR

Traditionally this would be made using mustard oil; however, I find this overpowering so I use vegetable oil instead. I've compensated a little by using mustard seeds in the tempering.

1. Boil the potatoes in a large pan of water – they should be cooked through but not too soft. Drain and allow to steam-dry.

2. Meanwhile toast the sesame seeds in a dry frying pan, on a medium to high heat. Don't let them burn. You'll be able to smell when they are ready, as the sesame aroma will waft up. Transfer to a pestle and mortar, and allow them to cool before grinding to a coarse powder.

3. In a small bowl, mix the ground sesame, chilli powder, green chilli, salt and Szechuan pepper.

4. Transfer the cooked potatoes to a large mixing bowl, and evenly sprinkle the dry spice mix all over them while they are still warm. Give everything a stir.

5. For the tempering, heat the vegetable oil in a small to medium frying pan, on a medium to high heat. Once it's at temperature, add the mustard seeds, and after about 30 seconds the chilli pieces. When the mustard seeds start to crackle, add the fenugreek seeds and cumin seeds and after 30 seconds remove from the heat. Add the turmeric and asafoetida. You don't want these spices to burn, as they will turn bitter. Swirl the pan, and after a few seconds carefully drop the sizzling spices on to the potatoes.

6. Stir to evenly distribute the tempered spices, season with a squeeze of lemon or lime, and garnish with coriander leaves.

- - - - - - - - - - - - - - - - - - - -

SERVES 4–6

700g potatoes, peeled and cut into 3cm pieces (about 4 medium potatoes)

Dry spice mix
1 tablespoon sesame seeds
1 teaspoon chilli powder
1 green finger chilli, finely sliced
1 level teaspoon sea salt
½ teaspoon crushed Szechuan pepper (or timur, if you can get it)

Tempering
4 tablespoons vegetable oil
¼ teaspoon mustard seeds
1–2 dried red chillies, broken into pieces
½ teaspoon fenugreek seeds
¼ teaspoon cumin seeds
½ teaspoon ground turmeric
pinch of asafoetida (hing)

Garnish
lemon or lime juice
fresh coriander leaves

CHILLI PANEER (OR TOFU) AND CHILLI CHICKEN

This is my version of the famous dish. Typically making chilli paneer (which you can replace with tofu) and chilli chicken involves coating the paneer, tofu or chicken pieces with a thick spicy batter and deep-frying them. You stir these battered and deep-fried morsels through a tangy and spicy sauce spiked with soy sauce, vinegar and ketchup. It's a serious commitment to deep-fried food, which to be honest I find a bit sickly, so I've stripped it back. I use the sauce in the c: momos recipe on page 124 as a 'mother sauce', as it were, and use it in other dishes too (see cook's note). Serve with egg fried rice, plain rice or noodles. The Nepali noodle of choice is Wai Wai, which you can purchase online (standard medium egg noodles are fine) – it's a national obsession. Nepalis love them, and use these noodles to make omelettes, pakoras and Chinese kathi rolls!

CHILLI PANEER (OR USE TOFU)

1. Make the chilli sauce and have this on standby. Include the optional sriracha sauce.
2. Mix the cornflour, Szechuan pepper, chilli powder and salt together on a flat plate.
3. Cut the paneer or tofu into bite-size cubes. Roll and coat each piece in the seasoned cornflour.
4. Shallow-fry the paneer or tofu in a couple of tablespoons of vegetable oil on a medium to high heat – shaking off any excess flour – on all sides, until golden. You'll see a lovely little crispy crust form. You will need to do this in batches, and don't overcrowd your pan or they won't crisp.
5. Drain on kitchen paper.
6. Stir the crispy fried paneer or tofu pieces through the chilli sauce, garnish with finely sliced spring onion and coriander leaves, and serve immediately, with rice or noodles, and a wedge of lime.

SERVES 2–3

c: momo chilli sauce (see page 124)

3 heaped tablespoons cornflour

½ teaspoon crushed Szechuan pepper (or timur, if you can get it)

½ teaspoon mild Kashmiri chilli powder

½ teaspoon ground sea salt

300g paneer (or extra-firm tofu)

vegetable oil, for cooking

Garnish

finely sliced spring onions

fresh coriander leaves

lime wedges

COOK'S NOTE Vegetables Manchurian is an identical dish. These are vegetable 'meatballs' that are deep-fried, and again you can use the 'mother sauce' to stir them into. You can use the same ingredients as in the filling for the vegetable and paneer momos (see page 120), except omit the paneer and increase the vegetable quantities to equal parts (e.g. 60–70g each), and use 1 teaspoon of dark soy sauce as a seasoning. Bring the mixture together with 2 tablespoons cornflour and 1 tablespoon plain flour, plus a splash of water if need be to make a pliable mixture from which you can make little 'meatballs'. Deep-fry or air-fry the 'meatballs' until cooked and golden, and stir them into the prepared chilli sauce.

CHILLI CHICKEN

1. Make the chilli sauce ahead and have this on standby. Include the optional sriracha sauce.
2. Cut the chicken breasts into flat strips, using your knife at an angle – you don't want thin strips but you do want fairly thin, wide slices.
3. Mix the cornflour, Szechuan pepper, chilli powder, salt and ginger together on a flat plate.
4. Coat the chicken in the seasoned cornflour, then shallow-fry in a couple of tablespoons of vegetable oil on a medium to high heat – shaking off any excess flour – until cooked and golden. It will take about a minute on each side to cook, depending on how thick the slices are – don't overdo it, as dry chicken is not pleasant. You will need to fry in batches, and don't overcrowd your pan or the chicken won't crisp.
5. Drain on kitchen paper.
6. Stir the crispy fried chicken through the chilli sauce, garnish with finely sliced spring onion and coriander leaves, and serve immediately, with rice or noodles, and a wedge of lime.

SERVES 2–3

c: momo chilli sauce (see page 124)
300g chicken breasts
3 heaped tablespoons cornflour
½ teaspoon crushed Szechuan pepper (or timur, if you can get it)
½ teaspoon mild Kashmiri chilli powder
¼ teaspoon ground sea salt
¼ teaspoon ground ginger
vegetable oil, for cooking

Garnish
finely sliced spring onions
fresh coriander leaves
lime wedges

COOK'S NOTE You could easily turn this into a tray bake. Use skin-on, bone-in chicken thighs, and coat them in a dredge using the same spices – chilli powder, Szechuan pepper and salt – but use 50/50 cornflour and plain flour. Oven bake in a 200°C oven for 25–30 minutes (you can turn the chicken halfway through), then cover with the chilli sauce and bake for another 10 minutes. Carpet with sliced spring onions and coriander, and serve with rice or noodles.

This is not Nepali, but this Indo-Chinese mash-up is incredibly popular on my food service menu, and it's not hard to understand why. My homage brings together my obsession with soft and pillowy bao buns with another all-time favourite – butter chicken. The sharp and sweet pickles cut through the richness of the butter chicken, resulting in a taste explosion, with crispy onions and crushed toasted nuts for texture. You can of course use shop-bought baos; on days when I need a shortcut I buy frozen oyster shell or sandwich-style buns from my Chinese wholesaler, which can be steam cooked from frozen in 8–10 minutes. Though for days when you want to immerse yourself in the kitchen, I've adapted a lovely recipe from Chinese chef Michael Lim, so you have the 'know-how'. Each element of this recipe can be made ahead.

BUTTER CHICKEN BAO BUNS

SERVES 4–6

tandoori marinade
(see page 36)
1kg boneless, skinless
chicken thigh fillets
makhani gravy (see
page 36)

Bao buns
560g plain flour
11g instant dried yeast
½ teaspoon salt
1 teaspoon baking
powder
30g caster sugar
320ml whole milk
30ml vegetable oil

**Pickled cucumber and
chillies**
100g caster sugar
a pinch of salt
125ml white wine
vinegar
2 teaspoons coriander
seeds, toasted, then
lightly crushed in a
pestle and mortar
4 mild green chillies,
finely sliced and
de-seeded
½ a large cucumber,
finely sliced on a
mandolin

Garnish
toasted and crushed
peanuts and cashew
nuts
crispy fried onions
(shop-bought)
finely sliced strips of
spring onion
fresh coriander leaves
lime wedges

Note
For the bao buns you
will need a steamer and
some greaseproof or
parchment paper, cut
into individual small
squares (8cm x 8cm).

1. Make the tandoori marinade, then add the chicken and marinate it overnight, or start marinating in the morning if you plan to make the recipe in the evening. The meat needs 8–10 hours marinating, ideally.
2. For the bao buns, mix the ingredients in a free-standing mixer, using the dough hook on the lowest speed for 1 minute to combine. After a minute increase the speed to the next level and mix for a further 6 minutes to work the gluten.
3. Remove the dough from the mixer and knead into a ball on your work surface. Place in a lightly greased bowl, cover with a damp cloth, and place somewhere warm to double in size (this will take 1½–2 hours).
4. Meanwhile make the pickles. Dissolve the caster sugar and salt in the vinegar in a medium mixing bowl, then add the toasted and crushed coriander seeds. Add the chillies and cucumber, cover and refrigerate.
5. Make the makhani gravy and set aside.

→

6. Once the bao dough has doubled in size, gently lift it out on to a floured surface and roll it into a long sausage shape. Cut the dough into equal pieces, using scales – 65g each will give you nice-sized buns. Shape each piece of dough individually. Flatten with the base of your palm to make a flat disc, then bring the edges into the centre to form a tight ball. Turn over so it is smooth side up, and cup with your hand while using a rotating action to shape it into a smooth ball. Place on an 8cm x 8cm square of greaseproof, for the second prove. This will take 30–40 minutes – just leave them on your work surface. The greaseproof and bun will then be placed in the steamer together.

7. Steam the buns for 8–10 minutes. Don't overcrowd the steamer, as the buns are going to almost double in size. Note: If you make them ahead on the day, you can zap them in the microwave for about 30 seconds to heat up, or just refresh them in the steamer. If I'm batch-making, I freeze them once steamed.

8. When you are ready, grill the chicken thigh fillets on the highest heat of your oven grill, as close to the hot grill as possible to get a nice char. Lay the fillets flat so they cook evenly. They will take 4–6 minutes on each side, depending on their thickness. You can cut the thickest part to check it's cooked through and juicy.

9. Meanwhile reheat the makhani gravy. Add the cooked chicken to the reheated sauce to give it a nice glaze and to keep it moist before assembly.

10. Slice the buns in half, and stuff them with the butter chicken, pickled cucumber and chillies, toasted crushed nuts, crispy onions, sliced spring onions, coriander leaves and a squeeze of lime. Serve with spicy potato wedges, Nepali slaw (see page 118) and a pot of the makhani gravy! I find it best to lay out all of the elements on the dining table and serve this family style.

I found that Indian sweets (mithai) are very popular in Nepal – gajar ko halwa, barfi, kheer, rasgulla. Rajiv tells me that there isn't really a dessert culture, and Nepalis tend to finish a meal with fruit salad. Sel roti, which is almost a cross between a doughnut and a bagel, isn't a sweet and is eaten as a snack during festivals and on auspicious occasions. So what we have here is a carrot cake that meets gajar ko halwa (which is also known as gajrella in the Punjab). Gajrella is a dish of grated carrot cooked down in milk, sugar, ghee and cardamom, and which is also studded with sultanas and sliced almonds. I've transferred these flavours on to one of my favourite cakes!

CARROT CAKE TRAY BAKE

SERVES 10–12

240g plain flour
240g light brown sugar
1½ teaspoons ground cinnamon
1 teaspoon ground ginger
1 teaspoon baking powder
1 teaspoon bicarbonate of soda
½ teaspoon sea salt, ground in a pestle and mortar
225ml vegetable oil
3 eggs
½ teaspoon vanilla extract

240g grated carrot
50g sultanas
50g flaked almonds

Cream cheese frosting

300g icing sugar
10 green cardamom pods (bruise to release the seeds, then pound the seeds into a powder)
75g softened unsalted butter, at room temperature
180g cream cheese

Garnish

dried rose petals, or shop-bought jalebis for the really sweet-toothed (optional)

1. Set your oven to 170°C and grease and line a 30cm x 23cm x 5cm baking tin or similar.
2. In a large mixing bowl, mix together the dry ingredients: flour, sugar, cinnamon, ginger, baking powder, bicarb and salt.
3. In a separate bowl, whisk together the oil, eggs and vanilla.
4. Pour the wet ingredients into the dry ingredients and mix well. Stir in the carrots, sultanas and almonds. Transfer the mixture to your lined baking tin and bake for about 50 minutes (check after 30 minutes as ovens vary), until the cake springs back to the touch and if you insert a cocktail stick in the middle it comes out clean. Leave to cool in the tin, then transfer on to a wire rack to cool completely.
5. Meanwhile make the frosting. Your butter really must be soft and at room temperature. First mix the powdered cardamom through the icing sugar, using a whisk so it's evenly distributed. Then, using either a free-standing mixer or a hand-held electric whisk, beat the butter into the icing sugar, followed by the cream cheese. Be careful not to overmix, as the frosting can start to become liquid.
6. Adorn your carrot cake with the frosting and your choice of decoration.

LEICESTER

LEICESTER MARKET

GUJARATI COMMUNITY

Leicester has been predicted to become Britain's first minority majority city, and is celebrated for its diversity. Described as 'the world in microcosm' by LSE (London School of Economics) researchers, it is made up of diaspora communities from across the world – as exemplified by the array of shops and businesses on Narborough Road. We are going to focus on the Gujarati Hindu community. Leicester has a significant Gujarati population, the largest outside London, with a notable contingent that first emigrated from East Africa in the 70s. In the UK you will meet two types of Gujaratis, with heritage from either East Africa or India. Those from India tend to be vegetarian and have more of a plant-based diet; those from Africa tend to eat more meat. I will focus on the vegetarians in this chapter. The Gujarati community is made up of a number of different minority faiths, including Muslims, Sikhs, Jains and Christians, but the predominant faith is certainly Hindu. Leicester hosts one of the largest Diwali celebrations outside India. Diwali is the Festival of Light, which is celebrated by Hindus, Sikhs and Jains; it marks new beginnings and the triumph of light over darkness, good over evil. It attracts around 40,000 visitors to Leicester's 'Golden Mile' – famous for its Indian restaurants and shops – to see spectacular firework displays, and for food, music and dancing.

DR PYAL PATEL (AGED 38)

NHS doctor

Pyal was born in south-east London and is currently based in Surrey; however, her father originally came to Leicester in the late 1960s. He was born in Tanzania and came to the UK as a teenager, part of the mass exodus from East Africa. He graduated from De Montfort University, and his family remained in Leicester for a number of years before moving to Twickenham. Pyal's mother came from India in the 1970s; both parents are Gujarati. I asked Pyal if being a doctor and GP was something she always aspired to do or was encouraged to do: 'Growing up it was always drilled into me that you'd have to do something that's respectable. A lifelong career, a field where there'll always be employment, always needed in the society or the community that you're in.' But this kind of projection can give youngsters huge insecurities. Pyal recalls that, growing up, she didn't always believe she could do it. But she did do it, having a natural affinity towards subjects like biology, maths and chemistry. We joke about the three acceptable career options being doctor, lawyer or engineer.

'It was a bit of an indoctrination but not to the extent that I've seen some of my friends and family go through. I think my parents were right – it is a very fulfilling job, when you enjoy it. There are certain aspects of general practice in the NHS that I don't enjoy, but most of it is quite fulfilling and rewarding. There's a great community feel, a lot of continuity with patients. The thing I enjoy the most is that you're constantly learning new things. I don't think there's ever been a boring stage in my career. There're always new things and new courses.'

However, Pyal does tell me about a 'wobble' she had during the first Covid lockdown, something she is still working through. A global pandemic was enough for us all to question our life choices. She explains that this ultimately comes down to a conflict of being a creative in a professional field with few creative outlets. I hope Pyal finds what she is ultimately looking for, the calling that gives her that sense of completion that she hopes she can do alongside her medical career. We each have our own 'kismat' or destiny. The key is to meet your own expectations.

Pyal relates her Gujarati identity to food. She's not hugely religious, and to her being a Gujarati Hindu is more about a way of life: a way of eating, a way of cooking, a way of living: 'We as a culture are a quirky group of people. And our food is unique to us. We're predominantly vegetarian, traditionally. Growing up, we didn't eat things like pasta or what the other kids were eating.' Identity was a real struggle for Pyal as the only Indian in her class at school. Her parents were shop owners, and at that time her biggest issue was that they used to live above the shop. They didn't have a conventional house as her friends had, so she was embarrassed about living above a corner shop: 'But now I wonder why, I mean what was there to be embarrassed about? We had a home, we were privileged, we had money, so why was I embarrassed? And I still can't figure it out to this day. I genuinely loved being Indian, the food, the clothes, the music, since I was a kid. But we couldn't openly have a tiffin, with roti and shaak or whatever. It was always: cheese sandwich. I wasn't even allowed to have a ham sandwich, as my mum is vegetarian, so it was just hard.'

Like many of us, Pyal lived with her grandparents too, who had a hands-on role in raising her. The extended family network was vital in enabling parents to work and earn back then. There were many African Indian influences at mealtimes – like eating meat, for example – but every Sunday the family would eat a traditional Gujarati thali in lieu of a roast (which ironically her two girls eat now). Helping her grandmother and mother with meal preparation evokes sweet nostalgia. Especially the plethora of ways in which Gujaratis use besan (chickpea flour) to make snacks, which is stretched to ingenious levels, quite frankly. Farsan is the collective term for these snacks, which can be deep-fried or steamed. Most Gujaratis batch-fry once or twice a month, she tells me. Everything from sev and chevdo (like Bombay mix) to khandvi (chickpea flour and water cooked down into thick paste, cooled on a flat surface, rolled, then topped with a tarka), dhokla (a savoury semolina cake) or dhokli (a thick flat noodle cooked into dhals). These are all made from store-cupboard ingredients, not fresh, because of the droughts and long periods of dry weather in Gujarat. So there is a reliance on store-cupboard ingredients, which is reflected in the cuisine. However, her father didn't allow any cooking during shop opening hours, as he felt this would offend customers.

'My dad was very "English". We still ate the Indian food, but my mum wasn't allowed to cook until the shop was closed because of the smells. When we do a tarka it's a very pungent smell. So my dad was like, Definitely not, and if you do do it, you have to lock the doors and make sure the extractor fan is on full blast. So that filtered down to me, and I'm thinking, Well, hold on, what's so embarrassing about it? You know I don't think anybody ever came in and said: Do you know, I don't like that smell! People were very curious and were like, What is that you're cooking? But my dad was like, Oh my gosh, they're picking on me, they don't like this smell. But they were just curious. I can look back now and see that.' Pyal understands that her father was just doing what fathers do, sheltering and protecting his family, but it's also clear how her feelings of cultural embarrassment in her younger years stem from this. She tells me she went through an identity crisis of sorts, almost like living a 'dual life': life at home and life at school: 'I felt I had the biggest problem at school . . . I had to watch *Neighbours* and *Home and Away* just to keep up with the Joneses. But really what I wanted to talk about was the latest Bollywood movie, because that's what we were watching at home. But I didn't have Indian friends, or Gujarati friends, as I grew up in a very white town . . . As a teenage girl you don't want to stick out, you just want to fit in – look like everybody else, feel like everybody else and that's when the struggle starts.'

It wasn't until she went to university that Pyal felt able to embrace the Indian side of her identity, to talk about it without feeling self-conscious, to talk about her identity with pride. Ultimately it's about acceptance, and finding the confidence to be at ease in your own skin, which comes with time and experience.

We segue on to the topic of linking food with wellness. There's a lot of traction behind this notion of culinary medicine; it's not entirely new – we've had an ancient tradition of Ayurveda in India for centuries. 'Wellness for me is an all-round feeling, a level of being: mind and body and digestion all being linked together. As long as I'm eating what I enjoy, but in a balanced plate . . . so I'm going to have a protein, I'm going to have vegetables, I'll have a salad, and then I'm going to have my dhal. Wellness is about balance, in diet, in exercise, in mental health. As a second generation Gujarati I think that is how we have evolved; understood what we needed to do to remain healthy. We saw a lot of the generation above having the heart attacks and the diabetes. And as a GP that's where I come in and tell my Asian patients that while you think this is good for you, and it's very tasty, we don't need to eat like that any more because we're not living in a place where there can be drought. Our palates have been accustomed for decades to eating this kind of food but we need to adapt and do things alongside.'

Lifestyle medicine is a topic Pyal is most passionate about. Ayurveda, and Ayurvedic medicine, is something we both know a fair amount about, but neither of us ever studied it. It strikes me that it is passed on intuitively as an oral tradition, particularly principles around digestion, and taught in an inherent way. As Pyal says, 'I will sometimes drink saunf tea [fennel], in just hot water, which aids digestion. I sometimes drink tea with ajwain [carom seeds], as it releases all the gases. My grandmother would say, Don't eat without drinking anything first thing in the morning. These Ayurvedic schools will teach you as soon as you get up you must drink something to aid your digestion, start off with a little warm water. All of that.'

Ayurveda is a healing system based on the premise that health and wellness depend on a balance between mind, body and spirit, and originates from ancient India.

SPICES AND WELLNESS

Written with Katy Petter, Cheshire-based nutritionist

There are continuous research and studies into so-called 'superfoods', and here are some spices I use regularly. Of course, eating for wellness is about achieving a balance, and involves portion control, water intake, exercise and mental health.

* TURMERIC: A powerful anti-inflammatory and a strong antioxidant, which helps against ageing. It can help with conditions such as arthritis, irritable bowel, cognitive decline, heart disease and back pain.

* GARLIC: Helps to purify the blood and flush out toxins. Also an aid to controlling acne. Though not used in Ayurvedic cooking, used more as a medicine. Proven to be helpful with atherosclerosis, high blood pressure and cold prevention.

* GINGER: Boosts immunity, helps digestion, enhances metabolism and increases blood circulation. It's also known to aid the absorption of nutrients. Medicinally it is used to calm upset stomach and irritable bowel, reduce inflammation, boost immunity, balance hormones and support liver function.

* CHILLI: Enhances metabolism, is rich in vitamin C and is needed to develop the immune system.

* CUMIN: Aids digestion and helps to minimize/reduce water retention.

* AJWAIN/CAROM SEEDS: Used to maintain digestive health, and used liberally by Indian mothers for their miraculous ability to cure tummy upsets, pain or indigestion.

* FENNEL SEEDS: Used to aid constipation, indigestion and bloating/gas. Used in herbal medicine to improve digestive symptoms such as colic, irritable bowel syndrome, reflux and heartburn.

* CORIANDER SEEDS: Possess antiseptic properties; used to treat inflammation.

* CINNAMON/CASSIA BARK: These have antioxidant and anti-inflammatory properties. Many positive effects on metabolic processes, such as blood sugar balance and digestion, and anti-fungal properties.

* CARDAMOM: Aids digestive health and increases blood circulation.

When you start looking closely at world cuisine, you notice certain cross-overs or variations of the same thing. A chapatti is strikingly similar to a tortilla or soft taco in many ways, and when you wrap your sabji, meat or tandoori grill into a chapatti – well, the similarities are uncanny. Thepla is a spiced Gujarati flatbread made with yoghurt and fresh fenugreek. Here's my variation.

FISH TACOS IN A THEPLA FLATBREAD

SERVES 4

Taco dough or thepla
500g Greek set yogurt
2 tablespoons cumin seeds
3 teaspoons sea salt
2 tablespoons Kasuri methi (dried fenugreek)
270g chapatti flour or atta
approx. 160g plain flour
vegetable oil, for frying

Green chutney
30g fresh mint
4–5 spring onions
1–2 green finger chillies, or to taste
1–2 tablespoons vegetable oil
salt
a squeeze of lemon juice, and a little zest

Tandoori spice mix
½ teaspoon ground turmeric
1 teaspoon garam masala
⅓ teaspoon garlic granules

1 teaspoon ground cumin
1 teaspoon ground coriander
½ teaspoon mild or medium Kashmiri chilli powder
⅓ teaspoon fennel seeds
1 teaspoon sea salt

White cabbage slaw
finely shredded white cabbage (about ¼ of a cabbage)

Fish
4 skinless white fish fillets (approx. 500g total weight; I use cod)
juice of 1 lemon
2–3 tablespoons panko breadcrumbs

Garnish
sour cream
garam masala
fresh coriander leaves
finely chopped red onion
pickled or fresh green chillies, finely sliced
lime wedges

1. Start by making the dough. Mix the yoghurt, cumin seeds, salt and methi in a large bowl. Test the seasoning here. If it's good, add the chapatti flour, mix, then add enough plain flour to make a relatively firm dough (you can add a splash of water if it gets too dry). Give it a good knead on your work surface until smooth, then place in a clean bowl, cover and pop into the fridge to rest.

2. Now make the green chutney. Pick off the mint leaves, roughly chop the spring onions (green parts too), and destalk and roughly chop the chillies. Place all the chutney ingredients in a blender and blitz until smooth. You can add a splash more oil if it needs loosening. Taste and adjust the seasoning if necessary, then set aside.

3. To make the tandoori spice mix, just mix all the ingredients together and place in a little dish.

→

4. Shred your cabbage into a bowl, and coat generously with the green chutney. Cover, then set aside at room temperature.

5. Prepare your sour cream. Place a couple of tablespoons in a bowl, and season with a pinch of garam masala. It's as easy as that. Place in a piping bag or squeezy bottle if you want to be fancy, and pop into the fridge.

6. Slice the fish into 2cm thick strips or goujons, and give these a good lick of lemon juice – this will allow the spice mix and panko to stick to the fish.

7. Place the spice mix on a large flat plate and mix with the panko. Now take the fish pieces and coat them in the spicy 'dredge'. Set aside. You could refrigerate at this point if you want to prep ahead.

8. Heat a frying pan or tawa on your hob on a medium heat, giving it a few minutes to come to temperature.

9. Now divide the dough to make the tacos, which shouldn't be too big. You're aiming for an 11–12cm diameter, so your dough balls should be about half or two-thirds the size of a golf ball. You can refrigerate any leftover dough in an airtight container and make flatbreads with this.

10. Take a dough ball and roll it into a thin round disc on a lightly dusted surface. Lift the rolled taco and pat it from hand to hand to shake off any excess dry flour (as this will burn). Place it directly on to the dry frying pan or tawa. Cook on each side for approximately 2 minutes using tongs to flip. Batch-make all the tacos (or as many as you need), wrapping them in foil to keep them warm. You can then transfer them to a 170°C oven to keep warm before serving.

11. Set your table and lay out all the condiments: slaw, sour cream and garnishes. Tacos are best served 'family style'. The self-assembly of tacos is a really convivial way to eat.

12. Finally, fry the fish. Heat a little vegetable oil in a large frying pan on a medium to high heat. Add the fish goujons, placing them as you would the dials of a clock, starting at number one – as you then know which pieces will be cooked first. Fry on each side until cooked and golden – it will only take a couple of minutes (in total) – and transfer to a warmed serving dish. You may need to fry them in batches. Take immediately to the table, and retrieve your tacos from the oven. The way I assemble is to take a taco, add a little slaw, then add the fish pieces, a squeeze of sour cream, adorn with coriander leaves, a sprinkle of chopped red onion, chillies, a kiss of lime juice and apply to face. Enjoy!

You can get a whole host of weird and wonderful Southeast Asian vegetables at Leicester market. Gujaratis love gourds, of all kinds. One such gourd reminds me of a crocodile, a gourd called a karela, and it is lip-puckeringly bitter! An acquired taste, let's say, often stuffed with keema. I remember my mum painstakingly sewing these up when I was little; they are said to be very good for diabetes, though it's the powder or juice that has most medicinal value. It is said that okra, or bhindi, also has medicinal properties. It often gets a bad rap for being slimy, but as with all things in life you have to prep it and treat it right to get the best results. You could also make onion rings (soak in milk beforehand).

BEER-BATTERED OKRA FRIES

SERVES 4 AS A STARTER

vegetable oil, for deep-frying
approx. 300g okra

Beer batter
100g chickpea flour (besan), plus extra if you want a thicker coating of batter
¼ teaspoon ground turmeric
1 teaspoon ground cumin
1 teaspoon chilli powder
1 teaspoon garam masala
½ teaspoon ground coriander
1 teaspoon sea salt
1 x 330ml can of cold IPA (you won't need all of this), or sparkling water if you prefer

chaat masala

1. Heat oil in your deep fryer or kadhai to 180°C.
2. Wash the okra under cold running water, then – this is very important – dry them thoroughly. I do this individually with kitchen paper to do a proper job. Set aside.
3. Put the chickpea flour, turmeric, cumin, chilli powder, garam masala, ground coriander and salt into a mixing bowl and whisk together. Slowly whisk in the pale ale or sparkling water. You want a double-cream-like consistency, and you won't need the whole can.
4. Top and tail the okra, and split the bigger ones vertically in half. If you want a thicker batter, roll the okra in some dry gram flour first, which will help the batter to stick. (Put a couple of tablespoons of gram flour on a plate, so you can easily roll the okra in it.) If you prefer a lighter batter, put the okra straight into the prepared batter.
5. Deep-fry the okra until cooked, crisp and golden, being careful not to overcrowd when frying. Drain on kitchen paper.
6. Sprinkle with a light hit of chaat masala, and serve with your choice of ketchup, firecracker mayo (see page 206) or chilli sauce.

Leicester is home to the largest crisp factory in the world, so I wanted to pay homage to that and tie it in with the Gujarati love of snacks. Inspired by the famous triangular-shaped corn chips – except in England we call them crisps – and in a token effort to be healthy, I give you my avocado and spinach rotli 'crisps'. You can serve them with a variety of dips: smoked aubergine raita (which also goes very well with tandoori lamb chops or kebabs), tarka houmous, mango chutney, lime pickle and grilled halloumi or okra fries. You can make the rotlis ahead (if they last) and can switch up the flavour and colour – maybe try a spiced beetroot flavour, or carrot and coriander, or even plain. Crisps and dips, a match made in heaven.

ROTLI 'CRISPS' } WITH SMOKED AUBERGINE RAITA DIP

SERVES 4–6

Smoked aubergine raita dip
1 aubergine (approx. 450g)
200g thick and creamy full-fat Greek yoghurt
½ teaspoon sea salt, or to taste
¼ of a clove of garlic, grated
chopped fresh mint or coriander (optional)
a pinch of ground cumin

Spinach and avocado rotli
300g plain flour (you can also use chapatti /atta flour)
½ teaspoon sea salt
1 teaspoon cumin seeds
2 tablespoons vegetable oil
1 tablespoon chopped fresh coriander

1 avocado (mine weighed 235g whole, 146g prepped)
1 teaspoon minced green chillies
juice of ½ a lime
50g young leaf spinach
25ml water

1. Preheat your oven to 200°C and line a baking tray with baking paper.
2. First, make the raita. Char the aubergine on an open flame – I use the biggest ring on my gas hob. Use tongs to turn and ensure every centimetre is charred. The skin will look black and burnt. Transfer to the lined tray and roast for 10–15 minutes, until cooked through and soft to the touch. Allow to cool completely.
3. Cut the aubergine in half from top to bottom, then scoop out the flesh on to a chopping board and discard the charred exterior. Finely dice the flesh, then transfer to a mixing bowl.
4. Stir in the yoghurt, sea salt, garlic and chopped herbs if you are using them. Taste, and adjust. Try not to eat it all here and now! Cover and place in the fridge.

5. Now make the dough for the rotli. Mix together the flour, salt, cumin seeds and oil in a large bowl, then stir in the chopped coriander. Put the avocado flesh, minced chillies, lime juice (which will prevent oxidization), spinach and water into a blender, or use a stick blender, and blitz to a smooth purée. Add the purée to the seasoned flour and bring together, using a spatula to scrape out every last bit. Knead for about 5 minutes, to a soft, smooth dough. You may need a touch more flour. Cover and rest at room temperature for 30 minutes.

6. When you are ready to make your rotli, heat your tawa or non-stick frying pan (I use a 30cm frying pan) on a medium to high heat. It needs to be hot.

7. Divide the dough into six equal portions. Dust your work surface with a little flour. Take one portion of dough, roll it between the palms of your hands until smooth, then flatten the dough ball into a disc.

8. Roll the disc into a thin circle with a rolling pin and pat it from hand to hand to shake off any excess dry flour. This is an important step as any excess dry flour will burn and spoil your rotli.

9. Place the rotli directly on the dry frying pan or tawa. Using tongs, flip after 30 seconds. You will start to see little bubbles form. Take a clean dry tea towel and roll it into a ball, then gently pat the rotli all over with it – this will encourage greater bubbles to form. After about 1½–2 minutes you'll be ready to flip the rotli over (and it should be cooked through on one side).

10. Remove the rotli from the heat and stack them inside a clean tea towel or chapatti warmer while you make the rest. When they are all done, cut and divide your rotli stack into sixths, as you would a pizza.

11. Put your smoked raita into a serving bowl, and sprinkle a little ground cumin over the top. Serve with your rotli 'crisps', and any other accompaniments. The crunch from the okra fries (page 149) is a great contrasting texture.

> **COOK'S NOTE** Of course you have a gorgeous rotli recipe here in itself to eat with your dhals, shaaks or thalis. I like to use them as wraps and fill them with either vegetable bhajis, or grilled halloumi along with a crunchy slaw and mango chutney. The layers of flavour and texture will bounce around your mouth like the ball in a pinball machine!

Shaak is what Gujaratis call their sabjis or veggie curries – sometimes these have a hint of jaggery or tamarind to add sweetness or sourness, according to what will complement that particular vegetable. The shaaks tend to be quite dry, and can swing from quite mellow and sweet to hot and spicy, depending on which area of Gujarat you find yourself in. The inclusion of nuts – which Gujaratis are very fond of – also adds another dimension and texture. This is lovely as a side dish or as part of a thali ensemble. You can also use new or baby potatoes in this recipe.

HASSELBACK POTATO SHAAK

SERVES 4–6 AS A SIDE

1kg small Vivaldi salad potatoes (these are naturally creamy and don't need butter – choose a similar variety if you can't get these)

vegetable oil, for cooking

50g cashew nuts

1 teaspoon cumin seeds

1 teaspoon poppy seeds (khus khus)

½ teaspoon sesame seeds

½ teaspoon ground turmeric

1 teaspoon chilli powder

½ teaspoon sea salt, plus an extra sprinkle for roasting

lemon juice, to taste

fresh coriander leaves, to garnish

1. Preheat your oven to 200°C and line a baking sheet with baking paper. Rinse the potatoes under cold water and remove any eyes.
2. To prep the potatoes you will need a wooden spoon and a sharp knife. Place each potato in the cavity of the spoon, and make deep and narrow cuts all along the potato without cutting the whole way through; the edges of the spoon will prevent this. You're aiming for about the thickness of a pound coin, but don't worry, it doesn't have to be exact.
3. Place the potatoes in a large mixing bowl, and toss them with a little vegetable oil. Then place the hasselbacks, cut side up, on the lined baking sheet, so they fan and concertina out during roasting and will take on more spices later. Season with sea salt and roast for 25–30 minutes, or until cooked and golden. Remove from the oven and drain on kitchen paper.
4. Heat 3 or 4 tablespoons of vegetable oil in a wok or kadhai on a medium to high heat. Sauté the cashews for a minute or so, until golden (take care, as nuts can catch very quickly), then add all the spices: cumin seeds, poppy seeds, sesame seeds, turmeric, chilli powder and salt.
5. Allow the spices to toast for a few seconds, then add the potatoes to the pan and stir-fry until they are all coated. Season with a good squeeze of lemon juice.
6. Remove from the heat, garnish with a little fresh coriander and serve.

Right, so this isn't exactly a puran poli, which has a sweetened dhal filling, I hold my hands up; but it's inspired by this sweet/savoury stuffed bread and uses the best of Leicester ingredients – yes, that cheese! I do love a paneer paratha, and rather than making my own cheese I've used English cottage cheese, which I've hung to drain out the liquid. Who doesn't like a shortcut? And I also think it's more flavoursome than paneer – which is very neutral. I love the layers of flavour in this filling: a bit of tang, a bit sweet and sour, creamy, and a hint of heat.

COTTAGE CHEESE AND CRANBERRY 'PURAN POLI'

MAKES 5 'PURAN POLI'

Rotli dough

300g chapatti flour or atta (use a medium blend)

a pinch of salt

2 tablespoons vegetable oil

approx. 150–200ml just-boiled water

Filling

300g full-fat cottage cheese

50g grated Red Leicester cheese

¼ teaspoon chilli powder

¼ teaspoon garam masala

salt, to taste

¼ teaspoon amchoor (dried mango powder) or chaat masala

20g dried cranberries, chopped

2 spring onions, green parts only, finely sliced

1 tablespoon chopped fresh coriander

melted ghee or vegetable oil, for cooking

1. You need to plan ahead as the cottage cheese needs an overnight 'hang'. Place a tea towel or a large piece of muslin cloth in a sieve, positioned over a bowl. Tip in the cottage cheese, then gather up the edges and wring out the liquid. Place the tied 'cheese ball' back into the sieve. Pop a plate on top to weigh it down and leave in the fridge overnight; you could also weigh it down with a tin of tomatoes or something similar.

2. To make the dough for the rotli, mix together the atta/flour, salt and oil in a large bowl. Add 150ml of just-boiled water, and use the end of a wooden spoon to bring everything together. Slowly add the rest of the hot water a little at a time (add a little extra if need be). When you can see that you have added a sufficient amount of water and the dough is 'balling', use your hands to knead for 5 minutes or so, until you have a smooth, soft dough. Cover and set aside at room temperature to rest for at least 30 minutes.

3. Meanwhile make the filling. Take your cottage cheese out of the fridge and open up the muslin or tea towel – you'll have crumbly dry cheese. Scrape it all out into a large mixing bowl and crumble with a fork, then add the Red Leicester, chilli powder, garam masala, salt, amchoor or chaat masala, cranberries, spring onions and coriander. Taste, adjust and set aside.

4. You will need a large non-stick frying pan or tawa, which you should heat in advance on a medium to high heat.

5. Divide the dough into five equal portions. Dust your work surface with a little dry flour. Roll a portion of the dough between the palms of your hands until smooth, then flatten the dough ball into a disc. Lightly dust your work surface with a little atta/flour (or you can use veg oil) and roll the disc into a thin circle with a rolling pin.

6. Place a couple of tablespoons of the filling mixture in the centre of the rotli, then bring in the edges to seal the mixture in – you'll have a hexagon shape.

7. Cup the sharp edges with your hands to soften them into a round disc, then gently roll out, turning as you go. The filling will be revealed the thinner you roll, like a stained glass window, deep red and green flecks, with golden strands of Red Leicester. Don't roll it too thin – you don't want to create a hole in your stuffed bread. Roll to about 18cm in diameter and 4mm thick.

8. Place the rolled 'puran poli' directly on to the dry frying pan or tawa. Using tongs, flip after 30 seconds, then brush this side with melted ghee or oil, flip again, and cook for about 2 minutes. Brush the other side with ghee or oil, then flip and cook that side for about 2 minutes.

9. Drain on kitchen paper. Serve immediately.

COOK'S NOTE You could have this on its own with a little onion marmalade or mango pickle – Gujaratis love their pickles – or as part of an extravagant thali.

I was quite intrigued when I first came across this traditional Gujarati dish. Ravaiya, to give the dish its proper name, is Gujarati soul food. It can be dry, or served in a tomato sauce or gravy, in which case it is called ravaiya bharela. The masala stuffing tends to be made from a mix of either toasted peanuts and spices or toasted chickpea flour and spices. There are always variations – some people use both and others also include grated coconut. Ravaiya could refer to any stuffed vegetable, and the Gujarati word for aubergine is 'ringan'. I've stuck to tradition with this one, pretty much anyway.

BABY AUBERGINE STUFFED } WITH PEANUT MASALA

SERVES 4

Tomato sauce
vegetable oil, for cooking
½ teaspoon cumin seeds
1 bay leaf
1 small brown onion, finely diced
½ teaspoon ground turmeric
½–1 teaspoon chilli powder
1–1½ teaspoons garam masala
1 teaspoon sea salt
1 x 400g tin of chopped tomatoes, blitzed into a purée
200–300ml water
½ teaspoon sugar (optional)

Stuffed aubergine
150g blanched unsalted peanuts, toasted
30g fresh coriander, stalks and all
10g ginger, grated
10g garlic, grated
1 teaspoon ground cumin
1 teaspoon ground coriander
½ teaspoon sea salt
½ teaspoon amchoor (dried mango powder)
pinch of asafoetida (hing) (optional)
1–2 tablespoons sriracha sauce
1 tablespoon vegetable oil
8 round baby aubergines (approx. 800g, black or purple ones are just fine)

fresh coriander, to garnish

1. Start with the tomato sauce. Heat a few tablespoons of vegetable oil in a large lidded ovenproof sauté pan or casserole dish on a medium to high heat, and add the cumin seeds and bay leaf. When they start to release their aromas, tip in the onions, reduce the heat and cook low and slow until golden.

2. Add the ground spices: turmeric, chilli powder and garam masala, and the salt. Toast them a little, then pour in the blitzed tomatoes and the water. Increase the heat and bring to a simmer. Give the sauce a quick taste – you can add a little sugar if you like. Remove from the heat and set aside.

3. Set your oven to 200°C. While it's heating up, make the aubergine stuffing. Blitz the toasted peanuts and coriander to a fine crumb in a food processor, then transfer to a large mixing bowl and combine with the ginger, garlic, cumin, coriander, salt, amchoor, asafoetida, if using, sriracha and oil.

4. Quarter each aubergine, starting at the base and without cutting through the stem, therefore leaving them intact. You'll end up with a cross-shaped

opening at the base of each aubergine – gently tease this open with your fingers and stuff each aubergine with the peanut masala.

5. Bring the tomato sauce back to a simmer and add the stuffed aubergines. Increase the heat to maximum to create some steam, then put the lid on and carefully transfer to the hot oven.

6. After 30 minutes remove the lid and bake for a further 15 minutes uncovered, or until the aubergines are soft and meltingly tender.

7. Garnish with coriander leaves and serve with kachumber salad (page 48), yoghurt and fresh buttered rotli (page 221).

Gujaratis adore dhal, and unsurprisingly there are specific dhals for certain occasions. As wedding dhal featured on Dr Pyal Patel's all-time thali, I had to include this. It's made with toor dhal, also known as split pigeon peas. This dhal does not contain onion or garlic, an omission which is rooted in Ayurvedic guidance and in some cases religious reasons; asafoetida or hing is used as a substitute. It is also 'khatti-meethi', which means sweet and sour: the sweetness often comes from jaggery or dried fruit, the sourness from kokum, tamarind or lemon juice. As always, there are many variations – some cooks include yam or peanuts, for example, but the spicing in this dhal is most distinct and will almost always have flavours of mustard seeds, cinnamon, cloves, asafoetida, curry leaves and fenugreek seeds.

GUJARATI WEDDING DHAL

SERVES 6–8

2 cups toor dhal (split pigeon peas)

6 cups water

1 teaspoon ground turmeric

1 whole green finger chilli, pierced but kept intact

1½ teaspoons sea salt

Tarka

50g butter or 3–4 tablespoons ghee

1 teaspoon black mustard seeds

1 teaspoon cumin seeds

2–3 whole cloves

5cm cassia bark or cinnamon

8–10 curry leaves

5g ginger, grated

1 teaspoon Kashmiri chilli powder

1 teaspoon shaak masala or garam masala

½ teaspoon asafoetida (hing)

200ml passata

1 teaspoon tamarind paste

1 teaspoon jaggery, or to taste (granulated or caster sugar is fine)

400ml water

a pinch of Kasuri methi (dried fenugreek)

lemon juice, for serving

1. Place the toor dhal in a large bowl and thoroughly rinse under cold water – you'll need about four changes of water. Put the washed dhal into a large saucepan along with the 6 cups of water. Bring to the boil, then reduce to a simmer.

2. Add the turmeric, whole pierced green chilli and salt, and simmer, covered, for 25–30 minutes, or until cooked. You may need to add extra water and skim off any scum that forms. Don't let the pan dry out. Set aside.

3. Start the tarka about 15 minutes before the dhal is cooked. It HAS to be cooked in either ghee or butter. Melt the ghee or butter in a large sauté pan or saucepan on a medium heat, then add the whole spices – mustard seeds, cumin seeds, cloves, cinnamon/cassia and curry leaves – and let them start to release their aromas.

4. Add the ginger and allow to cook out, followed by the ground spices: chilli powder, shaak or garam masala and asafoetida. Toast these for 30 seconds, then add the passata and bring to a simmer.
5. After a few minutes taste the masala, then add the tamarind paste and jaggery. Cook out a little more, then taste again and adjust accordingly.
6. Now mix in the cooked dhal and an additional 400ml of water. Gently stir, making sure everything is mixed together, and increase the hob heat. Add the crushed methi at this point too.
7. Once the dhal is at temperature, have a final taste – you may wish to add a touch more salt. Simmer for a further 15 minutes or so, to allow the flavours to develop. You may also like to add more water – some folks like their dhal to be very fluid.
8. Serve as part of a thali, or with the cheesy puran poli (page 154) or spinach and avocado rotli (page 150). I'm a bread over rice kind of girl. An extra squeeze of lemon will elevate the flavour.

> **COOK'S NOTE** A thali is a large metal plate or tray filled with small tapas-style dishes (these small bowls are called katoris). Here is Pyal's dream thali: wedding dhal, rice, tinda (stir-fried round gourd), khandvi (a rolled snack made from chickpea flour), puri (fried bread), pickles, poppadoms or papad, and magas besan barfi (a fudge made with chickpea flour – Pyal promised to convince me on that one!).

Gujiyas are sweet little pastries, most commonly filled with mawa/khoya (evaporated milk solids), sugar and nuts. They are traditionally made for Diwali and Holi festivals, and, depending on which part of India you find yourself in, they have a range of fillings from coconut, or poppy seed paste, to semolina. They are almost always a crescent shape, and often deep-fried. I'm making an oven-baked savoury version, much like an empanada, filled with mushrooms and using a shortcrust pastry. If you prefer to deep-fry them, use samosa pastry instead (see page 24 for the recipe). I was inspired by the wares at the Leicester market – it has a vast array of vegetables and produce and is said to be the largest covered market in Europe. Gujiyas can be made to look ornate by using a gujiya mould, or simple by twisting and crimping the edges, as you would with a miniature Cornish pasty.

MUSHROOM MASALA GUJIYAS

MAKES 16–18

Pastry
250g plain flour
125g cold unsalted butter, grated (use the coarsest side of your box grater; by grating you minimize handling)
1 teaspoon sea salt
approx. 100ml cold water (may be more or less, depending on the flour absorption)

Mushroom filling
vegetable oil, for cooking
250g button mushrooms, finely sliced (wipe or brush mushrooms clean, never rinse)
250g chestnut mushrooms, finely sliced
a pinch of salt
1 bay leaf
5cm cassia bark

4 green cardamom pods (bruise to release the seeds)
1 large brown onion, finely sliced into half-moons
2 green chillies, slit in half lengthways
10g garlic, grated
½ teaspoon ground turmeric
1 teaspoon garam masala
½–1 teaspoon sea salt, or to taste

50ml water
1 tablespoon chopped fresh coriander
1–2 tablespoons mayonnaise

Turmeric milk wash
20ml milk
⅛ teaspoon ground turmeric

1. First, make the pastry. Place all the pastry ingredients – except the water – in a food processor and pulse until you have a sand-like consistency. The fats should be kept as cold as possible, either coarsely grated or cut into small cubes. Add the cold water a little at a time, using the pulse setting; the dough will begin to ball and you may not need all the water (you want a play-dough texture). Remove the dough from the food processor and shape into a thick disc, handling it as little as possible, then wrap in cling film or an alternative and rest in the fridge for 30 minutes.

2. Now make the mushroom filling. To build the flavour and texture, the mushrooms must be sautéed on a high heat, 10 out of 10 high. Mushrooms actually benefit from some abuse on that front, so heat

→

a few tablespoons of vegetable oil in a large frying pan, kadhai or wok and chuck in the sliced mushrooms. Sprinkle generously with salt and sauté for 8–10 minutes, stirring from time to time. The salt draws out the moisture and will prevent the mushrooms from burning. The volume will reduce by about half, and you want some colour on them. Transfer them to a plate and set aside.

3. Wipe your pan if necessary. Heat a little more vegetable oil on a medium to high heat, and add the whole spices: bay leaf, cassia and cardamom. Add the onions and slit chillies, and reduce the heat to medium. Allow the onions to cook out and take on a light golden colour. This will take 10 minutes or so.

4. Add the grated garlic and cook out for a minute, then add the ground spices: turmeric and garam masala, and the salt. Toast these a little, then add 50ml of water, which will prevent the spices from catching.

5. Return the mushrooms to the pan and give everything a good mix, while bringing all the ingredients back up to temperature. Finally stir through the chopped coriander. Remove from the heat and allow to cool completely. Once cooled, stir in the mayonnaise.

6. Set your oven to 190°C and line two baking sheets. Roll out your pastry to the thickness of a 20p piece on a lightly floured work surface, then, using a 9cm round cutter, cut 16 pastry discs. Place a teaspoon of filling in the centre – don't be tempted to overfill. Brush a little water around the edge, which will act as glue. Now fold the pastry over the filling, to create a half-moon/semicircle. Crimp the edges with a fork. Transfer the gujiya on to the lined baking sheets, eight per sheet. Repeat, re-rolling the pastry as necessary.

7. Make the turmeric milk wash by mixing the milk and turmeric together in a small bowl, then brush on to the gujiyas. Bake for about 12–15 minutes, or until cooked and golden. Gobble!

COOK'S NOTE Add a dash of cream rather than mayo to the mushroom mixture and use it as a filling in a puff pastry vol-au-vent.

I've riffed on a recipe from my days at Ashburton Chefs' Academy here. Kulfi is a time investment: there are shortcuts with evaporated or condensed milk, but they can't match the flavour that time and loving care impart. For fun with the kids I make a pistachio praline with popping candy, for a Sherbet Dib Dab vibe. And for a dinner party you could freeze the mixture in a loaf tin lined with cling film and make a semi-freddo. Either way it's worth the effort.

CARAMEL KULFI ICE LOLLIES

MAKES 6 ICE LOLLIES

Kulfi
1 litre whole milk
80g caster sugar
5 green cardamom pods, bruise and split

2 teaspoons Carnation caramel, or to taste (you can drizzle a little extra over your lollies too)

Popping pistachio praline
100g caster sugar
60g pistachios
vegetable oil, for greasing
1 teaspoon popping candy

1. You will need an ice lolly/popsicle mould and wooden sticks to make these. Use a premium food grade silicone for the best results.
2. Place the milk, sugar and cardamom pods in a heavy-bottomed sauce-pan. Gently stir until the sugar has dissolved, then simmer on a moderate heat until the volume has reduced by half, stirring from time to time. This will take about 2 hours, or less, dependent on the pan you are using.
3. Allow the mixture to cool, then whisk through the caramel. Have a taste – note it will taste VERY sweet, but bear in mind that freezing will dial down the flavour. Strain through a sieve and decant into your moulds/ a suitable container.
4. Freeze for at least 4 hours, or ideally overnight.
5. To make the popping pistachio praline, lightly grease some greaseproof paper and lay it on a baking sheet. Heat the sugar in a heavy-bottomed saucepan over a medium heat, until it dissolves and turns a caramel colour – do not be tempted to stir at any point or the sugar will crystallize. Add the pistachios, then pour the mixture on to the greased paper and allow to cool. Once hardened, break into small fragments with a rolling pin, or pulse in a processor if you want it to be finer. Now mix with the popping candy. Place in an airtight container.
6. Allow the lollies to stand for a couple of minutes out of the fridge before unmoulding – they will slide out more easily. Serve immediately, with the popping pistachio praline.

LONDON & HARROW

LONDON — PARSI COMMUNITY

·—··—··—··—··—··—·

'Parsi' is the Gujarati word for Persian. The Parsi community is synonymous with the modern-day café culture of Bombay – now known as Mumbai. The Parsis came from Persia, and a large number emigrated to India – predominantly to Gujarat, which had a heavy influence on the cuisine – to escape religious persecution of their Zoroastrian faith. The exact date of migration is unknown but could be as far back as the eighth century. Many eventually settled in Bombay, and played a dominant role in the seventeenth century when Bombay came under the control of the British East India Company.

The Parsis are a small and close-knit community; the diaspora population in the UK is concentrated in London and is estimated to be around 5,000, according to the Zoroastrian Trust Funds of Europe, UK. Immigration came in two main stages, from India and Pakistan in the 60s, then from East Africa in the 70s.

ZARINA DHILLON, NÉE SHROFF (AGED 44)

Recipe developer

Before I even speak to Zarina, it strikes me how little I know about the Zoroastrian faith. I'm quite ashamed to admit it. So I take it upon myself to learn. Founded by its prophet, Zoroaster (also known as Zarathustra), Zoroastrianism is one of the oldest practised monotheistic religions, believing in one God. It is based on 'dualistic cosmology', which is the struggle between good and evil, as well as the divinity in seeking wisdom. Zoroastrianism dates back to ancient Persia, its birthplace, and was the religion of that once mighty empire. Zoroastrians live by three core values:

'Good Thoughts, Good Words, Good Deeds.'

The natural elements are of great significance, and fire and water in particular are important symbols of purity – which is required to defeat evil. Fire temples maintain sacred fires to represent the light and purity of God (Ahura Mazda), and rituals and ceremonies cannot be performed without the presence of a sacred fire. I find myself quite fascinated. You can't convert to Zoroastrianism but must be born into it, which is why it's a dying faith with a declining population. Zoroastrianism is the smallest of the nine recognized world faiths in the UK, which has one of the oldest established Zoroastrian communities outside India and Iran. There is a long history of eminent Parsis in Britain: in fact Dadabhai Naoroji, an important political leader and scholar, was the first Indian to be elected as an MP in the UK parliament, in 1892, as member for Finsbury (Liberal Party).

We start with a little background. Zarina is truly international and was actually born and raised in Hong Kong. Her mother was born in Bombay, her father was born in Shanghai and moved to Hong Kong as a teenager; both Parsis. They married in Bombay, then emigrated to Hong Kong together, where they remain to this day. Zarina moved to Switzerland as a teenager to study hotel management, then secured an internship at a famous hotel group in Atlanta, USA. She moved to

London six years later, where she met her husband – a Punjabi Sikh – with whom she has three children. It takes me a few minutes to follow the chronology and globe-trotting! Naturally her food style has global influences as a result. Zarina grew up in multicultural communities – religion was never pushed on her and there was always a respect for other religions. In many ways Zarina exemplifies the global dispersion of the Parsi population. She tells me how important it is to her that her children, who are thirteen, eleven and five at the time we speak, have a connection with their Parsi heritage. We talk about the Navjote ceremony, which is an initiation ceremony or coming of age where a child is accepted into the Zoroastrian fellowship; a rite of passage that takes place before puberty, at around ten or eleven years old. Her two older children have had these ceremonies, as she wanted to give them the option to practise the faith. Normally Orthodox Zoroastrian priests would refuse this, on the grounds that both parents are not Parsi; but this is a sign of how the community is evolving in response to the modern multicultural global age we live in, as a way of preserving the culture. They have been brought up understanding both religions, and attend both temples. Education is so vital, or else that Parsi inheritance is lost. I feel this sense of responsibility to act as custodians for future generations.

I ask Zarina about Parsi food. There are no restrictions on food and drink – Parsis will eat pork, for example – but it's more a case of eating certain dishes and food types at certain times and to mark certain occasions. It sounds quite complicated. I've included a recipe for one of the most famous Parsi dishes, the dhansak – understanding the context around the dish was very interesting. There aren't many Parsi-specific cookbooks, but Zarina does refer to a book called *Vividh Vani* by Meherbai Jamshedji Wadia, which was first published in the 1860s and is essentially an encyclopedia of Parsi food culture and history. Funnily enough, this was around the same time the famous tome written by Mrs Beeton was published: *Book of Household Management*. Perhaps a zeitgeist of that era.

There is a famous story in Parsi folklore about 'the sugar in the milk'. The way the story goes is that when the Parsis arrived in Gujarat, King Jadhav Rana sent the Parsi priests a glass brimming with milk. Lack of a common language was a barrier between the two communities, so this was sent as a gesture to convey that he could not accept the refugees, in a land already full of people. The priests added sugar to the milk, to send back a message that they would make the land richer and more prosperous with their values of good deeds, good thoughts and hard work. The king, so impressed, granted asylum and welcomed the Parsis into his kingdom. Not only have Parsis blended into India like sugar in milk, they have done the same in Britain. Zoroastrian centres and societies undertake many charitable and philanthropic projects, often working with other faiths. Zoroastrians in the UK have become leaders in business as well as in various professions, in some cases acknowledged with national awards and honours.

Breakfast is one of the most important meals of the day, and when it comes to weekends, how lovely is it to have a lie-in and a luxuriant full English? Except that this version isn't exactly English. Parsis have a well-documented love affair with eggs, akuri being a famous scrambled egg dish, so that's how we MUST have the eggs. As for the other components, well, we can make this vegan, vegetarian or made to pork-fection! Mix and match to your taste. The sausages must be something spiced, like a peppery Cumberland. The eggs can be replaced with crumbled tofu, and any dairy with non-dairy ingredients. I love the freshness and zip that a little avocado 'sambal' brings. I could eat this dish at any time of day. If you are lucky enough to have leftover masala baked beans, these are wonderful with cheese on toast! A fried egg on top of a potato cake is also a thing of beauty.

FULL BELLY-BUSTER 'BRINDIAN' BREAKFAST

SERVES 4

vegetable oil, for cooking

Roasted tomatoes

2 large tomatoes, cut in half across the middle

sea salt and black pepper

Avocado 'sambal'

1 large ripe avocado

juice and zest of 1 lime

¼ of a red onion, finely diced

1 finely chopped chilli, or to taste

chopped fresh coriander, to taste

sea salt, to taste

Potato tikkis (makes 4)

½ a large brown onion (approx. 65g), grated (use long sweeps with a box grater, we don't want a mush) and the liquid squeezed out using a muslin cloth/tea towel

1 teaspoon cumin seeds

1 teaspoon garam masala

1 teaspoon sea salt

1 teaspoon minced chillies

a pinch of Kasuri methi (dried fenugreek)

1 tablespoon chopped fresh coriander

2 medium to large potatoes (400g prepped weight), peeled, cut into large dice, boiled, drained, mashed and cooled

1 tablespoon cornflour or rice flour

Scrambled eggs 'akuri'

1½ teaspoons cumin seeds

1 large brown onion, finely sliced into half-moons

1 green finger chilli, split in half lengthways

1 teaspoon garam masala

½ teaspoon ground turmeric

1 teaspoon sea salt flakes, or to taste

6 baby plum tomatoes, halved

8–10 eggs, beaten

1 tablespoon chopped fresh coriander

a knob of butter (optional)

Masala baked beans

1½ teaspoons cumin seeds

1 brown onion, finely diced

1–2 green finger chillies, split in half lengthways

1 large garlic clove, grated

grated ginger (equal volume to the garlic)

1 teaspoon garam masala

¾ teaspoon ground turmeric

sea salt, to taste

4 baby plum tomatoes, quartered

2 x 400g tins of baked beans

a good knob of butter

Sautéd mushrooms

butter

4 large flat mushrooms, sliced

½ a clove of garlic, grated (optional)

sea salt and pepper, to taste

Sausages and bacon

4 large Cumberland sausages (or vegetarian/vegan alternatives)

4 rashers of bacon (streaky or back bacon, to taste)

→

COOK'S NOTE The potato cake is amazing in a chickpea chaat. Top with a couple of tablespoons of chana masala (see page 30), a drizzle of yoghurt, a drizzle of tamarind ketchup, diced red onion, pomegranate seeds, fine crispy sev, fresh coriander leaves and a dollop of mint chutney. It's also great simply topped with a fried egg – runny yolk, of course!

1. Heat your oven to 180°C and line two baking trays with greaseproof paper.
2. Gently massage a scant amount of vegetable oil on to your tomato halves, and season with sea salt and a good crack of black pepper. Place on one of your lined baking trays, cut side up, and set aside.
3. To make the avocado sambal, halve the avocado, remove the stone, then dice the avocado flesh, mix it with the rest of the sambal ingredients in a small mixing bowl, cover and set aside at room temperature.
4. To make the potato tikkis, mix the squeezed grated onion, cumin seeds, garam masala, salt, chillies, methi and chopped coriander together in a large mixing bowl. Check the seasoning and adjust as required. Mix in the cold mashed potatoes and the cornflour or rice flour. Divide the mixture equally into four and shape your tikkis into round, flat potato cakes. You can make these ahead and refrigerate them, which also makes them firmer and easier to shallow-fry. To shallow-fry the potato tikkis, heat some vegetable oil in a medium to large frying pan. The oil should be 3cm deep, and you want it heated to 170°C – so it's a fairly high heat. Gently place the potato tikkis in the pan and colour until golden, a couple of minutes on each side.
5. Drain the tikkis on kitchen paper and place on your second lined baking tray to finish cooking in the oven. Put your tomatoes in to roast at the same time. This will take about 15–20 minutes, and you can reduce the oven temperature to keep them both warm while you finish the other components.
6. Next, make the tarkas for the eggs and beans. First the eggs: heat 3 tablespoons of vegetable oil in a large frying pan, then add the cumin seeds. Toast until they start to release their aromas, then tip in your sliced onions and chilli. Sauté on a moderate heat until softened, then add the garam masala, turmeric and salt. Toast for 30 seconds, then add a splash of water to prevent the spices from burning. Add the baby plum tomatoes and allow these to break down to form a sauce – again you may need to add a touch of water to help the process along. Now have a taste. Adjust the seasoning and set aside. You'll reheat this and mix through the beaten eggs or crumbled tofu to make a scramble at the end.
7. Repeat the process to make the tarka for the beans (or do both simultaneously if you can multi-task) in a large saucepan, adding the garlic and ginger this time. Mix in the beans, add a good knob of butter, increase the heat to melt and incorporate it, then reduce to a simmer.
8. Meanwhile, sauté your sliced mushrooms in a little butter and vegetable oil – the oil prevents the butter from burning – adding your grated garlic if using, and seasoning with salt and pepper.
9. Grill the sausages, then the bacon.
10. When you are ready, reheat the tarka for the eggs. Once simmering, fold through the beaten eggs and stir until scrambled. Scatter over the chopped coriander leaves, and run a knob of butter through for an extra gloss, if you like.
11. Serve and enjoy! You may want a dollop of tomato ketchup or brown sauce too. You might also need to lie down again once you've eaten!

There are a couple of ways we could serve this dish, but it has to include an egg element, which is what 'per eedu' denotes. I love a keema pau, which is a very popular street food; a pau or pav is a light and soft dinner roll, and to make keema pau you stuff this roll with keema. You could also make this by cooking the eggs into the keema – create wells in your cooked keema and place a cracked egg in each, lid on, steam cook. A bit like a shakshuka. As with all keema it's very versatile (and healthier than lamb or beef mince). I like this in a crunchy corn shell taco, with grated carrot, fresh coriander leaves and a drizzle of yoghurt or raita over the top. Or just with plain roti (chapatti).

CHICKEN AND SWEETCORN KEEMA PER EEDU

SERVES 4–6

4–6 eggs
dried chilli flakes, nigella seeds and salt, to sprinkle

Chicken keema
vegetable oil, for cooking
1–2 bay leaves
1½ teaspoons cumin seeds
5cm cinnamon or cassia bark

4 green cardamom pods (bruise to release the seeds, then crush the seeds in a pestle and mortar)
½ teaspoon crushed black peppercorns
1 large red onion, finely diced
2–3 spring onions, green parts only, finely sliced
15g ginger, grated

15g garlic, grated
1–2 green finger chillies, or to taste, split in half lengthways
1 level teaspoon ground turmeric
1½ teaspoons garam masala
1–2 teaspoons Kashmiri chilli powder
2 teaspoons sea salt, or to taste

1 large tomato, peeled and diced (or 4 tablespoons passata)
500g minced chicken (needs to have a good fat content, so should be thigh meat ideally)
1 small tin of sweetcorn, drained (140g drained weight)
5–6 fresh mint leaves, finely sliced
juice of ½ a lime, or to taste

1. Heat 4 tablespoons of vegetable oil in a large lidded saucepan or sauté pan on a medium to high heat, then add the bay leaf and the whole spices: cumin, cinnamon/cassia bark, cardamom and black pepper. Beware, the bay leaf may spit. When they start to release their aromas, tip in both types of onion, reduce the heat and allow to soften for a few minutes.

2. Add the ginger, garlic and green chillies to the pan and cook out, then add the turmeric, garam masala, chilli powder and salt. Mix well and allow the spices to toast for 30 seconds – add a splash of water if the mixture starts to catch.

3. Add the diced tomatoes, using your wooden spoon or spatula to help break these down, with a splash of water to help them along. You want

→

a thick sauce consistency. Passata will give you a darker, richer sauce. Check the seasoning.

4. Now add the minced chicken to the pan and sauté and seal over a high heat, again using your spoon to break down the meat. Reduce to a simmer and cover with a lid. Check after 10 minutes – the chicken should be cooked by this point. Fold in the sweetcorn, and simmer for another 2–3 minutes so the corn can warm through. Sprinkle with the finely sliced mint leaves, add a squeeze of lime, and make any final adjustments to the seasoning.

5. Fry your egg just how you like it – sunny side up for me with a runny yolk! I season with the merest sprinkle of chilli flakes, salt and nigella seeds.

6. Serve your fried egg on top of a pile of keema with a dollop of brown sauce or tamarind ketchup on the side. Garnish with fresh coriander leaves.

COOK'S NOTE Make a keema pau by stuffing the keema into a soft, buttered dinner roll. Add a few straw fries kissed with salt and chaat masala for extra indulgence!

Continuing with the breakfast/brunch theme, here is my Parsi spin on this classic poached egg dish. English muffins, halved and slathered with butter, topped with creamed spinach (saag), a poached egg and curried hollandaise sauce. You could make this an eggs Benedict by replacing the spinach with bacon or ham. Personally it's the saag that really does it for me!

DESI EGGS FLORENTINE OR BENEDICT

SERVES 4

creamed saag (see page 36 – you may not need it all but it keeps and freezes well)
4 English muffins
spreadable butter
paprika, to garnish

Poached eggs
4 fresh eggs (8 if you want a poached egg for each muffin half – there is enough sauce)
1 teaspoon white wine vinegar

Curried hollandaise
150g unsalted butter
2 egg yolks (egg whites are freezable, save for making meringue)
1 teaspoon white wine vinegar
½–1 teaspoon mild curry powder, or to taste
sea salt, to taste
lemon juice, to taste

1. Make the creamed saag. If you make it ahead, it will keep in the fridge for 3 days. I very often have a batch in the freezer, which I can defrost the night before. Now, poach the eggs. I know it might sound weird, but you'll thank me, as it saves last-minute rushing to pull everything together. It's a common practice in commercial kitchens, and I learned this hack at chefs' school. Bring a saucepan of water to the boil. It should be quite deep.
2. Meanwhile crack your eggs into individual ramekins. When the water has boiled, reduce it to a rapid simmer (equivalent of 7 out of 10 in terms of heat). Add the vinegar, then gently put in the eggs, no more than two at a time. Set your timer to 3 minutes and 30 seconds.
3. Meanwhile prepare a big bowl of iced water to plunge the poached eggs into. This will halt any further cooking.
4. Take a slotted spoon and lift one of the eggs out. Check by gently pressing the yolk – you want a runny yolk but not too runny, so there should be a wobble, and the whites should be firm. You may need another 15–30 seconds, but no longer. It depends on the size of your eggs. Plunge them into the cold water, and set aside.

5. Let's make the hollandaise. Melt then clarify your butter. I find the easiest way to do this is to sieve it through a muslin cloth. Place in a jug and set aside.
6. Place a glass or Pyrex bowl over a saucepan of simmering water. Do not let the water touch the bottom of the bowl.
7. Immediately put in the yolks, along with the vinegar, and whisk until pale, quite thick and the mixture forms ribbons. Make sure the bowl doesn't get too hot – you can take the pan on and off the heat if need be. It will take 6 or 7 minutes. Turn the heat off.
8. Whisk in the clarified butter a little at a time – you want a double cream kind of consistency. If you add the butter too quickly the sauce can split – a splash of hot water can bring it back, though.
9. Season with the curry powder, salt, and a touch of lemon juice. Cover with cling film and set aside while you bring everything together.
10. Reheat the creamed saag. Trim any loose egg whites from the poached eggs. Reheat the eggs by placing them in boiling water for 45 seconds. Drain on kitchen paper.
11. Split, toast and butter your muffins. Add a little creamed saag to four of the halves, rest a poached egg on top, and crown with a spoonful of curried hollandaise. It looks pretty with a pinch of paprika sprinkled over the top. Place the other half muffin alongside or on top, or load that up too if you prefer.

COOK'S NOTE When poaching eggs, you really need to make sure they are good quality and fresh. Fresh eggs have a large amount of thick albumen and therefore less chance of spreading in the water. You can test if an egg is fresh by placing it in a bowl of cold water – if it sinks it is fresh, and if it floats it is not.

I got to thinking about Bombay duck – which is actually a fish – and it gave me a strong inclination to cook a dish with duck as the star ingredient. I'm not a massive lover of duck, but at chefs' school I was converted to the beauty of confit duck. The secret to the best results is the curing process or marinade, prior to the confit. I had a simple cassoulet in mind but with a Parsi accent not French. Once you have mastered confit duck, there are so many things you can do with it. You could shred the meat and make a terrine, or a hash, tacos, spring rolls, pancakes, waffles – the options are limitless!

SPICED CONFIT DUCK

SERVES 4

Cure
1 star anise
½ teaspoon whole black peppercorns
1 stick of cinnamon, broken into small pieces
2 whole cloves
½ teaspoon coriander seeds
1 dried Kashmiri chilli
2 bay leaves
2 teaspoons sea salt
½ teaspoon granulated/caster sugar

20g garlic
10g fresh coriander
5cm piece of orange zest (optional)
a pinch of ground mace (optional)

Confit duck
4 duck legs, skin on, approx. 880g total weight (I used Gressingham)
duck fat, to cover (I used 3 x 320g jars, and a 22cm saucepan)
15g garlic, unpeeled and smashed
3 bay leaves

4 green cardamom pods (bruise to release the seeds, then crush the seeds in a pestle and mortar)

Beans
vegetable oil, for cooking
1 brown onion, finely diced
10g garlic, grated
10g ginger, grated
1 green chilli, split in half lengthways
1 teaspoon garam masala

½ teaspoon ground turmeric
½ teaspoon Kashmiri chilli powder
1–1½ teaspoons sea salt, or to taste
½ x 400g tin of chopped tomatoes, blended (or 200ml passata)
2 x 400g tins of cannellini beans, drained
200ml water
1 tablespoon chopped fresh coriander

1. The confit process is very easy, but long, so you need to factor this in to when you'd like to serve it.
2. Put the whole spices for the cure into a dry frying pan over a medium to high heat – star anise, black peppercorns, cinnamon, whole cloves, coriander seeds, Kashmiri chilli and bay leaves – until they start to release their aromas. Then transfer to your mortar, pound with the pestle to crush and break them up, then add the salt and sugar and grind together into a coarse powder. Smash in the garlic cloves (no need to peel), then smash in the fresh coriander until it starts to become a coarse paste. Add a couple of splashes of water to help it along to a spreadable consistency. You can add the optional zest, which should be lightly pounded into the mixture to release its oils, and a pinch of mace, if using.
3. Smother the duck legs with this mixture, then place in a freezer bag or

similar, seal and refrigerate. Marinate for 24 hours, or overnight.

4. Set your oven to 140°C. Gently warm the duck fat in a saucepan on a low heat. Scrape off the marinade from the duck legs. Put them into either an ovenproof saucepan or an ovenproof dish, one that you can snugly place the duck legs in, then pour over the melted fat, making sure the legs are completely submerged. Add the garlic, bay leaves and crushed cardamom seeds.

5. Place a cartouche (circle of greaseproof paper) over the duck/surface area, and carefully put in the oven. Allow to slowly cook for 2–3 hours, until the duck is tender and can be easily pulled away from the bone. Set aside to cool. (See cook's note.) Meanwhile make the beans. Heat about 4 tablespoons of vegetable oil in a medium to large saucepan and sauté the onions until softened. Add the garlic, ginger and green chilli. Once these have turned golden, add the ground spices: garam masala, turmeric and chilli powder, and the salt. Let these toast, then tip in the tomatoes. Bring to the boil, then reduce the heat and simmer for about 10 minutes.

6. When you see the oil separate on the surface of the masala, taste and adjust the seasoning. Now mix in the cannellini beans, along with the water. Simmer for 15–20 minutes, then stir in the chopped coriander, take off the heat, cover and set aside. Reheat before serving if need be.

7. Gently lift the duck legs out of the dish and drain on kitchen paper. Transfer them to a lined baking sheet and reheat in the oven at 200°C, which will render any excess fat and allow the skin to go crispy. It will take 6–8 minutes. You could sprinkle the duck with a scant amount of garam masala and salt before placing in the oven if you wish – but I think it has enough flavour.

8. Assemble the dish: first the beans, then the confit duck, and finally a carrot and coriander salad (see below). You could replace the beans with a bhaji rosti and serve with a strained masala sauce if you wanted to push the boat out! Experiment.

> **COOK'S NOTE**
> Confit duck legs can keep in the fridge for a number of weeks, covered with fat and stored in an appropriate sterilized jar or airtight container. You can also strain the cooking fat – use a muslin cloth to catch any sediment – then refrigerate and re-use.

CARROT AND CORIANDER SALAD

SERVES 4–6

4 small round shallots, finely sliced into half-moons
1 large carrot, grated
20g fresh coriander leaves
1 tablespoon vegetable oil
lemon juice, to taste
salt and black pepper

1. Put the shallots, carrot and coriander into a serving bowl.
2. Whisk the oil, lemon juice and seasoning to make a simple dressing, pour over and serve.

Here's another way with eggs – we're boiling them this time, for my Parsi-inspired Scotch eggs. In this dish we have gorgeous soft-boiled eggs, encased in an onion and potato bhaji batter. I warn you, these are seriously addictive, and for me they have to be served with a generous helping of mango chutney, and eaten in a quiet corner of a room, by myself, without any interruptions!

ONION BHAJI SCOTCH EGGS

MAKES 4 SCOTCH EGGS

4 eggs
3 heaped tablespoons yoghurt
1 tablespoon cumin seeds

2 teaspoons sea salt, or to taste
1 teaspoon garam masala
2 teaspoons minced chillies, or to taste

1 heaped tablespoon chopped fresh coriander
100g chickpea flour (besan)
1 medium potato

1 large onion, finely sliced into half-moons
vegetable oil, for deep-frying
extra chickpea flour, to roll the boiled eggs in

1. Boil the eggs for 5 minutes in boiling water, then place in a large bowl of ice-cold water to halt the cooking process. Set aside.
2. Stir together the yoghurt, cumin, salt, garam masala, minced chillies and chopped coriander in a large mixing bowl, then mix in the gram flour – you want a thick batter/moist paste. Set aside.
3. Peel the potato and grate on the coarse side of a box grater, using long strokes – you want long strands, not a mush. Place the grated potato in a tea towel or muslin cloth and squeeze out all the moisture. Tip the grated potato into the bowl of batter along with the sliced onions, and use your hands to bring everything together. Set aside.
4. Heat oil in your deep fryer or kadhai to about 160°C.
5. Carefully peel your eggs, then put a few tablespoons of extra gram flour into a flat bowl.
6. It's going to get messy. Take an egg and roll it in the dry gram flour, then cover the egg with the thick bhaji mixture, ensuring it is completely encased. You may find it easiest to take a quarter of the batter, shape it into a disc on the palm of your hand, sit the egg in the centre and gradually wrap the egg. Do whatever works for you.
7. Place on a large spoon and gently lower into the hot oil. Fry until golden and cooked through, which should take approximately 4 minutes but may vary. You don't want to fry more than two at a time.
8. Using a slotted spoon, remove the Scotch eggs from the oil and drain on kitchen paper.
9. Serve with mango chutney, and savour every morsel!

This is my version of the much-loved Parsi dish that often comes in the form of mutton, slow-cooked with lentils and vegetables. It's pure comfort. Dhansak is actually a mourning dish, prepared on the fourth day after a loved one passes; there must be an abstinence from meat for the first three days. In Parsi homes, this dish is often made on a Sunday, as it involves a lot of prep and slow cooking. My version is stripped down and simple. It's always served with caramelized onion rice, so I'm going to respectfully observe the traditions on this one.

LAMB AND BUTTERNUT SQUASH DHANSAK

SERVES 4–6

Masoor dhal
1 cup masoor dhal (split red lentils)
4–5 cups water
½ teaspoon ground turmeric
1 green finger chilli, left whole but skin pierced with the tip of a knife
1½ teaspoons sea salt

Lamb masala
vegetable oil, for cooking
2 red onions, finely sliced into half-moons
a pinch of salt
20g garlic, grated
20g ginger, grated
1 teaspoon ground turmeric
2 teaspoons garam masala or dhansak masala

2 teaspoons Kashmiri chilli powder
1 teaspoon sea salt
½ x 400g tin of whole tomatoes, blended until smooth
500g lamb neck fillet, cut into big bite-size pieces
approx. 50ml water
½–1 teaspoon Kasuri methi (dried fenugreek)

Roasted butternut squash
approx. 400g butternut squash, peeled and cut into 2.5cm cubes
vegetable oil
a sprinkle of sea salt
approx. 1 teaspoon cumin seeds

1. Set your oven to 200°C and line a baking sheet with baking paper.
2. We'll start with the dhal. Masoor or split red lentils don't often require a pre-soak. Rinse them a couple of times under cold water, using a sieve. Put them into a large lidded saucepan along with 4 cups of water, the turmeric and the whole pierced green chilli. (We only want the flavour from the chilli, not the heat. The heat is in the seeds and inner membrane and is released when chopped.) Bring to the boil, then simmer with the lid on for 25–30 minutes. Keep an eye on it, and don't let the lentils go dry – you may need another cup of water.
3. Meanwhile slow-cook the onions for the lamb masala. Heat a few glugs of oil in another large lidded saucepan on a medium heat and add the onions – you want to caramelize these low and slow for 20–25 minutes. Add a pinch of salt – this will draw out the moisture and prevent the onions from burning. Toss the diced butternut squash with a little vegetable oil and season with sea salt and the cumin seeds. Transfer to your lined baking sheet and roast for 30 minutes, or until cooked and golden. Drain on kitchen paper and set aside.

4. Check on the dhal – it should be cooked by now. Season with 1½ teaspoons of sea salt, or to taste. Remove from the heat and set aside.

5. Add the garlic and ginger to the caramelized onions, cook out for a couple of minutes, then add the ground spices: turmeric, garam masala and chilli powder, and the salt. Toast the spices for 30 seconds, then tip in the tomatoes. Bring the masala to a boil, then reduce the heat and simmer for 10 minutes or so. You'll see the oil separate on the surface when it's ready, at which point taste and adjust the seasoning as necessary.

6. Gently mix the lamb through the masala over maximum heat. You want to ensure all the pieces are coated and sealed. Reduce the heat and simmer for 30–35 minutes, or until the meat is meltingly tender. Keep a close eye: you want a dry masala but don't let the meat catch – you may need to add about 50ml of water to prevent this.

7. Once the lamb is cooked, pour in the lentils, mix together, then add the roasted butternut squash. Give everything a good stir, then add the Kasuri methi. Simmer for another 2–3 minutes, or until everything is piping hot.

8. Serve with caramelized onion rice (see below) and a kachumber salad (page 48).

CARAMELIZED ONION RICE

1. Start by rinsing the rice to remove any excess starch. Place in a bowl and cover with cold water, give it a swish to agitate it, then rinse three or four times, using a fine sieve. Cover with cold water again and set aside for at least 30 minutes.

2. Heat 3 or 4 tablespoons of oil in a medium to large lidded saucepan, add the green cardamoms and sauté until they release their aromas, then tip in the onions and allow them to cook low and slow for 20 minutes or so, until golden and caramelized.

3. Strain the rice and add to the onion mixture, stirring to coat thoroughly. Mix in the saffron and salt. Now add 4 cups of water. It's always a 1:2 ratio for the absorption method. I use boiling water from the kettle. Give everything a good stir and check you are happy with the seasoning. As soon as the water reaches boiling point, put a tight-fitting lid on the pan (you can wrap the lid in a tea towel if need be) and reduce to a simmer. It needs 10–12 minutes – you can check after 10 minutes but not before – then remove from the heat.

4. Allow to stand for another 10 minutes with the lid on. Before serving, fork the rice through (not a spoon – it will break the long grains).

▪ ▬ ▪ ▬ ▪ ▬ ▪ ▬ ▪ ▬ ▪ ▬ ▪ ▬ ▪ ▬ ▪ ▬ ▪ ▬ ▪

2 cups basmati rice

vegetable oil, for cooking

4 green cardamom pods (bruise to release the seeds)

1 large brown onion, finely sliced into half-moons

a pinch of saffron threads, or ¼ teaspoon ground turmeric

1–2 teaspoons sea salt, or to taste

4 cups water

This should be called a dope-iaza as I have totally amped up the 'piaz', which is the Hindi word for onion. Dopiaza is Persian in origin and means two onions, though this refers to the two-way method of cooking the onions as much as anything. Now cheese and onion is my favourite flavour of crisps – it is a perfect combination, and that applies in this curry too. I am dedicating this one to 'Squeak the Guinea Pig' – a friend that I love dearly and on whom I conducted vegetarian recipe experiments! Loves a dopiaza does Squeak, but also likes curries to pack some heat. Parsi dishes tend to be quite mellow, with sweet and savoury flavours. The onions bring the sweetness and you can decide how much heat you fancy. I like to garnish with lots of finely sliced mild red chillies to add a pop of colour, bite and flavour.

PANEER DOPIAZA } WITH CHARRED SHALLOT PETALS

SERVES 4

Shallot petals
8–10 small round shallots
vegetable oil, for cooking
sea salt

Masala sauce
vegetable oil, for cooking
1–2 bay leaves
1 whole dried Kashmiri chilli

5cm cinnamon or cassia bark
4–5 green cardamoms (bruise to release the seeds, then crush the seeds in a pestle and mortar)
2 whole cloves
1 red onion, finely diced
5 spring onions, finely sliced, including the green part (keep green and white parts separate)

15g ginger, grated
15g garlic, grated
1–2 green finger chillies, to taste, split in half lengthways
1 teaspoon ground turmeric
1½ teaspoons garam masala
2 teaspoons sea salt, or to taste
1 x 400g tin of chopped tomatoes, blended until smooth

400–450g paneer
a drizzle of double cream (approx. 3 tablespoons)
a pinch of Kasuri methi (dried fenugreek)
3–4 pinches of chaat masala
100g young leaf spinach (optional, see cook's note)

Garnish
lots of fresh coriander
2 mild red chillies, finely sliced

1. Set your oven to 200°C. Cut the shallots vertically in half, through the root and keeping each half intact. Peel off the outer skin and first layer if necessary. Massage the shallots with a scant amount of vegetable oil. Place them on a lined baking tray, cut side up, and roast for 15–20 minutes, or until cooked through. Remove from the oven. The next step is to char. You can use your oven grill set on the highest heat, placing the shelf as close to the hot grills as possible, or use a chef's blowtorch. Alternatively place the shallots cut side down in a very hot dry frying pan for the same effect. Set aside to cool.

2. To make the masala, heat 3 or 4 tablespoons of vegetable oil in a large lidded saucepan or sauté pan on a medium to high heat, then add the bay leaf and the whole spices: dried chilli, cinnamon/cassia, cardamom

→

and cloves. Be careful, the bay leaves will spit. Once they start to release their aromas, add the red onion and the white parts of the spring onions, then reduce the heat and allow to soften for a few minutes.

3. Add the ginger, garlic and green chillies and cook out for a couple of minutes, then tip in the ground spices: turmeric and garam masala, and the salt. Mix well and allow the spices to toast for 30 seconds – add a splash of water if the mixture starts to catch.

4. Pour in the tinned tomatoes, give everything a good mix, and crank up the heat to bring the masala to the boil. Then reduce the heat to medium and simmer for 8–10 minutes, covered.

5. Meanwhile prepare the paneer. If you are using shop-bought paneer, which tends to be firmer, soak it in a bowl of boiling water for a couple of minutes. This will make it lovely and soft, like home-made paneer. Drain and pat dry on kitchen paper (any moisture will spit when fried, so do be thorough with this step). Cut into bite-sized cubes.

6. Your masala will be about ready now, and you should see the oil split on the surface. Drizzle in the cream, mix through, then bring to a simmer once more and taste. Adjust the seasoning as necessary, sprinkle with the methi, then take off the heat.

7. To shallow-fry the paneer you don't need much oil in the frying pan. Fry in batches until golden on all sides, on a medium to high heat. Be careful in case it spits – which it shouldn't as long as you've done a good job in removing the moisture and your oil isn't too hot. Place on kitchen paper to drain. Season with a little sea salt while it's still hot, and a sprinkle of chaat masala, then fold it through the masala sauce along with the green parts of the spring onions. Put the saucepan back on the hob on a medium heat.

8. Separate the cooled shallots into petals and season them with sea salt. Reserve the prettiest petals for presentation and fold the rest in with the paneer, to warm through. Simmer for a further 2–3 minutes, so all the flavours can become acquainted. This is the point at which you should wilt the spinach through the dopiaza too, should you wish to add it.

9. Garnish with the shallot petals you held back, plenty of fresh coriander and finely sliced red chilli. Serve with naan flecked with onion seeds, hot buttered rotlis or even hot buttered pitta bread or rice.

COOK'S NOTE The addition of the spinach gives this a saag paneer vibe, or you could use charred red pepper from a jar, which is another delicious combo.

So this is my pain perdu à la Parsi. Now I don't want to under-egg the Parsi love of, well, eggs! We've had a Scotch egg, scrambled egg, poached egg, fried egg, and now we're going to finish with eggy bread. I've adapted this recipe from one I learned at Ashburton Chefs' Academy. We made our own brioche, which was divine, but don't stress it, shop-bought is just fine. It's the heady rose water flavour in the yoghurt that take me off to Persia. This would also work as a dessert with pistachio ice cream; pistachios are of course native to Iran.

FRENCH TOAST } WITH WHIPPED ROSE WATER YOGHURT AND SPICED FRUITS

SERVES 4–6

Spiced fruit compote
300g frozen fruits
20g stem ginger in syrup, finely diced
a generous pinch of ground mixed spice
caster sugar, to taste

Whipped rose water and honey yoghurt
300g Greek yoghurt
½–1 teaspoon rose water, or to taste
90ml double cream
2 tablespoons honey, or to taste

French toast
2 eggs
200ml whole milk
1–2 teaspoons vanilla extract
100g caster sugar
6 x 3cm thick slices of brioche (buy an unsliced loaf so you can control the thickness)
40–60g unsalted butter, for cooking

Garnish
toasted and chopped pistachios (optional)

1. Make the fruit compote first. Place the frozen fruits, stem ginger and mixed spice in a small to medium saucepan and bring to a simmer. Reduce to a thick sauce over a medium heat – this will take at least 5 minutes – then sweeten with sugar, to taste, or you can use the syrup from the stem ginger. Set aside. You can make this ahead and chill, if you like.
2. To make the whipped yoghurt, whip all the ingredients together – you're aiming for a soft peak. Cover and refrigerate.
3. Prior to making the French toast, heat your oven to 170°C and line a baking tray with baking paper.
4. In a large mixing bowl whisk together the eggs, milk, vanilla extract and sugar.
5. Place the slices of brioche in the egg mixture and allow to soak for a minute, then repeat on the other side. Meanwhile melt a little butter in a frying pan – you may have to fry in batches. When the butter is foaming, add the brioche and fry for 2 minutes on each side until golden – be mindful not to burn the butter.
6. Place the brioche slices on your lined baking tray and bake for 5 minutes. Drain on kitchen paper to remove any greasiness before serving.
7. Serve your French toast with the spiced fruit compote, a dollop of whipped yoghurt and a sprinkle of toasted pistachios, if using.

COOK'S NOTE
You can replace the Greek yoghurt with 200g mascarpone to make this more indulgent, but sweeten to taste with icing sugar rather than honey.

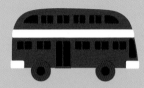

LONDON — SRI LANKAN COMMUNITY

London has the largest Sri Lankan community in the UK, who have been settled there since the 1960s. The onset of the Sri Lankan civil war in the summer of 1983 led to immigration in greater numbers in the 1980s and 90s, to escape the unrest.

Sri Lankan food culture is often described as pan-Asian and has a number of influences – from South India, Malaysia, Indonesia and China. It's markedly different to that of mainland India. Rice crops make up the largest part of Sri Lanka's plantations (formerly known as Ceylon, of course it is famed for its tea plantations too), and rice pancakes called hoppers are a national dish, as well as rice noodles called string hoppers. Many ingredients are unique and indigenous to Sri Lanka, and it's so lovely to see that these are readily available in Britain, enabling us to recreate this most exciting cuisine; be warned, though, it can be very hot and fiery!

MANGA THARMA (AGED 36)

Founder, Senna's Collections

Civil war between the majority Sinhalese and minority Tamils has blighted Sri Lanka's recent history. This was a bitter, bloody and vitriolic campaign that lasted for 26 years, between 1983 and 2009, with tens of thousands of innocent lives lost on both sides. Sri Lanka gained independence in 1948. It wasn't until 1956–8 that violent rioting started, mainly in Colombo, and this then spread to all parts of the island. However, the root of the troubles can be traced back to the Ceylon Citizenship Act 1948, passed by the Ceylon government post-independence, which effectively made hundreds of thousands of Indian Tamils stateless; state-sponsored discrimination against the minority Indian Tamils ensued, with heinous consequences. Ultimately all Indian Tamils were granted citizenship, but only as recently as 2003.

Manga was born in Sri Lanka – her family came from Jaffna, in the northern region of the island. She was two years old when her family were forced to flee after a life-threatening incident: her parents had to leave their home abruptly with minimal food and clothing to seek shelter in a temple. This was the moment they took the heart-breaking decision to leave their motherland, which they loved dearly, when they realized they couldn't protect themselves or their children. Most of the family lived in India for four subsequent years, before moving to the UK when Manga was six. It took time to gain the refugee status needed to emigrate. Her father came to the UK first, before he could call his family over. The family was cruelly split. Manga, her mother and brother moved to Chennai in India to wait for her father to send for them. The extended family – from her mother's side – all lived in an apartment block while seeking asylum. One by one the families left as they were granted asylum all over the world: France, Switzerland, Canada, some to the UK. Manga was one of the last to leave. I can't imagine the horrors of having to leave your home so suddenly, not having all your belongings, giving up your property, having your lifestyle ripped away from you.

Thankfully the family were able to settle in north-west London. Manga grew up in Alperton, in Wembley, which she describes at that time as being 'Little India', as the whole street was either Sri Lankan or Indian. Memories of when she moved to the UK are still sharp:

'Coming to the UK was difficult. The culture was so different and I absolutely hated the food. It was so bland in comparison to what I was used to. I couldn't speak the language . . . there's certain things I remember when I was at school. I had left my coat in the cloakroom, and it was VERY cold. I just wanted to go back in the building to fetch my coat but I didn't know how to tell the teachers in the playground. I was speaking to them in Tamil, which they didn't understand. I still remember that day so clearly, just heartbroken and wondering, what am I doing here? I don't understand why I've been left in this school where nobody understands me.'

Manga has school dinner nightmares about eating bland and cold mashed potato to this day. After a while, her mum sent her in with a packed lunch. These would be bog-standard sandwiches – ham, bread and butter, jam – so that Manga didn't stand out, and to help her and her brother to blend in, although occasionally she'd get tuna, potato and chilli toasties! Manga was able to pick up the language pretty quickly – in about six months – after which she thrived.

We talk about identity. Manga's parents were very keen for their children to learn about their Sri Lankan heritage; arts, literature, dancing and poetry are highly esteemed within the culture. Every Sunday she would go to Tamil school and learn the language, and about the arts and music. She learned Bharatanatyam, a form of Tamil classical dance, and how to play an instrument called a veena (which is similar to a sitar), as well as how to sing classical Tamil songs. Having these after-school classes throughout the week helped her to be rooted in her Sri Lankan and Tamil culture, which she feels is very vibrant, and easy to fall in love with. Of course there was always the collision of cultures in her teenage years, but we all experienced that – the phenomenon of the daytime raves and not always being where you told your parents you were. The obligations to attend family functions and endless rounds of visiting each other's houses was stifling for all of us. I ask Manga about any balancing of cultures and what she admires most about British culture:

'I feel like my parents very heavily pushed towards study, study, study, be academic, then go and get a good job . . . a lawyer or a doctor . . . Whereas British people really help you to open up your eyes and see that that's not the only route for you. If you're passionate about something else and you really enjoy it, you should follow your dreams. Do what makes you happy, and do what you enjoy. Maybe it's the British in me that's coming out now. I never did that before and always listened to my parents. I was always a "good girl"; they said to study and I did. The most rebellious I had been was that my dad wanted me to be a doctor, and I said no I'm not going into medicine but I went down the finance route instead [Manga is a qualified chartered accountant] as I didn't feel I had any other options, and this was the least boring out of what was expected. So I forced myself to go down that avenue.'

I find it so sweet that Manga's idea of rebellion was to become an accountant rather than a doctor – she is a credit! It was when she went off to university that the balance swung very much the opposite way, connecting with Western culture and more diverse friendship groups:

'I don't feel 100 per cent British. I feel Sri Lankan–British or British–Sri Lankan. I feel very bi-cultured.'

I wonder, are we bi-cultured or is our identity more complex than that? With the global influences we consume through various media on a daily basis – together with gender, race, religion and sexual orientation – I'm not sure binary covers it, rather something much more fluid. What I am certain about is that Manga does much to preserve her culture while at the same time embracing Britishness; she's equally proud of her heritage and of her adopted homeland, and quite rightly.

And Manga has indeed followed her dreams. While on maternity leave (Manga is mum to a two-year-old and an eleven-month-old), not only did she relocate to the countryside in Hampshire but also decided to turn her back on her career and launched her own 'bi-cultured' children's clothing business in 2021.

Manga is very grateful for the massive risks that her parents took to safeguard her future. Our parents took different kinds of risks to those we take today – like the bold and intrepid steps it takes to turn your back on a profession and start your own business.

Hoppers are a wonderful thing – I tried them for the first time while researching this book and have very much wondered where they've been all my life! They are thin, crispy, bowl-shaped pancakes that can be enjoyed for breakfast or dinner, though they are most commonly associated with street food. There are a myriad ways to make the batter: some folks use only rice flour, others a combination of rice flour and plain flour, some add eggs, and I've even tested recipes with sliced bread blended into the batter. I've made a few trips to that famous namesake restaurant in London to help me decipher the best recipe, and these trips have inspired some of the other recipes in this chapter too. For hoppers the fermentation process is the key to the best results, and I think overnight is best. These are my breakfast hoppers, served with a bacon 'sambal', which is the perfect hangover cure. You can also have hoppers for dinner and serve them with your choice of curries and sambals inside; though you've got to always include the egg, in my humble opinion!

EGG HOPPERS } WITH BACON 'SAMBAL'

MAKES 12–15 HOPPERS

Hoppers
300g rice flour
50g plain flour
5g easy-blend dried yeast
5g caster sugar

approx. 300ml water (36–40°C temperature)
200ml full-fat tinned coconut milk
approx. 100ml water (36–40°C temperature)
a pinch of salt
vegetable oil, for the pan

1 egg per hopper
sea salt and dried chilli flakes

To serve
bacon 'sambal' (see page 194)
finely sliced spring onions
fresh coriander leaves

Note
You will need a non-stick Sri Lankan hopper pan, with a lid and accompanying spatula. These are easily available online. Choose a deep demi-dome shape, not the flatter style. My pan is 18cm in diameter, about 6cm in height.

1. I've tried to design a hopper recipe that will fit around day-to-day life. I find it's best to start the process after you've had your dinner, done the washing up and are relaxed. Place the rice flour in a large mixing bowl, sieve in the plain flour, then add the yeast and sugar (you won't need to bloom easy-blend yeast).

2. Using a wooden spoon, start to mix in the warm water, creating a thick paste. You'll need about 300ml. Cover the bowl with cling film and move to a warm dry place to kickstart the yeast (I place it on a windowsill above a radiator). After 2 hours, place the bowl/mixture in the fridge; we don't want to over-proof and this will slow things down. Go to bed and forget about it, and let the yeast do the work. Overnight fermentation is the key to great hoppers.

→

3. You can make your hoppers for breakfast, lunch or dinner. Just take your fermented mixture out of the fridge 30 minutes to 1 hour prior to making the hoppers.

4. Make the bacon 'sambal'. You'll note this recipe title is in inverted commas, as it is by no means authentic.

5. Mix the coconut milk into the fermented mixture with a balloon whisk, then whisk in 100ml of warm water a little at a time – you may not need all of it. You want to achieve a double cream consistency – so not too thick, which is why we're letting it down with water to achieve the desired result. Add the salt at this point too.

6. Let's make some hoppers! You will need a direct flame, so use a gas hob. Put a scant amount of vegetable oil in your hopper pan and use kitchen paper to wipe round the pan and ensure the whole surface is very lightly coated. You want a hot pan, so heat it on the maximum temperature, then reduce to a heat that's equivalent to 8 out of 10.

7. The heat is really important to get right. You don't want a limp, anaemic hopper in a pan that is too cold, but if the pan is too hot the batter will congeal before you can swirl it around the pan. You will be a hopper champ after a couple of attempts, I assure you.

8. Break an egg into a ramekin and set aside. Take a ladle full of the batter – don't overload – and place in the centre of the hot hopper pan, then lift the pan with both handles and swirl the batter around the inside to create that pancake bowl – take this as high and as close to the rim of the pan as possible, and do a double swirl with the batter if need be as you don't want too much batter pooling at the bottom. Put the pan back on the heat, then drop your egg into the middle of the pan and pop on the lid immediately to trap the steam. Set a 2-minute timer, then lift off the lid; the egg should be set. Season with a pinch of salt and a few flecks of chilli flakes. Replace the lid and give it another 10–15 seconds (or less if you want a runny egg).

9. Remove from the heat and gently tease the edges away with the spatula, then slide on to your serving plate.

10. Serve with the bacon 'sambal', finely sliced spring onions and fresh coriander leaves. Repeat.

COOK'S NOTE You can make this dish more hearty by adding home fries – boil the potatoes, cut into 3cm dice, shallow-fry until crisp, and season – and a caramelized onion (seeni) 'sambal' (see opposite). Also you can use any leftover coconut milk to make pol roti (page 198). The dough keeps and is yummy!

SAMBALS AND CONDIMENTS

Sambals are an intrinsic condiment in Sri Lankan food. They are often very spicy – though there are mellow ones – and some would argue a meal is incomplete without this flavour grenade. Pol (coconut) sambal is revered as a national dish by many and is ubiquitous – this is made with grated/scraped coconut, flavoured with chillies, red onion, lime juice and chilli powder (see coconut chutney, page 278). Now I have taken a few liberties with my sambals here, and added a second-generation twist. Of course Sri Lankan hot sauce and ketchup are also important condiments to mention, and you can easily purchase these online if you don't live near a Sri Lankan grocer.

CARAMELIZED ONION (SEENI) 'SAMBAL'

So versatile and gives any dish a burst of flavour – have this with cheese on toast, as a burger relish, stirred through rice, with cheese and crackers or pâté. Simply reheat in the microwave. Oh, and of course you can have this the traditional way with curries or hoppers too.

- - - - - - - - - - - - - - - - - - - -

coconut oil, for cooking

5 green cardamom pods (bruise to release the seeds and grind the seeds slightly)

2 whole cloves

6cm cinnamon stick

6 curry leaves

5cm pandan leaf, torn (leave this out if you are unable to find it)

3 large red onions (approx. weight 590g), finely sliced into half-moons

1 anchovy fillet (easier to source than dried crumbled Maldive fish, of which you need a good pinch)

2 teaspoons tamarind paste

1 teaspoon chilli powder

1½ tablespoons caster sugar

½ teaspoon sea salt, or to taste

1. Melt and heat a good amount of coconut oil in a large lidded saucepan – I use cold-pressed oil – say about 4 tablespoons. Add the whole spices – cardamom, cloves, cinnamon – and when they start to release their aromas, add the curry leaves and torn pandan if you have any.

2. Tip in the onions and give everything a good mix. Reduce the heat to medium and let the onions sauté for 10 minutes until lightly golden.

3. Add the anchovy fillet and let it melt in the heat, then add the rest of the ingredients: tamarind, chilli powder, sugar and salt. Ensure everything is well mixed, and have a little taste. Make any adjustments, then leave the onions to simmer on a low to medium heat, partially covered, for 25–30 minutes, to a marmalade consistency. Don't let anything catch.

4. Cool, decant to a sterilized jar and refrigerate. Will keep for weeks.

BACON 'SAMBAL'

Completely inauthentic but great with egg hoppers!

– · – · – · – · – · – · – · – · – · –

500g smoked bacon lardons

3 small to medium brown onions, finely sliced into half-moons

vegetable oil, for cooking

20g garlic, grated

2 hot green finger/bird's-eye chillies, split lengthways

4 tablespoons light brown sugar

½ teaspoon hot/extra hot chilli powder

½ teaspoon ground turmeric

½ teaspoon chilli flakes

4 tablespoons white wine/cider vinegar

2 tablespoons maple syrup

1. Sauté the bacon lardons in a large frying pan until crisp and brown. Decant to a plate and set aside.
2. In the same pan sauté the onions in a little vegetable oil on a medium heat. You want it to cook slowly and turn golden to really develop the flavour – it's going to take a while, so don't rush this, it will take about 15–20 minutes.
3. Add the garlic and chillies to the pan and allow to cook a little, then add the sugar and the spices: chilli powder, turmeric and chilli flakes. Return the bacon to the pan and mix everything together, then deglaze with the vinegar and sweeten with the maple syrup. Cook down for another 10–15 minutes, or until reduced to a jammy consistency.

CHARRED PINEAPPLE 'SAMBAL'

Yes, I've taken liberties, but I like this as a fruity alternative to pair with mutton rolls instead of a hot sauce.

– · – · – · – · – · – · – · – · – · –

½ a pineapple (about 180–200g prepped)

½ a red onion, finely diced

½ teaspoon grated ginger

½–1 green chilli, finely diced (depends how hot you like it)

¼ teaspoon black mustard seeds, toasted

juice and zest of ½ a lime

2 teaspoons scraped or unsweetened desiccated coconut

1 tablespoon chopped fresh coriander (or mint if you prefer)

salt, to taste

1. Top and tail the pineapple, slice off the outer skin, quarter, and slice away the woody core. Then cut lengthways into three slices – as much as needed for the recipe – and char on both sides on a screeching hot griddle pan.
2. Remove the pineapple from the pan and finely dice. Set aside.
3. Mix all the sambal ingredients together in a bowl.

How could I do a chapter on Sri Lanka without paying due respect to this iconic and much-loved dish? Interestingly it's also known as 'black chicken', and if you look at the root word, 'kalu' translates to 'black' and of course 'pol' is 'coconut'. Traditionally this is made as a curry, using a whole chicken cut into pieces. The chicken is marinated, then added to a spicy sauce loaded with a fair amount of ground black peppercorns. The tamarind adds to the dark colour also. I've decided to cook a whole chicken using the beer can method – with a delicious IPA, naturally – as it keeps the bird moist. This is necessary as I've removed the skin. I'm not a fan of marination with the skin kept on the bird, as all the flavour sticks to the skin and can't really penetrate the meat; an added bonus is that it's healthier as well as being more flavoursome!

BEER CAN KALUPOL CHICKEN AND PEPPERCORN SAUCE

SERVES 4

1 whole skinned chicken (approx. 1.6kg)

1 x 330ml can of Indian pale ale (choose a tropical flavour)

Chicken marinade

2 tablespoons extra hot chilli powder

1 teaspoon ground turmeric

3 tablespoons Sri Lankan roasted curry powder (use Madras/hot curry powder if you can't get your hands on this)

1½ teaspoons salt

1 teaspoon whole black peppercorns, pounded to a powder using a pestle and mortar

3 heaped tablespoons coconut oil (I use cold-pressed)

2 tablespoons tamarind paste

Masala powder

1 tablespoon uncooked rice

2 tablespoons unsweetened desiccated coconut

1 teaspoon black mustard seeds

1 teaspoon fennel seeds

1 teaspoon cumin seeds

1 teaspoon black peppercorns

2 dried Kashmiri chillies

Peppercorn sauce

vegetable or coconut oil, for cooking

6cm cinnamon stick

5cm pandan leaf, torn (leave this out if you can't source it)

8–10 curry leaves (dried is OK if you can't get fresh)

1 large brown onion, finely sliced into half-moons

15g garlic, grated

15g ginger, grated

2 green chillies, split in half lengthways (if you'd like a milder sauce, leave these out)

50ml brandy (optional)

1 teaspoon sea salt, or to taste

400ml thick full-fat coconut milk

250ml water/chicken stock (don't add salt if you use stock)

1–2 teaspoons green peppercorns in brine

Garnish

2 limes, cut in half across the middle

1. Make 2cm deep slashes on the breasts of the chicken, and the thighs and legs. Mix all the dry marinade ingredients in a large mixing bowl, then add the melted coconut oil and the tamarind and bring together into a paste. Smother the chicken with the paste, then put it into the mixing bowl and cover with cling film. Marinate overnight ideally or for

→

a minimum of 4 hours in the fridge (allow to come to room temperature for 1 hour prior to roasting).

2. When you are ready to roast the chicken, heat your oven to 180°C fan. You will need to remove the middle oven shelf – the chicken will be standing tall, as it were, so you'll need space.

3. Pour half the IPA into a glass – either drink this, or give it to somebody you love along with a packet of crisps. Place the chicken on top of the opened beer can – the cavity will fit over – and put both on a large roasting tray. Wrap loosely in foil (this will prevent the spices from burning) and roast in the oven for an hour. Keep any leftover marinade (the coconut oil will have firmed up), as we will use it for basting the chicken in the last 15–20 minutes of cooking.

4. To prepare the masala powder, toast the rice in a dry frying pan until it turns golden – taking care that it doesn't burn – then set aside. Do the same with the desiccated coconut. Add the mustard seeds, fennel seeds, cumin seeds, black peppercorns and dried chillies to the hot pan, and when they release their aromas, put them all into a small bowl and mix together. Set aside to cool. Once completely cooled, blitz to a powder using a coffee grinder. Do this in two or three batches, as necessary.

5. For the peppercorn sauce, heat 3 or 4 tablespoons of vegetable/coconut oil in a large saucepan on a medium to high heat and add the cassia bark/cinnamon. When it starts to release its aromas, add the pandan leaf and curry leaves. Reduce the heat to medium and tip in the onions, followed shortly by the garlic, ginger and the split green chillies if you want your sauce to pack real heat. You need to cook the onions really slowly, about 20 minutes, until golden.

6. Now pour in the brandy if you are using it – let some of the alcohol 'burn off' but not all. Add all of the masala powder you have just prepared and the salt (unless you plan on using chicken stock) and give everything a good mix. Allow to cook out for a short while, then add the coconut milk and water/stock and simmer for 15 minutes or so. The toasted rice will thicken the sauce somewhat. Add your peppercorns in brine 5 minutes before the end of simmering. They don't add heat like the black peppercorns, but they give a lovely burst of flavour.

7. Remove the foil from the chicken and brush with the reserved marinade (which you will need to heat and melt). Roast, uncovered, for a further 15–20 minutes, or until the chicken is cooked. This timing will vary according to the weight of your chicken.

8. Char the lime halves on a hot griddle pan cut-side down and serve with pol roti (page 198), plain basmati rice, a crispy salad and a choice of sambals. You could replace the rice with chips, though, as I often do – yum!

Bread or roti is important to each community, indeed country, each having its own particular spin on this basic and fundamental staple. As a self-confessed bread lover – which I will take over rice all day long – this roti is a real treat, so packed with flavour that I could happily eat this naked; fully clothed, I hasten to add, I mean by itself. You HAVE to try this.

POL (COCONUT) ROTI

MAKES 8 ROTIS

375g plain flour
80g unsweetened desiccated coconut
1 teaspoon sea salt
1 small (or ½ large) red onion, finely diced

2 green finger chillies, finely chopped
3 spring onion tops, green parts only, finely sliced
1 tablespoon chopped fresh coriander

2 fresh curry leaves, shredded (optional)
2 heaped tablespoons coconut milk (4 tablespoons if your coconut milk is more liquid and you can't heap)

approx. 235ml water
approx. 4 tablespoons coconut oil, for cooking (I use cold-pressed: if solid, warm and melt it in the microwave)

1. Place the plain flour, desiccated coconut and salt in a large mixing bowl. Use a balloon whisk to mix everything together.
2. Add the diced onion, chillies, spring onions, coriander and curry leaves (if using) to the bowl.
3. Mix the coconut milk with the water and add this to the bowl too. Bring the ingredients together and knead for 3–5 minutes until you have a fairly firm dough – you may need a touch more water. Transfer to an airtight container and place in the fridge to rest for at least 30 minutes.
4. When you are ready to make the rotis, place a large non-stick frying pan or tawa on a medium to high heat.
5. Divide the dough into eight equal parts – each roughly the same size as a golf ball. Take a dough ball and roll it into a thin disc, not much thicker than a chapatti, on a lightly floured surface. (Note: if you would prefer thicker pol rotis, just adjust the cooking time accordingly – it will take longer.) Mine were about 18cm in diameter and 3mm thick.
6. Place the roti on the hot frying pan/tawa. Flip with tongs after 30 seconds, and brush this part-cooked side lightly with coconut oil. Then flip again and repeat on the other side. Your rotis need a couple of minutes on each side to cook through. You want lovely golden and burnished flecks on each side.
7. Repeat with the rest of the dough balls. Every now and again, wipe the pan with kitchen paper to prevent any residue oil from smoking. Wrap the rotis in foil or place in a chapatti warmer while you make the rest.
8. Enjoy with kalupol chicken and peppercorn sauce (page 195). You can pair these rotis with any curry, not necessarily a Sri Lankan one either!

Inventive use of leftovers is a vital part of home economics. The ability to transform leftovers into something as exciting and appetizing as the original dish is something you need to have in your locker. Kottu roti – you can have this with any leftover curry: seafood, paneer, lamb, any vegetable curry – is an excellent example of this. It's also exactly the kind of comfort food you crave the morning after the night before.

CHICKEN KOTTU ROTI

SERVES 4–6

350–400g chopped chicken (from leftover curry)

approx. 300ml leftover curry sauce (more for gravy lovers)

coconut oil, for cooking (I use cold-pressed)

½ teaspoon black mustard seeds

8–10 curry leaves (use dried if you can't get fresh)

½ a large red onion, finely sliced into half-moons

15g garlic, grated

15g ginger, grated (equal volume to garlic)

2 green chillies, slit in half lengthways

70g leeks, finely sliced

100g Savoy cabbage, finely shredded

90g grated carrot

salt and black pepper, to taste

3 parathas, cut into 2cm squares/ diamonds

3 eggs, beaten

90g beansprouts

fresh coriander leaves and charred limes, to serve

1. Take the leftover curry out of the fridge 20–30 minutes before you start – you can then separate the chicken from the sauce more easily. Chop the chicken and put it into a bowl. Reheat the sauce in a separate pan, and have ready on standby.

2. Heat 3 tablespoons of coconut oil in a large frying pan or wok. Add the mustard seeds and curry leaves, and, when they start to release their aromas, throw in the red onion. Treat this as a stir-fry and keep everything moving over a medium to high heat.

3. After a minute add the garlic, ginger and chillies, followed shortly afterwards by the leeks. Sauté for a minute, then add the cabbage and carrots. Season with salt and pepper, then stir through the chopped chicken and the pieces of paratha; you want to get some heat through these.

4. Mix in the eggs, and scramble them with the vegetables, chicken and pieces of paratha.

5. When all the ingredients are well mixed and hot, stir through the hot leftover curry sauce, along with the beansprouts.

6. Scatter with coriander leaves and serve with charred limes and extra curry sauce if you fancy it. Enjoy!

COOK'S NOTE For a vegan alternative I would replace the chicken curry with a tofu or jackfruit version. You can also replace the paratha with roti, or even flour tortillas, if you need a shortcut.

You'll note the use of Sri Lankan roasted curry powder in this recipe. Most Sri Lankans have their own house blend – much like Punjabis with our garam masala. It tends to be a mix of such spices as coriander seeds, cumin seeds, black peppercorns, black mustard seeds, cloves, green cardamoms, Sri Lankan cinnamon, fennel and toasted uncooked rice. Always heavy on the coriander. You can make this chicken curry vegetarian/vegan by replacing the chicken with tinned jackfruit or firm tofu.

SRI LANKAN HOUSE CURRY

**SERVES 4
(WITH LEFTOVERS AND
GRAVY FOR KOTTU ROTI)**

approx. 3 tablespoons coconut oil, for cooking (I use cold-pressed)

1½ teaspoons cumin seeds

6cm cinnamon stick

7 green cardamom pods (bruise to release the seeds, then slightly pound the seeds)

1 teaspoon black mustard seeds

3 whole cloves

10–12 curry leaves (dried is OK if you can't get fresh)

5cm pandan leaf (leave it out if you can't get your hands on it)

1 large brown onion, finely sliced into half-moons

2–3 green chillies, split lengthways

25g garlic, grated

25g ginger, grated

1 teaspoon ground turmeric

1½ teaspoons Sri Lankan roasted curry powder (use Madras/ hot curry powder as an alternative)

1 teaspoon hot chilli powder (use mild if you prefer)

1 teaspoon black peppercorns, pounded to a powder using a pestle and mortar

1–2 teaspoons salt, or to taste

400ml passata

1–1.25kg skinless and boneless chicken thighs, cut into pieces

approx. 250ml water

100–150ml thick coconut milk

1. OK, the chicken kottu roti recipe on the previous page calls for leftover chicken curry, so let me run you through how to whip up a quick Sri Lankan house chicken curry. Melt and heat the coconut oil in a large saucepan or sauté pan. Once hot, add the whole spices: cumin seeds, cinnamon, cardamom, mustard seeds and cloves. Once they start to release their aromas, add the curry leaves and pandan leaf (tear this to release the flavour), followed by the onions. Allow these to sauté long and slow, at least 20 minutes on a medium heat, until golden.

2. Add the split chillies, garlic and ginger and cook out for a few minutes.

3. Now add the ground spices: turmeric, curry powder, chilli powder, ground pepper and salt. Give everything a good mix, so the spices can toast a little, but don't let them burn – add a splash of water if need be.

4. Add the passata and increase the hob heat to bring the mixture to a

simmer. After a few minutes you'll see the tell-tale separation of the oil on the surface, so taste and adjust the seasoning if you need to.

5. Add the chicken pieces to the pot, or the jackfruit or tofu if you are making the vegan version (see the introduction and cook's note). Turn the heat to maximum, stirring all the time to ensure the meat pieces are sealed, then pour in the water. Bring to the boil, then reduce to a simmer on a medium heat.

6. Finally, after 5 minutes or so, mix through the thick coconut milk. Simmer the chicken for a further 25 minutes, or until cooked and tender. Gauge the level of sauce – you can add a touch more water if you'd like extra sauce for the kottu.

COOK'S NOTE To make a tofu version of this curry, coat the tofu pieces with a spiced dredge – made from 3 tablespoons of cornflour, a teaspoon of curry powder and seasoning – coat, shallow-fry and add to the sauce/gravy towards the end of cooking.

Stuffed and rolled sole is a bit European retro, and I quite like a throwback, so I've taken inspiration from that. Kiri hodi is a very mild coconut 'gravy' not dissimilar to Keralan moilee (Kerala is located on the west coast of India, at the bottom tip, neighbouring Tamil Nadu on the east coast, which neighbours the island of Sri Lanka), and is often served with string hoppers. String hoppers are fine noodles made from red rice and steamed. Normally kiri hodi would be flavoured with curry leaves and toasted fenugreek seeds, but I've neutralized my version so it doesn't overpower the sole. I love this dish – it's very much an East meets West mash-up that still allows the delicate fish to take centre stage!

ROLLED SOLE IN A 'KIRI HODI' SAUCE

SERVES 4 AS A STARTER

'Kiri hodi'
vegetable oil, for cooking
6cm cinnamon stick
1 level teaspoon fennel seeds
1 large onion, finely diced
1 green chilli, slit lengthways
10g ginger, grated
10g garlic, grated
1 level teaspoon Sri Lankan roasted curry powder (use Madras or hot curry powder as an alternative)
1 level teaspoon ground turmeric
1 teaspoon sea salt, or to taste
1 x 400ml tin of full-fat coconut milk
lime juice

Rolled sole
4 equal-sized skinless sole (or plaice) fillets, about 70g each (to ensure they take the same amount of time to cook)
lemon/lime juice
salt and pepper
4 bamboo knotted cocktail sticks (any cocktail stick will do)
100g samphire
a little butter

Garnish
chilli oil
fried curry leaves (see page 206)
toasted coconut flakes

1. Heat 3 or 4 tablespoons of vegetable oil in a medium to large pan. Add the whole spices first – cinnamon and fennel seeds – and when they start to release their aromas, tip in the onions and green chilli, and sauté for 10–15 minutes on a medium heat.

2. Add the ginger and garlic, cook out until they turn golden, then add the powdered spices: roasted curry powder and turmeric, and the salt. Don't let the spices catch – add a little water if need be.

3. Once the spices have toasted for a minute, pour in the coconut milk, mix everything together and bring to a simmer. Allow to simmer, covered, for 10 minutes, then season with a little lime juice, taste and make any adjustments.

4. Meanwhile prepare the fish, to which we are going to do very little. Lay each fillet out, season with a little lemon/lime juice, salt and pepper. Then roll up each fillet, starting at the thicker end, and skewer into position with a cocktail stick. Gently place the rolled sole fillets in the kiri hodi sauce, and trap the steam by replacing the lid on the pan to aid poaching. The fish will take about 6 minutes to cook – the time will vary

depending on the size of your fillets. After 3 minutes, turn the rolls over and baste with the sauce, then cook for another 3 minutes. You can tell the fish is cooked when it becomes opaque and firm to the touch. With the samphire, the easiest method is to cook it in boiling water for 2–3 minutes. Drain thoroughly, and season with a hint of butter and cracked pepper. It's already salty, so it won't need any more.

5. I serve this in a deep plate/bowl: first a pool of kiri hodi, then a little nest of samphire on which to sit the rolled sole. Garnish with chilli oil, crispy curry leaves and toasted coconut shavings. You could have a little pol roti (page 198) on the side to make this more substantial – which I think I've become addicted to . . .

A 'short eat' is what Sri Lankans refer to as an equivalent to afternoon tea or tiffin really; not so much about sandwiches and cakes, more all things spice and salt, which can be had with a lip-smacking chai or tipple of choice. ALL Indians love a tasty snack. The first time I had a mutton roll, I couldn't help but think of the Findus crispy pancakes of my youth – but this is its Sri Lankan cousin: tall, dark, handsome and out of control! Woof! Now you could make your own pancakes, but Chinese spring roll pastry is a wonderful shortcut. You can prep ahead and these will keep in the fridge overnight in an airtight container, to be deep-fried and devoured the next day.

SRI LANKAN 'SHORT EAT' MUTTON ROLLS

MAKES 9–12 ROLLS

Keema filling
500g peeled potatoes, cut into 3cm dice (prepped weight)
vegetable oil, for cooking
6cm cinnamon stick
1 teaspoon black mustard seeds

8–10 curry leaves (dried is OK if you can't get fresh)
1 large brown onion, finely diced
2 green chillies, slit in half lengthways
15g ginger, grated
15g garlic, grated
2 teaspoons Sri Lankan roasted curry powder (or hot Madras curry powder)

1 teaspoon mild chilli powder
½ teaspoon ground black peppercorns
1 teaspoon ground turmeric
1 teaspoon sea salt, or to taste
500g mutton or lamb mince
50–75ml water
juice of ½ a lime

For the rolls
Chinese spring roll pastry sheets (215mm x 215mm – these are usually frozen, so defrost them)
approx. 100g seasoned flour
2 eggs, beaten
approx. 150g golden breadcrumbs
vegetable oil, for deep-frying
lime wedges, to serve

1. Boil the potatoes until tender, then drain and allow to steam-dry.
2. Meanwhile start the masala. Heat 3 or 4 tablespoons of vegetable oil in a medium to large sauté pan on a medium to high heat, then add the whole spices: cinnamon/cassia, mustard seeds and curry leaves. When they start to release their aromas, reduce the heat to medium, tip in the onions and chillies and allow the onions to soften.
3. When the onions are soft and translucent, add the ginger and garlic. Once these are toasted and starting to turn golden, add the ground spices: curry powder, chilli powder, black pepper and turmeric, and the salt. Give everything a good mix and cook out for 30 seconds. You may need a splash of water to prevent the spices from catching.
4. Now add the mince. Use the bottom of your wooden spoon to break up the meat – you want to seal and brown it, so increase the hob heat to do so. Add the water and simmer, covered, for 25–30 minutes, or until the meat is cooked. You may need a touch more water so it doesn't catch, but note that it needs to be a dry filling.

5. Add the potatoes to the pan, and mix them through, smashing them as you do so. You want a little texture, though, not complete mash. Check and adjust the seasoning, and add the lime juice. Cool completely.

6. When you are ready to assemble the rolls, cover your pastry with a damp tea towel so it doesn't dry out. Take a single sheet and position it as a diamond on a work surface in front of you. Take a couple of tablespoons of filling and place this about 8cm below the top point of the diamond in a little sausage shape.

7. Fold that 8cm section of pastry that's above the filling over it, thereby encasing it, then bring in each side to create an envelope shape, ensuring the filling is compacted in. Then roll over into that familiar cylinder shape. You can seal the tip with a dab of water if need be.

8. Panne/breadcrumb the rolls: seasoned flour first, then beaten egg, then breadcrumbs. It's easiest to set these out in three separate bowls so you can create a little production line.

9. Deep-fry at 170–180°C until piping hot, crisp and golden, no more than two at a time. Or you can fry for a couple of minutes until lightly golden, drain on kitchen towel, then finish cooking in a 180°C oven for 12–15 minutes. Serve with a ketchup or sambal of your choice, a colourful salad and lime wedges.

COOK'S NOTE For dramatic effect you could place a little block of stretchy cheese in the middle of the filling when assembling the rolls. You will have a very impressive cheese 'pull' this way. Like a Juicy Lucy burger.

Jaffna curry powder takes its name from the city of Jaffna, located near the northern tip of the island. Though this blend is used throughout Sri Lanka, and is often referred to as an 'all in one' curry powder, it's predominant in the cuisine of this region, which has the largest Tamil population. It has a hotter, deeper flavour than the roasted curry powder that's used in so many Sri Lankan dishes, the rich colour owing much to the ratio of red chillies in the blend. Jaffna curry powder is used in meat, seafood and vegetarian dishes, and brings a distinct intense flavour.

JAFFNA COCONUT PRAWNS } WITH FIRECRACKER MAYO

SERVES 4 AS A STARTER (5 PRAWNS EACH)

Firecracker mayo
150g premium mayonnaise
1 teaspoon white wine vinegar
¼ teaspoon paprika
¼ teaspoon cayenne pepper
¼ teaspoon ground cumin
¼ teaspoon ground coriander
a pinch of dried chilli flakes
1 tablespoon hot sauce
½ a clove of garlic, grated

1 teaspoon chopped fresh coriander leaves
a squeeze of lime juice
a pinch of salt

Coconut prawns
vegetable oil, for deep-frying
2 tablespoons cornflour
1 tablespoon rice flour (rice and cornflour are gluten free, a lighter coating than plain white flour, and also add a lovely crunch)

1 teaspoon Jaffna curry powder (you can buy this online or at an Indian grocer)
½ teaspoon salt
2 egg whites
approx. 75g unsweetened desiccated coconut
20 raw, peeled, de-veined king prawns (tails on) (approx. 400g)

Garnish
1–2 sprigs fresh curry leaves, for frying
50ml vegetable oil
lime wedges

1. The prawns are super quick and easy to whip up, so make the mayo first (which is very easy too). Whiz up all the mayo ingredients in a blender, make any seasoning adjustments, and ta-da, it's ready. Decant into a bowl or airtight container and refrigerate. (Have what's left over with gunpowder potatoes – see page 286 – scrummy!)

2. You can either deep-fry or shallow-fry the prawns – it's up to you. You do need to have the oil at the correct temperature, however – 160°C – as the coconut can easily burn.

3. Shallow-fry the curry leaves for the garnish in the vegetable oil on a medium to low heat. The leaves need to have had time to dry out, or they will really spit. So be mindful of that. They will turn the brightest green in

→

about 30 seconds. Remove from the oil and place them on kitchen paper. They will crisp as they cool. You can re-use this oil.

4. Mix both flours, the curry powder and salt in a mixing bowl – use a whisk.

5. In a second bowl whisk the egg whites until frothy. Finally, put the desiccated coconut into a third bowl.

6. I like to keep the tails on the prawns when it comes to finger food, as not only does it look pretty, but from a practical point of view it makes it easier to pick up the prawns. Dip the prawns first in the seasoned flour, then in the egg white, then in the coconut, and fry until cooked, crisp and golden.

7. Remove from the oil and place on kitchen paper.

8. Serve immediately, with the mayo, crispy curry leaves, lime wedges and an ice-cold IPA, or an Arrack cocktail – a fermented spirit made from . . . yes, coconut!

COOK'S NOTE You can use strips of white fish and make goujons if you prefer, or use chicken, or a plant-based meat alternative. Simply adjust the cooking time accordingly.

As you will know, Sri Lanka was known formerly as Ceylon, and is famed for its tea plantations. I wanted to pay homage to this history by way of tea and biscuits, but in a much more sophisticated pudding form! Earl Grey is a beautifully perfumed black tea that is flavoured with bergamot oil, from the rind of bergamot oranges; hence the delicate and floral notes. I could have gone down a classic English posset route; however, as bergamot oranges are grown commercially in Calabria, Italy, I wanted to pull in that influence. The shortbread, with original measurements, is my mother-in-law's famous recipe, which was bequeathed to her by her Aunt Enaus, whose father was a master baker in Glasgow.

CEYLON EARL GREY INFUSED PANNA COTTA } WITH STRAWBERRIES AND SHORTBREAD

SERVES 6, WITH SHORTBREAD LEFT OVER!

Panna cotta
3 x 2g sheets of leaf gelatine
vegetable oil, for greasing
600ml double cream
200ml whole milk

75g caster sugar
1 tablespoon loose-leaf Earl Grey tea
½ teaspoon vanilla extract (optional)

Shortbread
228g softened butter, at room temperature (8oz)

114g caster sugar (4oz)
a pinch of salt
grated orange zest (optional – see cook's note)
280g plain flour (10oz)
85g cornflour (3oz)
extra caster sugar, for sprinkling
a pinch of salt

Macerated strawberries
300g strawberries, hulled and cut into pieces – allow 50g per person
4–5 teaspoons icing sugar, or to taste
lime juice, to taste

1. First, 'bloom' the gelatine leaves by soaking them in cold water for 10 minutes or so.
2. Lightly grease six dariole moulds or ramekins with a scant amount of vegetable oil – wipe away most of it with kitchen paper. I occasionally use small ornate teacups if I'm being fancy, though I do like to unmould the panna cotta to see that all-important wobble in all its glory! It somehow tastes different unmoulded.
3. Meanwhile gently heat the cream, milk, sugar and loose tea leaves in a medium saucepan, stirring occasionally with a wooden spoon until the sugar has dissolved and it comes to a simmer. Add the vanilla extract too, if using; or simply let the flavours of the tea sing. Remove from the heat.
4. Squeeze out any water from the gelatine, then stir and melt the leaves through the hot liquid.

→

5. Place a sieve over a large jug and strain the cream mixture. Then pour this mixture into your moulds/cups/ramekins – don't worry if a little tea slips through, a few flecks look pretty. Allow to cool, then refrigerate for a minimum of 4 hours or ideally overnight.
6. On to the shortbread. Heat your oven to 150°C fan. Grease and line a Swiss roll tin (a 20 x 30cm baking tray). Cream together the softened butter, sugar and salt, then add both flours. Lightly knead into a dough, then evenly press this into the prepared baking tray. Use the back of a spoon or a small palette knife to smooth over the top.
7. Prick with a fork all over and bake in the oven for an hour. Check after 40 minutes, as ovens vary.
8. Cut the shortbread into bars or squares as soon as you take it out of the oven, and sprinkle with a little extra caster sugar and a cheeky pinch of salt. Allow to cool in the tin, then transfer to a wire rack. Any leftover shortbread will keep well in an airtight container.
9. To prepare your strawberries, simply season them with icing sugar and lime juice to taste.
10. Finally the unmoulding. Dunk the bottom of your moulds/ramekins into just-boiled water for a couple of seconds to loosen, then turn out on to your serving plates. Serve with the strawberries and shortbread.

COOK'S NOTE If you choose to use the optional orange zest in the shortbread – to pick up on the bergamot in the tea – cream together with the butter and sugar at step 6.

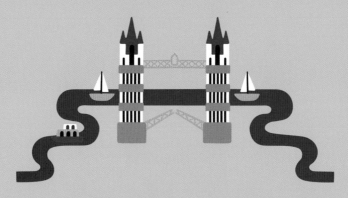

HARROW — AFRICAN INDIAN COMMUNITY

- - - - - - - - - - - - - - -

This community came to the UK in the early 1970s, after the expulsion of Indians from Uganda in 1972 by Idi Amin. Many Ugandan Indians settled in Harrow. There was also a significant diaspora from Kenya, where there had been much political volatility since independence in 1963. The Kenyan Immigration Act 1967 led to the mass exodus of tens of thousands of British-passport-holding Kenyan Indians – who had not acquired Kenyan citizenship by the deadline – and they settled mainly in Leicester and London. In this chapter I'm going to look at the unique confluence of Indian and African cooking styles and how these have crossed over to the UK. Unlike the experience of the first generation, all kinds of global produce is readily available today at greengrocers, supermarkets and online – accessibility to ingredients is no longer an issue – making these recipes really easy to recreate.

Karoga is the Kenyan word for 'stir', and karoga cooking today is quite a communal experience, which you can either sit back and watch unfold or play an active role in. This cooking style is said to have been introduced to Kenya and Uganda in the 1890s by Indian migrants, who were indentured by the East Africa Protectorate (formerly the Imperial British East Africa Company) to build the railway system. Labourers would start cooking early in the morning – in preparation for lunch – on an outdoor stove called a jiko, not dissimilar to an Indian tawa. Many people would have a hand in the process, adding ingredients and spices along the way, so that by mealtime the dish was fragrant and hearty, slow-cooked to perfection.

Today karoga is a popular food trend and it's a great way to socialize in large groups; some second-generation twists even include cooking pizza karoga style – though be careful not to get too tipsy as you wait for dinner to be ready!

GEORGE PARMAR (AGED 51)

Karoga Club chair

George's family came to the UK from Nairobi in Kenya in the early 70s – his father and uncle arrived in 1974 when George was four years old. Tens of thousands of Kenyan Indians fled the country, starting from the mid 60s, as a result of much political upheaval. Kenya gained independence in 1963 and there soon followed a policy of 'Africanization' introduced by the Kenyan government, which wanted Southeast Asians to take up Kenyan citizenship. The policy involved Kenyan citizens replacing non-Kenyan citizens across key sectors of government, the civil service and the economy. Those who retained their British status were discriminated against, and Kenyan Indians faced redundancy, marginalization and growing unemployment; many had to give up their businesses ultimately. Unlike Uganda it wasn't an expulsion, but life was made very hard for those who did not take up citizenship by the deadline.

In Kenya, George's family had a history as shirt-makers, and they have shirt factories there to this day – his cousin and parts of the family still live in Nairobi. Those Kenyan Indians who did take up Kenyan citizenship continued to lead successful lives. Once settled in the UK, his father and uncle set up a clothing and textile business, which led to opening a denim factory in Wembley – the segue into the fashion industry was only natural. They started off supplying to market stalls, then brands, and things really took off from there; they went on to be involved in founding Pepe Jeans. It's a common story and something to really celebrate. Once in the UK, Kenyan and Ugandan Indians had to start again, and as many had been business owners and self-employed in Africa, they came with the skills and expertise to start their own businesses here. Many came with trading links to Europe and America, so they already had the network, knowledge and determination to thrive. The reputation for being real entrepreneurs is well deserved.

George grew up in and was educated in Harrow. But the family always kept a close affinity to Nairobi. As a child he and his cousins would go back during the summer holidays for six weeks, and his Kenyan roots were embedded. This is very much reflected in his cooking style and love for all things karoga; he'd cook outdoors constantly if he could. When he moved from Harrow to Stevenage as an adult in 2005 – George wanted more of a country life for his young children – he found that there were very few Indian restaurants for dining out. Not knowing how to cook, and with drastic measures required, he took it upon himself to learn. This started off as inviting a few friends over for dinner, where he'd set up a karoga in the garden – jikos, tawas, etc. His friends enjoyed it so much they decided to host karoga dinner parties in each other's gardens, and take turns, with a different host rotating each month. This new karoga concept gathered such traction that they eventually outgrew themselves in terms of popularity and numbers and ended up hosting at a local rugby club every six weeks. Karoga Club members even have their own T-shirts and badges. What's particularly heart-warming is that this tradition is being passed on to the next generation – George's children love it! It's such a lovely way to preserve a unique heritage and identity, and the complexity of the different diaspora communities. In this case it brings three different cultures together: Gujarati, Kenyan and British.

SONALI MORJARIA

Harrow-based digital content creator

The conditions in which Indian diaspora communities were forced to flee Uganda were brutal and heart-breaking – there is no rose-tinting. Idi Amin was a ruthless dictator who seized power in 1971 after a military coup, and declared himself President. Amin accused Indians of 'milking Uganda's money' rather than viewing them as wealth creators who did much to drive economic growth. They were given only three months to get their affairs in order, uproot a lifetime, leave properties, good jobs, successful businesses and family ties. This was only the start of Amin's tyranny: over the course of his time in office until 1979 it is estimated that he murdered 300,000 African Ugandans, and brought the economy to its knees through mismanagement, corruption and cronyism. Yet when you speak to those who were displaced, there is nothing but genuine warmth and love towards their former homeland, which is passed on through their children.

Sonali's great-grandparents migrated to East Africa when the railway system was being built between Uganda and Kenya. Her mother was born in Kampala, Uganda, and came to the UK in 1968 with her brother to study – of course this was before Idi Amin declared the expulsion in 1972. Uganda had gained independence in 1962, and many Indians after that time decided to have UK savings and to educate their children in the UK as a result of Africanization policies. The two of them lived in a small flat in Golders Green. When the expulsion happened, there was very little warning. Suddenly all the family back home left in a hurry, able to leave with only what they could carry, and rushed to the UK.

'A family with nine children, squeezed into one flat. My grandfather didn't have the money to buy a house big enough for nine kids. It came as a shock to the system. On a human level, to be expelled from your homeland at a moment's notice, and have to take refuge in a country so far removed and foreign, was a real trauma . . . at a time when different communities weren't as understood or accepted in the UK. It was also a vast drop in the standard and quality of life. We don't even have pictures of Mum when she was little, as they could only leave with basic possessions.'

Coming from the vast open space and freedom of the family home in Uganda to being cramped in a flat in Golders Green must have been so challenging. I can't help but feel emotional while talking to Sonali about her family history – as I imagine my family in that same situation – yet the overwhelming feeling of loss, turmoil and grief was assuaged by the magical properties of food. 'It's the food that kept everybody connected, it's a cultural thing, everybody cooking together, everybody gathering around the table and keeping everything together.' I understand that feeling implicitly.

We go on to talk about what the essence of African Indian food means. Sonali talks fondly of her summer holidays spent in Nairobi – her father was born in Kenya, and his side of the family remained there: she was sent to Kenya from the age of five or six, with her brother, and would spend summers there with her paternal grandparents. One of her most vivid memories is of 'Mama Mboga' (mboga is the Swahili word for vegetables), a lady who would go from house to house selling an abundance of beautiful fresh and sweet vegetables. Mama Mboga would carry a bag full of vegetables on her back, with the strap of her bag around her head. She would shout out to announce her arrival and to sell her wares. Sonali's grandmother would come out and barter over the price of veg – much like my granny would! You can picture the scene. Shelling peas together is a treasured memory for her, too. For Sonali, it's the use of root vegetables like cassava, sweet potatoes and raw plantains that epitomizes African Indian food, staples while growing up and in her cooking.

It's important to know our history in order to understand why we are where we are now. Certainly most African Indians came from prosperous and privileged middle-class backgrounds, highly educated, and embraced life in Britain and the new opportunities it created, determined to succeed. These advantages helped them to thrive and earn a reputation as real entrepreneurs, and it is testament to how they overcame expulsion. Sonali feels it's important to share the family history with her young daughter, so that she can understand about how resilient, driven and successful they are as a community, and of course lucky to be living in the UK. Giving back to the host nation is a key motivation.

We Indians love finger food – it heightens the enjoyment as far as I'm concerned and this chicken is certainly finger-licking good! These wings are a great starter. You can easily veganize this recipe by replacing the chicken wings with cauliflower florets. Make a wet batter rather than a dry dredge by adding a little water – you want a double cream consistency – and reduce the roasting time accordingly. Both options are to be enjoyed with a cold beer or beverage of choice, perhaps while you wait for your karoga to cook.

STICKY AND SPICY MANGO CHICKEN WINGS

SERVES 4–6

1kg chicken wings

Dry dredge

150g plain flour, or enough to coat the wings

1 teaspoon ground turmeric

1¾ teaspoons garam masala

5 whole cloves, ground to a powder using a pestle and mortar

5 ground whole peppercorns

1 tablespoon Kashmiri chilli powder

2 teaspoons sea salt

6 green cardamom pods (bruise to release the seeds and grind the seeds to a powder)

1 tablespoon Kasuri methi (dried fenugreek)

1 teaspoon garlic granules

1 teaspoon ground ginger

Glaze

1 x 320g jar of premium mango chutney

1 tablespoon honey

1 tablespoon cider vinegar (you can use white wine vinegar instead)

3 tablespoons sriracha hot sauce, or to taste

a good glug of apple juice (enough so you have a nice sauce consistency)

1. Set your oven to 200°C.
2. Mix the dry dredge ingredients together in a bowl and coat the wings.
3. Shake off any excess and lay the wings out on two lined baking trays. Bake for 22 minutes, then turn the wings over with tongs and bake for another 22 minutes.
4. Meanwhile mix together the ingredients for the glaze, adding the apple juice last so you can gauge the consistency – about 1–2 tablespoons should do it. Set aside.
5. Remove the wings from the oven, coat evenly with the mango glaze and bake for another 10–15 minutes. Serve with charred lime halves, if you like.

This recipe is from the 'Karoga King' himself, George Parmar, and is intended to be cooked outdoors; weather permitting in Blighty of course. There is such a thing as an umbrella, though, if you choose to brave it! Karogas can be meat-based, vegetarian, vegan, seafood-based – it's simply a method of cooking. Here we have British lamb, meets Kenyan cooking technique, meets Indian masala, and all the guests have a hand in stirring the pot. Just have everything pre-prepared and measured out.

KAROGA LAMB MASALA

SERVES 4

1kg diced lamb leg meat, cut into 3cm pieces

Marinade

½ tablespoon garlic paste

½ tablespoon ginger paste

1 tablespoon ground cumin

1 tablespoon ground coriander

1 teaspoon garam masala

1 teaspoon chilli powder

1 tablespoon amchoor powder (dried mango powder)

4–5 tablespoons yoghurt

1 teaspoon sea salt

Masala sauce

6 tablespoons vegetable oil

1 teaspoon cumin seeds

2 star anise

3 black cardamom pods

5 green cardamom pods (bruise to release the seeds)

3 small cinnamon sticks

2 bay leaves

3 red onions, very finely chopped

1 tablespoon ginger paste

1 tablespoon garlic paste

1 x 400g tin of chopped tomatoes, blitzed until smooth (or use passata)

1 teaspoon ground turmeric

1½ teaspoons chilli powder

1½ teaspoons sea salt, or to taste

4 green finger chillies, finely chopped

1 tablespoon ground cumin

1 tablespoon ground coriander

a pinch of ground mace

40g chopped fresh coriander

40g salted butter

approx. 250ml water

2 tablespoons Kasuri methi (dried fenugreek)

1 teaspoon garam masala

1. Mix all the marinade ingredients together and evenly coat the lamb pieces. Place in an airtight container and marinate in the fridge for 48 hours.
2. Heat the oil in a large saucepan on your jiko (hot coals), or on a medium to high heat on your hob, and sauté the cumin seeds until sizzling.
3. Next add the rest of the whole spices – star anise, black and green cardamoms, cinnamon and bay leaves – to the pan and sizzle for 10 seconds to infuse the oil, then add the onions and cook for about 10 minutes, or until they are a caramel colour.
4. Move your pan to an area where the heat is lower, or turn down the heat to medium, and add the ginger and garlic pastes. Cook for 1 minute.
5. Add the tomatoes, followed by the turmeric, chilli powder and salt, and increase the heat a little. Simmer for 2 minutes.

6. Add the chopped green chillies, ground cumin, ground coriander, mace and half the fresh coriander, and cook out for about 5 minutes. Then add the lamb, together with the butter, and sauté over a high heat for 5 minutes or so, ensuring the lamb pieces are coated in the masala and sealed. Pour in half the water and bring to a simmer.

7. Put a lid on the saucepan and steam cook the lamb on a medium heat for about an hour, or until tender, stirring regularly and adding more water as necessary so the meat doesn't catch. You want a nice, thick and rich sauce.

8. Finally add the Kasuri methi and garam masala, cook for a further minute, then garnish with the remaining chopped coriander.

9. Serve with hot naan – you can heat shop-bought naan on the jiko, and even barbecue foil-wrapped sweet potatoes and corn on the cob as your karoga lamb cooks. Do slather both in butter, though.

COOK'S NOTE You can of course easily – worst-case scenario – cook this delicious lamb curry on your hob indoors. I would never judge! I have provided the necessary adjustments in the method. See page 70 if you'd like to make your own naan.

The Rolex is an iconic and much-loved Ugandan street food. There is a lot of debate over the origins of the dish, the most charming theory being that it's a mispronunciation of 'rolled eggs'; which has stuck! Others liken the vibrant colour of the diced vegetables to precious jewels. However it got its moniker, it's peng! I love the fact that it's a delicious way to reinvent leftovers, and it's incredibly versatile. It works great with leftover lamb curry, chicken and even keema. For vegetarians, black bean makhani or rajma (kidney beans) work particularly well – but whatever you use you must ensure the curry is dry, or you will get an ooze. For me the sweet chilli sauce is an essential component, as I feel the best street food is a combination of hot, sweet and savoury. You can use any Indian flatbread – parathas are really good – but I feel Gujarati rotli would be most authentic, as most of the diaspora emigrated from this region of India.

CHAPATTI ROLEX

MAKES 6 ROLEX

Rotli

300g plain flour
   (or chapatti/atta
   flour if you prefer)
a pinch of sea salt
2 tablespoons
   vegetable oil
approx. 150–200ml
   just-boiled water

Filling

approx. 2 cups leftover
   curry (if using a meat
   curry, remove any
   bones as appropriate
   and chop into pieces;
   if using beans/
   pulses, ensure it is
   dry without too much
   'gravy')
sweet chilli sauce,
   to taste

grated cheese
   (optional)
50g fresh coriander

Masala omelette

12 eggs (2 per
   omelette)
approx. 100g finely
   sliced white cabbage
½ a large red onion,
   finely diced
½ a large red pepper,
   cut into 1cm dice

2–3 spring onions,
   including the green
   parts, finely sliced
2–3 mild green
   finger chillies, finely
   chopped
sea salt, to taste
garam masala, a
   sprinkle per omelette
vegetable oil, for
   cooking

1. Start by making the dough for the rotli/chapatti. Mix together the flour, salt and oil in a large bowl. Then add 150ml of just-boiled water, and use the end of a wooden spoon to bring everything together. Slowly add the rest of the hot water a little at a time. When you can see that you have added a sufficient amount of water and the dough is 'balling', use your hands to knead for 5 minutes or so until you have a smooth, soft dough. Cover and set aside at room temperature to rest for at least 30 minutes.

2. If you're planning to make all six Rolexes at one given time, it will be best to batch-make all the rotlis beforehand and keep them warm in foil or a chapatti warmer. Divide the dough into six equal portions. Follow the standard method for making chapattis from step 3 onwards (see page 19) – except that there is no need to slather on butter at the end. You will need a large non-stick frying pan or tawa.

→

3. When you are ready to cook and assemble, heat your leftover curry in a saucepan.
4. Crack 2 eggs into a bowl and beat together with a little of the cabbage, red onion, red pepper, spring onions and green chillies. Season with a pinch of salt and garam masala.
5. Heat 2 or 3 tablespoons of vegetable oil in your frying pan on a medium to high heat, ensuring the surface is coated, then add the beaten egg mixture. This will naturally spread, but give it a helping hand by swirling the pan around if necessary – you want an omelette similar in size to the rotli (chapatti). Once cooked underneath, flip using a fish slice or large spatula. Place a chapatti on top of the omelette so it heats as the bottom cooks through for
a minute or so.
6. Turn the omelette out on to your plate or work surface, chapatti side down, omelette facing up. Drizzle with a little sweet chilli sauce, then thinly cover the area with the leftover curry – you'll need a couple of tablespoons – using the back of a spoon to spread. (If using cheese, place on top of the curry layer.) Next, carpet with a layer of fresh coriander, which we are using almost as a salad component.
7. Finally, roll your Rolex, ensuring that the filling is packed in tight. I find wrapping it in foil or greaseproof paper keeps the Rolex intact. Traditionally street vendors wrap it in newspaper. If you prefer to serve it on a plate, present it with the fold side down, and slice in half. Demolish with glee! Eat and repeat.

> **COOK'S NOTE** The Gujarati rotli is more pliable and soft than a Punjabi roti. This is because of the oil used in the dough and also the very hot water, which acts to destroy the gluten bonds in the flour, resulting in a soft bread. I use plain flour, as it's commonly used in Africa and you'll most likely have it in your store cupboard. You can replace the plain flour with atta/whole wheat chapatti flour to be fully authentic Gujarati.

Bunny chow is an iconic dish synonymous with South African Indian railway workers in Durban, who used hollowed-out loaves of bread as vessels to carry their lunch! Of course the inner bread should not be discarded, as it's perfect for dipping into the curry, so you want plenty of gravy! You really could use any curry in your 'bunny', but this was originally vegetarian. Jackfruit, or vegan 'meat' as it's become known, is indigenous to India; however, it is grown in many parts of Africa – predominantly in Uganda – so I felt it was somewhat poetic for this recipe. The African love of root vegetables is served well by the inclusion of sweet potatoes, and green beans bring a satisfying crunch. For the carnivores, a lovely lamb curry version is lip-smacking.

SWEET POTATO AND JACKFRUIT BUNNY CHOW

SERVES 4

1 x 565g tin of green jackfruit

vegetable oil, for cooking

1 tablespoon tandoori masala

4 small cob loaves or 2 farmhouse loaves, cut in half

Masala
1 brown onion, finely diced

1 Scotch bonnet chilli (use half if you don't want it too spicy), chopped

15g ginger, grated

15g garlic, grated

1 level teaspoon ground turmeric

1 teaspoon chilli powder

1 teaspoon paprika

1 teaspoon ground cumin

1 teaspoon coriander seeds, toasted, then finely crushed in a pestle and mortar

1½ teaspoons garam masala

1½ teaspoons sea salt, or to taste

1 x 400g tin of chopped tomatoes, blended until smooth (or use passata)

1 x 400g tin of full-fat coconut milk

2 small to medium sweet potatoes, peeled and cut into 3cm cubes

250ml water

125g fine green beans, trimmed and cut into 3cm pieces (you can use sliced runner beans or long-stem broccoli instead)

Garnish
unsweetened coconut yoghurt for vegans, or use full-fat Greek yoghurt if non-vegan

finely sliced red onion

fresh coriander leaves

charred lime halves (see page 196)

1. Set your oven to 180°C. Drain the jackfruit and cut it into small bite-sized pieces, then put it into a large mixing bowl and toss with a little vegetable oil and the tandoori masala, making sure all the pieces are evenly coated. Lay them out on a lined baking tray and roast for 15 minutes, then set aside. We want to create some deep flavour.

2. Now start the masala. Heat a few glugs of vegetable oil in a large saucepan on a medium to high heat, then drop in the onions and chopped chilli, followed by the ginger and garlic a few minutes later.

3. Once the onions have softened and become translucent, reduce the heat to medium and add the ground spices: turmeric, chilli powder, paprika, cumin, toasted crushed coriander seeds, garam masala, and the salt. Toast these a little, without catching – add a splash of water if need be.

→

COOK'S NOTE This is a gorgeous stand-alone vegan curry. Serve with plain rice, charred lime halves and shards of poppadom for added texture.

4. Pour in the blended tomatoes/passata and coconut milk, give everything a good mix, and crank up the heat so you can bring the masala to a simmer. After 5–10 minutes you'll see the tell-tale separation of the oil on the surface, which means it's ready to taste. Adjust the seasoning accordingly.

5. Add the sweet potatoes to the masala and stir to evenly coat. Simmer for 10 minutes, then add the jackfruit and about 250ml of water. The bread will soak up a lot of sauce or gravy, so you're going to need plenty of it. Bring to a simmer and cook, covered, for a further 10 minutes.

6. Finally lob in the green beans and simmer for a further 5–7 minutes – you want to keep these al dente. Check that your sweet potatoes are pretty much cooked through first.

7. Fill your hollowed loaves with curry and garnish with a good dollop of yoghurt, finely sliced red onion, coriander leaves, and charred lime halves.

This is possibly one of the most opulent kebabs ever, as it's made with rib-eye steak. Steaks are the best cuts for quick barbecuing and grilling because the meat is so tender – and we know how popular outdoor cooking and grilling is in Africa. The coal also imparts such a delicious layer of flavour. Sirloin or rib-eye would be great for this recipe, and you want a steak with a good marbling of fat to make it extra juicy. You can use a cheaper cut and use grated or liquidized papaya or kiwi to tenderize the meat – add just a couple of tablespoons to the marinade depending on how much meat you are marinating; overnight is best for tougher cuts. Rib-eye tends to be cut thicker, which is why I prefer it, as for mishkaki the meat is cut into chunks and I like these to be a decent size. This is a delicious Swahili-Indian mash-up made better by a side of mogo chips!

STEAK MISHKAKI AND MOGO CHIPS

SERVES 2

2 rib-eye steaks (500g), cut into 4cm chunks (see above)

Marinade

50ml vegetable oil

3 tablespoons white wine vinegar

1½ teaspoons tandoori masala

1 teaspoon chilli powder

1 teaspoon ground black pepper

½ teaspoon ground turmeric

15g garlic, grated

15g ginger, grated

1 tablespoon finely chopped fresh coriander

juice of ½ a lemon

For the kebab skewers

½ a red pepper, cut into 4cm chunks

½ a green or yellow pepper, cut into 4cm chunks

2 small red onions, each cut into 6 segments

Mogo chips

2 medium cassava

oil, for deep-frying

sea salt, to taste

To serve

1 lime or lemon, cut in half

firecracker mayo (page 206)

1. Mix all the marinade ingredients together in a medium bowl. Add the steak and smother all the pieces with the marinade, then cover and refrigerate. Take the steak out of the fridge an hour before grilling so that it can come to room temperature. You want to marinate rib-eye for about 4 hours, so that gives you lots of time to prepare the barbecue. The coals impart a lovely smoked flavour; if using wood, choose a hard wood like oak or hickory. You are ready to grill when the coals turn white and are scorching hot. (See notes if using an oven grill.)

2. Fried mogo is traditionally served with lemon juice and chilli powder; however, I like to have the mogo chips with my firecracker mayo, which is loaded with a citrus and chilli hit. Alternatively you can flavour plain mayo with lemon juice, chilli flakes, chilli powder and salt, to taste. Make it ahead and refrigerate. (You can have the chips with tomato or tamarind ketchup if you prefer.)

→

3. I use three 20cm metal skewers to grill the meat. You may wish to use four skewers if serving on the skewers to two people. If you are using wooden skewers you will need to soak them in cold water for 30 minutes before using, to prevent them burning on the barbecue or under the oven grill.

4. Next, prepare the mogo (cassava) chips. Cassava is a very dense and starchy root vegetable, with a lovely unique flavour not dissimilar to the humble potato. The easiest way to peel it is to cut the ends off, then run the tip of your knife along the outer skin from the top to the bottom. Use your knife blade to gently lift off the skin, which will pull away quite easily to reveal the smooth white interior. If your cassava is long and thin, cut it into two or three sections so it's easier to handle.

5. Cut the cassava into chip-shaped wedges, taking care to remove the woody fibrous core in the centre. You'll need a sharp knife. Parboil the cassava until tender but retaining its shape – the time will vary according to the thickness. Allow to steam-dry.

6. Meanwhile thread the steak on to the skewers, alternating with the pepper and onion segments. You can dab the vegetables with a little of the marinade.

7. The mogo chips are made while the steak is resting, so prepare your deep-fryer or kadhai (wok), heating the oil to 180°C.

8. When ready, grill the kebabs for 2 minutes on each side for the perfect blushing medium, as low to the coals as possible to get that all-important char. Grill the lemon or lime halves too. Allow the steak to rest for a few minutes before serving, covered loosely with foil. See separate note below if using an oven grill.

9. Fry the chips until cooked and golden, then transfer on to kitchen paper and season with sea salt.

10. Serve the steak mishkaki with the mogo chips, a colourful and crunchy rainbow salad and the charred lemon or lime.

NOTES ON USING AN OVEN GRILL: Set your oven grill to the highest heat. Grill the steak, placing the shelf as close to the hot elements as possible.

* For medium steak – about 4/5 minutes per side.

* For well-done steak– about 5/6 minutes per side.

* Rest the kebabs for 5 minutes after cooking.

* Heat a griddle or frying pan on your hob on the highest heat. Place the lemon or lime halves on it cut side down, lifting them off when charred.

COOK'S NOTE You can't have a barbecue without making s'mores for pudding. Sandwich giant marshmallows and blocks of chocolate between two Digestive biscuits and grill until the centre is gooey and melted. Heavenly!

Fufu means 'mash' or 'mix' in the West African Twi language. Fufu is a popular dumpling of sorts, eaten with soup or broth, and involves pounding boiled cassava and plantain together until a smooth dough is formed. My fried version is more akin to the Puerto Rican variation of fufu called mofongo. Mofongo involves pounding fried green plantain with raw garlic, chicharrón (crispy pork crackling), salt and olive oil. You could use bacon lardons instead of chicharrón, but I'm keeping my mash-up meat-free, and pairing it with a funky Indian peperonata. Of course it's not all about the fufu! Tilapia fish is eaten all over Africa, and is delicious simply marinated in a pili pili hot sauce and grilled. My recipe works well with bream or mackerel, which you could grill whole, butterfly or fillet if you don't wish to contend with fish bones – just reduce the amount of marinade and the length of the cooking time accordingly.

ROASTED SEA BREAM PILI PILI } WITH FRIED GREEN PLANTAIN FUFU

SERVES 4

4 whole bream, gutted and scaled, fins and gills removed (400–450g each)

Pili pili marinade
80ml vegetable oil
1–2 Scotch bonnet chillies
20g garlic
70g fresh coriander leaves
zest and juice of 1 lime or lemon
½–1 teaspoon sea salt, or to taste

Mint chutney
40g fresh mint leaves
1–2 green finger chillies, roughly chopped
6 spring onions, roughly chopped
1 small tomato, roughly chopped
sea salt, to taste

Stuffing for fish
1–2 lemons, thinly sliced
approx. 20g fresh coriander

'Peperonata'
vegetable oil, for cooking
7g garlic, grated
½ a Scotch bonnet chilli, chopped
1 large brown onion, finely sliced
1 teaspoon ground cumin
1 teaspoon ground coriander
1 teaspoon paprika
a large pinch of saffron (or 1 teaspoon ground turmeric)
1 teaspoon Kashmiri chilli powder

1 teaspoon sea salt, or to taste
1 red pepper, julienned/finely sliced
1 yellow pepper, julienned/finely sliced
1 tomato, chopped (approx. 125g)

Fufu
4–6 green plantains (approx. 800g unpeeled)
vegetable oil, for deep-frying
10-15g garlic
sea salt, to taste
3–4 tablespoons olive oil

1. Blitz the marinade ingredients together into a paste using a food processor. Use 1 chilli to start with, then taste – Scotch bonnets have a lovely fruity flavour – and if you prefer to go a little hotter, blitz in the second chilli. Set aside.

2. Blitz all the mint chutney ingredients together in a food processor with a splash of water. Place in an airtight container and pop into the fridge. I always have some of this in the fridge – it's an essential condiment and flavour grenade for Indian food.

3. To prepare the fish, make three diagonal slashes about 2cm deep along the fish on each side using a sharp knife – this is to allow the marinade to penetrate. Smother each bream with the marinade, being sure to work it into the slashes. Fill the cavity with thinly sliced lemon and fresh coriander. Set aside to marinate for 20–30 minutes.

4. To make the peperonata, heat 3 tablespoons of vegetable oil in a large saucepan and sauté the garlic and chilli on a medium heat. After a minute, add the sliced onions and soften for 4–5 minutes, then add the ground spices: cumin, coriander, paprika, saffron (or turmeric), chilli powder, and the salt. Give this a good mix and toast the spices for 30 seconds, then add the sliced peppers, followed by the chopped tomato. Cook on a medium to low heat for 25–30 minutes, partially covered. Don't let your pan go dry – you may need a splash of water. Remove from the heat.

5. Place your bream on two baking trays lined with greaseproof paper and roast in a 200°C oven for about 25 minutes, or until cooked through. Quick tip: the eyes will turn opaque when the fish is cooked, but you don't want these to be opaque and sunken, as that's an indication that they are overcooked. If you don't want to contend with fish bones when eating, use butterflied mackerel or fillet of bream instead. Obviously cooking time will be reduced and you won't need as much marinade.

6. Plantains are pretty tricky to peel. You can't peel them like a banana, for example. They should always be at room temperature. First, cut off the top and bottom tips, then carefully make one slit through the outer skin only, from the top to the bottom with the end of a sharp knife. For safety, now use the tip of a blunt dinner knife to slide under the skin to loosen and tease it open, without cutting the flesh. Then use your fingers to pull away the skin, in a side-to-side motion rather than vertical as with a banana. Remove any peel still clinging to the flesh, and cut the flesh into pieces just under 3cm long.

7. Deep-fry the plantain in oil heated to 175°C until cooked and golden (but not brown), for about 6–8 minutes, then drain on kitchen paper to soak up any excess oil.

8. Mash some of the garlic with a little salt in a pestle and mortar, mix in a little olive oil (traditionally a large wooden pestle and mortar is used, called a pilón), then add the fried plantain bit by bit and mash together. You will need to do this in batches, depending on the size of your pestle and mortar, or in individual portions. Season with sea salt as you are mashing. Once you have a homogenous mixture, you can turn it out. If you have a small mortar you can turn it out straight from that – giving you that dome shape – or use a small dome-shaped receptacle as a mould to create the same effect.

9. Serve the roasted bream, peperonata, and fufu with a little mint chutney – which acts as a zingy salsa verde – and a kachumber salad (see page 48).

COOK'S NOTE You could simply shallow-fry sliced green plantain instead of making the fufu. Alternatively you could give mofongo a bash, by mashing in a little chicharrón (crunchy pork crackling).

Mandazi is a much-loved triangular doughnut that's popular throughout East Africa, taken for breakfast or as a teatime snack with hot coffee or spicy chai. The dough is often made with yeast, similar to a beignet, but I wanted a super easy recipe that doesn't need a prove or indeed contain eggs. Now mandazi aren't sugar-coated, but mine HAVE to be. Freshly fried doughnuts coated in sugar are a thing of my childhood, from many a visit to the seaside and fairground. It's the ground cardamom that's the point of difference – and you need a lot of it to get a proper hit – you'll see the black flecks in the dough. These are best eaten fresh and still warm.

LEMON AND CARDAMOM MANDAZI DOUGHNUTS

MAKES 16 DOUGHNUTS

400g plain flour
100g caster sugar

1½ teaspoons baking powder
2 teaspoons ground green cardamom (or you could use ground cinnamon or mixed spice)

zest of 1 lemon
a pinch of salt
65g melted unsalted butter
100g yoghurt

approx. 100ml water
extra caster sugar, for rolling
vegetable oil, for deep-frying

1. Whisk the flour, sugar, baking powder, ground cardamom, lemon zest and salt together in a large mixing bowl.
2. Mix the melted butter through the dry ingredients – you're aiming for a texture similar to crumble. Then mix in the yoghurt – it will start to look like rubble – and finally add the water. You want a soft dough, but don't knead it or overwork.
3. Cover the dough and rest it at room temperature for 15–30 minutes.
4. Heat oil to 170°C in your deep fryer or kadhai (wok). Place a few tablespoons of caster sugar in a mixing bowl or on a shallow tray, and set aside; this is to roll the hot doughnuts in, once fried.
5. Cut your rested dough in half. Lightly knead one half on a scantly floured work surface, and re-cover the other half. You want a round dough ball without working the dough too much. Roll it into a thin disc, about 20cm in diameter and 6-7mm thick (a bit like a chapatti but thicker).
6. Now, using a sharp knife, cut the dough into eighths as you would a pizza. You want that triangle shape.
7. Deep-fry the mandazi for 2–3 minutes on each side until cooked, puffed and golden – be careful to place them away from you in the hot oil. Do this in batches, being sure not to overcrowd the pan.
8. Drain the cooked mandazi on kitchen paper, then immediately roll them in the caster sugar. Repeat the process with the rest of the dough.
9. Serve immediately and scoff!

Now I have no 'school-tie' loyalties, having attended a state school! However, the irony of including Eton mess – arch public school rivals to neighbouring Harrow of course – is not entirely lost on me. All that concerns me is that it's a super-tasty pudding, and what complements sugar more than a little spice? What's nice about this dessert is that shop-bought shortcuts are fully acceptable, as we want to get to the enjoyment as soon as possible! Though you could easily whip up some meringue and flavour it with a little ground ginger, were you so inclined. This recipe is fully loaded with stand-alone components. The ginger cake recipe has been adapted from a stellar Women's Institute cookbook that was bequeathed to me – I'm afraid my copy is barely held together, with some pages missing, but highly treasured!

ETON MESS KNICKERBOCKER GLORY

SERVES 4–6

Ginger cake
50ml whole milk
2 tablespoons black treacle
1 tablespoon golden syrup
115g coconut oil (cold-pressed)
200g plain flour
115g soft light brown sugar

2 teaspoons ground ginger
1 teaspoon ground cinnamon
1 teaspoon bicarbonate of soda
2 eggs

Caramel sauce
150g soft light brown sugar
50ml water
30g butter
150ml double cream

Candied pecans
150g whole pecan nuts
50g soft light brown sugar
¼ teaspoon sea salt
10g unsalted butter
¼ teaspoon ground spice (optional)

Chantilly cream
300ml double cream
1–2 tablespoons icing sugar
30g stem ginger in syrup, finely diced

You'll also need
shop-bought meringues (3–4 nests)
shop-bought salted caramel ice cream (or vanilla if you prefer)

1. Heat your oven to 150°C. Grease and line a 20cm x 20cm cake tin or similar, and line a large baking tray with greaseproof paper.
2. Warm the milk, treacle, syrup and coconut oil in a small saucepan.
3. Take a large mixing bowl and place in all of the dry ingredients: flour, sugar, ginger, cinnamon and bicarb. Give it a good mix together with a whisk. Pour in the wet mixture and beat together until combined, then beat in the eggs, one at a time, to a smooth and silky consistency. Pour into the prepared cake tin and bake on the middle shelf for 45–50 minutes. Check after 35 minutes as ovens vary.
4. To make the caramel sauce, combine all the ingredients in a heavy-bottomed pan and warm on a low heat until the sugar has dissolved and the butter has melted. Raise the heat slightly until you see bubbles trying

to break though the surface. Stir constantly for about 6 minutes – you will see the sauce starting to thicken. You may need to continue to heat for another 2 or 3 minutes. Be aware, the sauce will thicken further once cooled. To test, lift the spoon and allow to cool (it will be very hot), then drag your finger along the back of the spoon. If the line in the sauce you have made stays, you know the sauce is ready. Remove from the heat and cool completely.

5. For the candied pecans, toast your nuts in a large frying pan on a medium to high heat, being careful not to burn them. Transfer to a plate and set aside. Add the sugar, salt and butter to the pan, and the spice if using, then stir together and allow to melt. Return the pecans to the pan, stirring continuously so they are all coated in the sugary butter – do not allow it to burn. This will take about 3–5 minutes.

6. Transfer the nuts to your large lined baking tray, and immediately separate them – use a couple of forks or whatever you have handy – before they start to set. Allow to cool and harden for about 5 minutes or so.

7. To make the Chantilly cream, whisk all the ingredients together to a soft peak (don't make it too sweet, as you need to balance the sweetness of the meringue). You can fold through extra diced stem ginger should you want more of a hit. Next fold through shards of broken meringue.

8. Time to assemble. Take a conical-shaped sundae glass or small Kilner jar and first layer some caramel sauce, then ice cream scoops, then ginger cake cut into 3cm squares, then Chantilly cream, a final drizzle of caramel, and top with candied pecans. Divine!

COOK'S NOTE You have a 4-in-1 recipe here, and you can pick and mix the combinations:

∗ **Ginger cake, with salted caramel ice cream and caramel.**

∗ **Eton mess: ginger spiked cream, mixed with broken meringue, caramel sauce and candied pecans – just add blackberries or any other tart soft fruit.**

∗ **Plain and naked ginger cake to have with a brew.**

∗ **Candied pecans – great as a snack in themselves.**

I adore the candied pecans, they're great as a gift, and to make for special occasions. Have fun with the flavours; salty, sweet and spicy caramel is fab, or ground ginger or ground cinnamon with a pinch of cayenne! Experiment!

MANCHESTER

BANGLADESHI COMMUNITY

Large-scale Bangladeshi migration to the UK took place in the 1970s.
When the new state of Pakistan was established in 1947 after the partition
of India, Pakistan consisted of two territories. Bengal was split in half –
West Bengal remained part of India, while East Bengal became part of
the Dominion of Pakistan. Two territories, located 2,000 miles apart. The
partition of India was made along religious lines, and it's estimated that
over 70 per cent of the population of East Bengal practised the Muslim faith
at that time. The civil war between these two territories in 1970–71 resulted
in a split, creating modern-day Pakistan (formerly West Pakistan) and the
birth of modern-day Bangladesh (formerly East Pakistan).

Most migration to the UK came from the Sylhet region of Bangladesh,
to escape the civil unrest. The largest Bangladeshi community in Britain
is concentrated in East London – Brick Lane is famed for its restaurants.
Did you know that eight out of ten curry houses in the UK are actually
Bangladeshi? Rusholme is Manchester's 'curry mile', located along
Wilmslow Road, two miles south of the city centre. There is also a notable
Bangladeshi community in Oldham, where they began to settle from the
1950s and 60s to work in the local cotton mills. When the textile industry
went into decline in the 1970s, many Bangladeshis moved into the
restaurant business, spotting a gap in the market. However, I'd like to take a
closer look at some adaptations of traditional home-style cooking. There is
a huge amount of regional nuance in Bangladeshi cuisine – a cooking style
from one region of Bangladesh can differ greatly to that of the next, so it's
difficult to do it justice. The food history has had many influences over the
years, from Mughal, Persian, Turkish and Arabic to neighbours further East.
Inspired by the communities I've met here, and how they cook, I've added
a layer of British fusion too . . . which is most exciting!

HASINA ISLAM (AGED 41)

Board member of a Bangladeshi women's charity,
currently studying for a Master's degree in Social Work

Not only is Hasina in full-time education, she is a (single) mother to four children, aged 3, 10, 17 and 24, she's a board member of a Bangladeshi women's charity, very much involved in social activism, and she even squeezes in time to be part of a running club: 'I like to keep myself busy,' she tells me.

Now there's busy and there's Wonder Woman levels of keeping yourself occupied. Hasina lives in Old Trafford in Greater Manchester, and she has four siblings of her own, all sisters and very much a close-knit family. Both her parents came from Chittagong, in Bangladesh, one of the oldest ports in the world. Her father, who has now passed away, had the most colourful life. The family's journey to the UK started with him, 'Michael' Islam. He came here in the early 1950s, having run away from home at eight years old after his mother died, and his father remarried. His stepmother was very cruel and abusive, so he decided to leave home to escape her clutches, and ended up on a passenger ship; he worked from ship to ship, travelling the world. He learned how to cook and worked in the kitchens, working his way up to being a chef. Michael arrived in England at the age of 22, and it seems quite a Cinderella story that he ultimately ended up becoming a restaurateur. He was illiterate, never learned to read or write, but went on to become a very successful businessman.

In 2006 Hasina joined Ananna, which is a Bangladeshi women's charity (the word 'ananna' means unique). It was established in 1989 by a group of women who felt there was a lack of services catering for Bangladeshi women in the Manchester demographic. The charity was set up with support and funding from the council, and its core purpose is to be women-focused, service-user led, designed to 'enable'; in particular disadvantaged women who are survivors of domestic abuse or have struggled with mental health. They provide support in a number of ways that are community-led, ranging from education, employability, physical and mental well-being, social isolation and accessing statutory services. With an all-female board, the mantra is very much 'for women, led by women'. She's worked at the charity for over 15 years now: 'I'd like to think that I've shown that anybody can be resilient and how you can turn things around. Getting married very young, leaving school with no qualifications, people write you off, that you'll achieve nothing. When I had my first child that was the turning point – I decided I had to be the best example to my child. I went back to study, got into a red-brick university at Manchester, did a degree in Sociology, got a job at the end of it – which was a life-changing experience – and now I'm on the board.' Hasina is a powerful and fantastic role model. Her ultimate goal is to influence and change policy in relation to social care, to take into account different cultural needs.

I ask Hasina what Bangladeshi food culture means to her. 'For me it's a very important and integral part of my life, having grown up in the restaurant business with my dad, but also food being really central to my family. As in, when we were growing up it was about people coming over, about making big handis of biryani, sending them home with Tupperwares full of food. It's a very communal thing. I would say food is our love language.'

Hasina tells me how Bangladeshi food varies massively depending on which region you're from. Food from Sylhet is very different to food from Chittagong, for example, and people tend to stick to the food of their region. Spice or heat levels also vary: in Chittagong the food is very spicy, and because it's a port, fish is very popular, but particularly dried fish, which is an acquired taste. Being a port city there are a lot of different influences from the trade routes, Portuguese and Arab influences. She's keen to highlight a dish called kala bhuna, which is almost like a beef jerky. So why then do we not see more traditional Bangladeshi food in Bangladeshi-run restaurants? 'I used to go to the restaurant [as a child] every weekend, earn a few pennies there and buy my trainers with that. What Dad was making there was this very generic food. And I'd think, but our food is so much more different, and vibrant, and amazing at home . . . I used to find it almost like McDonalds', curry McDonald's, just the same old, same old.' It does seem a travesty that this same scenario is still played out up and down the country, even more so as Bangladeshi home food is so diverse and hyper seasonal.

Home cooking, and communal cooking and eating, is something that's been an incredibly positive outlet for the women at Hasina's charity. She tells me about the 'pitha parties' – pitha is a snack, which can be sweet or savoury. Each year they have a competition to mark the Bangladeshi New Year: 'Who has the best pitha?' The real game-changer came after they received funding for a community garden, and they started to grow fruit and vegetables in their allotment: '. . . the women grew Bangladeshi vegetables that we would then cook for a weekly lunch club. It was ace.'

Of course growing our own also connects us to seasonality and making the best of the seasonal ingredients available. I love that element.

Nihari is a very popular stew in Bangladesh, normally made with meat on the bone; a nalli nihari also uses bone marrow to enrich the gravy. It's often made as part of an Eid feast, and is sometimes cooked very slowly overnight and eaten for breakfast after morning prayers – 'nihari' is derived from the Arabic word for 'morning': 'nahaar'. Hotpot is also a famous and much loved stew, originating from Lancashire, so this dish is a blend of the two! There'll be no need to cook overnight, as I'm using some beautifully tender lamb neck fillet. Warning, this dish will make you weak at the knees!

LAMB NIHARI HOTPOT

SERVES 4–6

1kg lamb neck fillet, cut into 4cm pieces

2 tablespoons plain flour

vegetable oil, for cooking

2 teaspoons cumin seeds

3 whole cloves

5cm cassia bark or cinnamon

6 whole black peppercorns, crushed in a pestle and mortar

2 black cardamom pods

2 bay leaves

2 onions, finely sliced into half-moons

2–3 green finger chillies, or to taste, slit in half

5 small to medium carrots, sliced into 1cm thick rounds (approx. 300g prepped weight)

25g ginger, grated

25g garlic, grated

1½ teaspoons garam masala

1 teaspoon mild Kashmiri chilli powder

1 teaspoon ground turmeric

2 teaspoons sea salt, or to taste

2 tablespoons Greek yoghurt

500ml water

approx. 650g potatoes, peeled

30g butter

a sprinkle of nigella seeds

1. Put the lamb pieces into a large freezer bag or similar. Add the flour, close the seal or twist shut, and shake the bag so all the pieces of meat are coated. Heat 3 or 4 tablespoons of vegetable oil in a large saucepan on a high heat, then seal the lamb pieces in batches. Don't overcrowd the pan or the meat will just stew, not seal and brown. Place on a plate and set aside.

2. Heat a touch more oil in the pan and then add the whole spices: cumin, cloves, cassia or cinnamon, peppercorns, cardamom and bay leaves. When they start to release their aromas, tip in the onions, green chillies and carrots. Sauté for 5 minutes on a medium heat, scraping any sediment from the bottom of the pan with your wooden spoon.

3. Add the ginger and garlic, cook out for a couple of minutes, then add the ground spices – garam masala, chilli powder and turmeric, and the salt – and toast for a minute.

4. Return the lamb to the pot, and stir in the yoghurt and water. Bring to the boil, reduce the heat to a simmer for 5–7 minutes, then remove from the heat.

→

5. Heat your oven to 180°C fan. Transfer the hotpot to a casserole dish. I use a round one that's 28cm in diameter. Set aside.

6. Now prep the potatoes. Let's talk about starch – this helps the potatoes to stick together during cooking, so you don't want to wash it off. It's fine to rinse the peeled whole potatoes but DO NOT rinse the sliced potatoes. You want 3mm thick slices, and the easiest way to achieve this is by using a mandolin (but be careful of your fingers, and use the safety holder).

7. Layer the potatoes over the top of the hotpot. Make it look as pretty as possible. I like a potato rose, layering and overlapping the slices in a spiral working from the outside in. Use the larger slices around the outside and save the smaller slices for the middle. Double layer the edges with any leftover slices, using the tip of your knife to lift and make spaces, and gently tuck the extras into the gaps.

8. Dot the top with half the butter and a sprinkle of salt to taste. Either pop a tight lid on top or tightly cover with a double layer of foil. Transfer to the oven and bake for 45 minutes.

9. Carefully remove the dish from the oven. Gently lift off the lid or the foil, if using, and discard. Dot with the remaining butter and a light sprinkle of nigella seeds.

10. Turn the oven temperature up to 200°C fan, and bake for another 20–30 minutes, uncovered, until the potatoes are cooked through, crispy and golden.

11. Serve with a green salad (or indeed with charred hispi cabbage, see page 244) and a crusty baguette for dunking in the gravy!

Shatkora is a rich and spicy speciality from Sylhet. A shatkora is actually a citrus fruit and its zest adds a real depth of flavour to this dish. This curry should pack a real punch, so I'm using Thai bird's-eye chillies. Usually beef chuck or such like would be used to make this, but I'm opting for ox cheek instead. If you choose to use chuck meat, simply adjust the cooking time.

OX CHEEK SHATKORA

SERVES 4–6

1kg ox cheek, cut into 3cm dice

vegetable oil, for cooking

5cm cassia bark/ cinnamon

1 teaspoon cumin seeds

8–10 green cardamom pods (bruise to release the seeds)

5 whole cloves

1½ brown onions, finely sliced into half-moons

25g ginger, grated

25g garlic, grated

3–4 Thai bird's-eye chillies, or to taste

1 teaspoon ground turmeric

½ teaspoon crushed black peppercorns

1 teaspoon crushed toasted coriander seeds

1–2 teaspoons sea salt, or to taste

400ml passata

18–20g shatkora or grapefruit zest (you can source shatkora either fresh or frozen from most Asian green-grocers)

about 400ml water

1½ teaspoons garam masala

chopped fresh coriander, to garnish

1. First make the masala. Heat about 4 tablespoons of vegetable oil in a large saucepan on a medium to high heat. Add the whole spices – cassia, cumin, cardamom and cloves – and when they start to release their aromas, tip in the onions. Reduce the heat to medium and lightly caramelize the onions – this will take 10 minutes or so.

2. Add the ginger, garlic and chillies and cook for a few minutes, then add the ground spices – turmeric, pepper and crushed coriander seeds – and the salt, and let them toast for about 30 seconds.

3. Pour in the passata. Give everything a good stir, bring to the boil, then reduce to a simmer for a few minutes.

4. Meanwhile prepare the shatkora or grapefruit zest. Use a knife to cut strips of the zest, then stack these on top of each other and finely slice.

5. Add the meat and sliced peel to the masala, and increase the heat to seal the meat. Add enough water to cover – about 400ml. Bring to the boil, then reduce the heat to a simmer and cook, covered, for about 2–3 hours, until the meat is tender. Keep an eye on it to ensure the pan doesn't dry out. If it does, add more water.

6. Sprinkle over the garam masala and more salt, to taste. Your shatkora should have some oomph to it. Simmer for another 3–5 minutes, then remove from the heat.

7. Garnish with chopped coriander and serve. Bangladeshis like to have plain white rice to accompany their meals.

Bangladeshis LOVE fish. A jhol is a soupy gravy. Now this fish curry isn't exactly Bangladeshi, but is my ode to Dhaka, the capital city. Once described as 'the Venice of the East', it has known many different rulers throughout history and was once a vital trading hub, a strategic route connecting the Indian subcontinent and Central Asia thanks to the Grand Trunk Road. So I'm combining a number of different influences in this dish: of course mustard seeds, which are beloved by Bangladeshis, and lemongrass, and fish native to British waters. Rohu and hilsa are very popular fish in Bangladesh, and I have opted for hake, which isn't dissimilar. You could also use monkfish tail. As for prawns, well, they're Hasina's favourite!

HAKE AND PRAWN JHOL } WITH RUNNER BEANS

SERVES 4

Hake and prawns

600g skin-on boneless hake (or monkfish), cut into large 5cm chunks

¾ teaspoon ground turmeric

sea salt

juice of 1 lime

12 raw king prawns, peeled and deveined

vegetable oil, for deep-frying (optional)

Coconut gravy

1 stick of lemongrass

vegetable oil, for cooking

1½ teaspoons cumin seeds

6 green cardamom pods (bruise to release the seeds)

1 large brown onion, finely sliced into half-moons

2–3 green finger chillies, or to taste, split in half lengthways

15g garlic, grated

15g ginger, grated

1 teaspoon garam masala

½ teaspoon ground turmeric

2 teaspoons coriander seeds, toasted and ground

2 teaspoons white/yellow mustard seeds, toasted and ground

2 teaspoons sea salt, or to taste

1 x 400ml tin of full-fat coconut milk

approx. 200g sliced runner beans (see cook's note)

Garnish

lime pickle

crispy onions (shop-bought)

chopped fresh coriander

finely sliced red chillies

lime wedges

1. This curry is very quick to bring together. Pat the hake dry, then lightly sprinkle with ½ teaspoon of turmeric, a sprinkle of sea salt and the lime juice. Use your fingers to massage and evenly distribute the turmeric – you may want to use gloves to avoid staining. Do the same with the prawns, but using less turmeric, and place them on a separate dish. Don't leave them to stand for much more than 10 minutes, as the acid in the citrus will start to cook the fish.

2. The reason you retain the skin on the hake is so that it doesn't break up during cooking. An additional step to prevent this is to deep-fry the fish, which is common in Indian fish cookery. Heat the oil to 180°C in a deep fryer/wok/kadhai and add the fish – it will take no more than 3–5 minutes. Drain on kitchen paper. If you don't want to deep-fry you can poach the fish instead (see step 6) but handle it with care. Don't deep-fry the prawns – these will be poached.

3. Place the lemongrass stick on a chopping board and bash with a heavy saucepan. By breaking up the fibres more flavour will be released during cooking.

4. Heat 3 or 4 tablespoons of vegetable oil in a large saucepan on a medium to high heat. Add the lemongrass, cumin and cardamom to the hot oil, then tip in the onions and chillies. Reduce the heat to medium and allow the onions to lightly caramelize and soften – about 10 minutes.

5. Now add the garlic and ginger. Cook out for a couple of minutes, then add the ground spices: garam masala, turmeric, ground coriander, mustard and the salt, and toast for 30 seconds

6. Pour in the coconut milk. Increase the heat to maximum and bring to a simmer, then gently add your hake (if poaching), prawns and runner beans. (If you deep-fried the hake in step 2, start with the prawns and runner beans.) Put a lid on to trap in the steam and poach until cooked (if you fried the hake, add it 3 minutes later to heat through). The total poaching time will be 5–6 minutes. If you are poaching the hake you may also need a touch of water to ensure the fish is submerged and can poach properly.

7. Serve immediately, with plain boiled basmati rice and lime pickle. Garnish with crispy onions, chopped coriander and finely sliced red chillies for the heroes, and serve with lime wedges.

COOK'S NOTE Runner beans are very easy to grow, and are in season from midsummer through to autumn. To prep the runner beans, take a potato peeler and peel both edges of the runner bean – this is where the stringy bits can be, so we're removing them. Then finely slice the beans on a diagonal about 3mm thick – not too thick as you want them to cook in the same time as the fish.

Mashed potato equates to comfort food in any language, and that is certainly the case with Bangladeshi bhorta. Bhortas can be made with any vegetable or fish – dried fish is very popular – and the main ingredient is either mashed or crumbled, and flavoured with garlic, chillies and usually raw onion. The oil traditionally used is mustard oil, which I have an aversion to unless it's an achari dish and cooked to the point where you can't really taste it. So I use a combination of butter and veg oil. The addition of the charred hispi cabbage provides a lovely twist and is a great use of beautiful British veg.

CHARRED HISPI CABBAGE } WITH SWEET ALOO BHORTA

SERVES 4

Aloo bhorta

4–5 sweet potatoes, peeled and cut into 3cm pieces (about 650g prepped weight)

10–15g butter

1–2 tablespoons vegetable oil

½ teaspoon cumin seeds

½ teaspoon mustard seeds

1 large brown onion, finely sliced into half-moons

15g garlic, very finely sliced

2–3 Thai bird's-eye red chillies, or to taste

1 teaspoon salt, or to taste

Charred hispi cabbage

1 hispi cabbage (aka pointed or sweetheart cabbage)

vegetable oil, for cooking

5g butter

sea salt, to taste

a sprinkle of nigella seeds

Garnish

chilli oil

yoghurt raita

fresh coriander leaves

> **COOK'S NOTE** To make tandoori hispi cabbage, marinade the cabbage quarters for an hour (see tandoori marinade, page 36). Then roast at 200°C fan for 12–15 minutes. Brush with melted butter, then grill for a minute or two until charred.

1. Boil the sweet potatoes until tender, then drain and allow to steam-dry. (Or you could roast the potatoes and garlic, for a deeper flavour.)
2. Meanwhile, prepare the onions. Heat the butter and oil in a large frying pan, on a medium to high heat. Add the cumin and mustard seeds, and when they start to release their aromas, tip in the onions and reduce the heat to medium. After a few minutes add the sliced garlic and the chillies. You need to really caramelize these – it will take at least 15 minutes. Taste the mixture after 3–4 minutes – it should be quite spicy, so add more chillies if need be.
3. While the onions are caramelizing, set your oven to 180°C fan.
4. Remove any wilted outer leaves from the cabbage, then cut it into quarters. Heat a couple of tablespoons of veg oil in a separate frying pan on a medium to high heat, then place the cabbage quarters cut side down and sauté for 3–5 minutes on each cut side, until you achieve a golden crust. Hold the cabbage down, as it will have a tendency to curl up at the start. Once charred, transfer the cabbage quarters to a lined baking tray, dot with a little butter and season with a sprinkle of sea salt and a light sprinkle of nigella seeds. Bake for 10–12 minutes, or until the cabbage is cooked through.

5. Mash the sweet potatoes and season with the salt. Stir the mash into the onion and garlic mixture. Taste and check your seasoning. It may need a touch more salt – it should be spicy and garlicky. Remove from the heat and set aside, covered, to retain the heat while you wait for your cabbage.
6. Serve each quarter of hispi cabbage on a bed of sweet aloo bhorta, and dress with a drizzle of chilli oil. You may also like a little yoghurt raita on the side and a coriander leaf garnish.

A canny use of leftovers is a must for running a tight domestic ship! You could use any leftover curry in this recipe really. The trick is to distract your diners with a reinvention that looks and tastes completely different to the original. Thrifty and time-saving, what's not to like? Arancini are Italian risotto rice balls – the name actually translates to 'little orange', and that's the size to aim for, though you can also make a conical shape if you prefer. This is a Bangladeshi twist on a classic ragù arancini. Of course you could also use keema.

PULLED SHATKORA BEEF ARANCINI

MAKES 8

15g butter
1 tablespoon vegetable oil
1 small banana shallot, finely diced

approx. 800–900ml chicken or vegetable stock (you will need to add salt if using unsalted stock)
¼ teaspoon ground turmeric
300g Arborio risotto rice

vegetable oil, for deep-frying
200–250g leftover ox cheek shatkora (see page 241 – pull apart the meat with two forks, you only need a scant amount of sauce)

Dredge
4 tablespoons plain flour, seasoned with salt and pepper
2 eggs, beaten
120g panko breadcrumbs

1. To make the risotto, heat the butter and oil in a medium to large saucepan over a medium heat. Sweat the shallots until soft – you don't want to colour them, only soften, which will take about 5 minutes.

2. Meanwhile prepare your stock in a separate pan, and leave on standby on a low heat.

3. Add the turmeric to the shallots and toast for 30 seconds, then tip in the rice. Stir well, coating the grains, and watch them turn golden.

4. Add a ladleful of stock at a time to the rice, adding the next when each ladleful has been absorbed. I'm afraid risotto involves constant stirring and nursing, and will take around 20–25 minutes to cook. You're aiming for a sticky rice. Once all the stock has been absorbed and the rice is cooked, allow it to cool completely (or better yet, prepare this the night before and refrigerate).

5. Heat the oil in your deep fryer, wok or kadhai to 180°C. At the same time heat your oven to 180°C fan. Prepare three bowls or plates: one with seasoned flour, the second with beaten eggs and the third with the panko.

6. Divide the rice into eight portions. Take a portion and shape it into a flat disc in the palm of your hand. Place a spoonful of shatkora in the middle,

→

then encase it with the rice to form a ball. Ensure the mixture is fully encased.

7. Dip the arancini first in flour, then in beaten egg, then in panko. Set aside and repeat. You can prep ahead and refrigerate the arancini – these will easily keep for a few hours.

8. Gently and carefully place your arancini in the hot oil, using a slotted spoon, and fry until golden on all sides. You will need to do this in batches – I used a wok so I could do two at a time. Once golden, drain on kitchen paper.

9. Transfer the arancini on to a lined baking sheet and bake in the oven for 15–20 minutes, until piping hot right through to the centre.

10. Serve with leftover shatkora sauce, raita or even ketchup. If you make keema arancini, this is complemented nicely by a tamatar ka masala (see below).

TAMATAR KA MASALA

A versatile tomato sauce that you can make ahead and will keep in the fridge for 3–5 days.

FOR 8 ARANCINI

vegetable oil, for cooking
1½ teaspoons cumin seeds
2 black cardamom pods
3 whole cloves
5cm cassia bark
1 brown onion, finely diced
8–10g ginger, grated
8–10g garlic, grated
1–2 green finger chillies, slit in half lengthways
30–40g butter
1½ teaspoons garam masala
½ teaspoon ground turmeric
1–2 teaspoons salt
2 x 400g tins of chopped tomatoes, blended to a purée

1. Heat 4 tablespoons of vegetable oil in a medium saucepan on a medium to high heat. Add the whole spices – cumin seeds, cardamom, whole cloves and cassia – and sauté them in the hot oil until they start to release their aromas.

2. Tip in the onions and allow them to soften and become translucent. This will take a couple of minutes – you should drop the heat to medium so they don't burn.

3. Add the ginger and garlic and the slit chillies. Cook out for 2–3 minutes, then add the butter and the ground spices: garam masala and turmeric, and the salt. Toast the spices for 30 seconds, taking care not to burn them.

4. Pour in the blended tomatoes. Increase the hob heat and bring to the boil, then reduce the heat and simmer for 15 minutes. Taste and adjust the seasoning.

5. Serve with piping hot ox cheek arancini, and a dollop of thick set yoghurt.

Bangladeshis are quite partial to fish. Only natural, given that Bangladesh is known as 'the land of rivers'. British waters too are rich and diverse in fish stocks and I wanted to take the opportunity to celebrate an unsung and underrated store-cupboard item: tinned pilchards, which in the UK are classified as large sardines. Their robust flavour is a good counterpoint to the spice and makes a most appealing mash-up!

SARDINE AND CHANA TORKARI

SERVES 4

1 large potato (approx. 300g)
vegetable oil, for cooking
1 teaspoon cumin seeds

1½ onions, finely sliced into half-moons
1 x 400g tin of pilchards in tomato sauce
5g ginger, grated
5g garlic, grated

3–4 green finger chillies, or to taste, slit in half lengthways
½ teaspoon ground turmeric
1 level teaspoon garam masala

1 teaspoon sea salt, or to taste
1–2 tablespoons passata
approx. 50ml water
1 x 400g tin of chickpeas, drained
chopped fresh coriander

1. Peel the potato and slice it into 3–5mm thick rounds crossways. Rinse under cold water, then place in a bowl and cover with cold water. Set aside.
2. For the masala, heat 3 or 4 tablespoons of vegetable oil in a large saucepan on a medium to high heat. Add the cumin seeds, and as soon as they begin to crackle tip in the onions. Reduce the heat to medium and allow the onions to soften and lightly caramelize for 10 minutes.
3. Meanwhile decant the pilchards on to a plate. Gently separate the fillets and remove the central bone, splitting the whole fish into two fillets. Discard the bone but retain the tomato sauce the fillets came in. Set aside.
4. Add the ginger, garlic and chillies to the pan and cook out for a few minutes, then add the ground spices: turmeric and garam masala, and the salt. Toast them for about 30 seconds, then stir in the passata and the tomato sauce from the pilchard tin.
5. Simmer for 5 minutes, then taste so you can make any adjustments to the seasoning. Put the sliced, drained potatoes into the sauce along with about 50ml of water, ensuring the potatoes are covered in the sauce. Increase the heat and bring to the boil, then put the lid on to trap the steam and reduce the heat to medium. Simmer for 10 minutes, then add the chickpeas and simmer for a further 5 minutes, or until the potatoes are pretty much cooked through.
6. Gently fold the pilchards through the mixture, being careful not to break up the fish, and simmer for a final 5–7 minutes.
7. Garnish with chopped coriander, and serve with plain rice or buttered chapattis, and wedges of lime.

In Bangladesh a bhaja can refer to a deep-fried vegetable or fish. This recipe is dedicated to the ladies who tend the communal garden and allotment belonging to Hasina's women's charity. These bhajas celebrate allotment-heroes carrots and kale, again easy to grow in the UK. You can interchange the ingredients with whatever veg is seasonal, and even upgrade to a bhaja burger (see cook's note).

CARROT AND KALE BHAJAS

MAKES APPROXIMATELY 15 BHAJAS (OR 4 BURGERS)

vegetable oil, for deep-frying

3 tablespoons Greek yoghurt

1 tablespoon cumin seeds

1 tablespoon coriander seeds, toasted and crushed in a pestle and mortar

1 teaspoon garam masala

2 teaspoons sea salt, or to taste

½ teaspoon grated ginger

2–3 teaspoons minced chillies

a pinch of dried red chilli flakes

1 heaped tablespoon chopped fresh coriander

1 egg, beaten

100–150g chickpea flour (besan)

3 medium carrots (approx. 375–400g), peeled and grated (using the coarse side of a box grater)

60g curly kale, destalked and shredded

1 large brown onion, finely sliced into half-moons

1. Heat your oven to 180°C fan and line a large baking sheet with grease-proof paper.
2. Heat the oil to 180°C in a deep fat fryer, wok or kadhai.
3. Mix the yoghurt, cumin seeds, crushed coriander seeds, garam masala, salt, ginger, minced chillies, chilli flakes and chopped fresh coriander together in a large bowl. Taste, and adjust the seasoning.
4. Mix in the beaten egg, followed by the flour, to make a thick batter. Add the grated carrot, shredded kale and sliced onion to the batter, and use your hand to mix and squelch everything together (keep one hand clean). You may want to add a touch more chickpea flour for a thicker batter consistency.
5. Form golf ball-sized balls of the batter and roll between your hands, ensuring even distribution of the ingredients. Gently place three or four at a time in the hot oil, frying until golden. It will take 5 minutes or so, turning as necessary. You will need to batch-make these, being careful not to overload the fryer or wok.
6. Once fried and golden, place the bhajas on kitchen paper to absorb any excess oil. Now transfer them on to the lined baking sheet and bake until cooked through – another 10–12 minutes or so.
7. Eat immediately, with whatever sauces and chutneys take your fancy.

COOK'S NOTE You can make much larger bhajas, formed into the shape of a burger. These are best shallow-fried in a large frying pan. Again, don't overload the pan – do this in batches, perhaps two at a time given the size, and adjust the cooking times, which will be slightly longer. Serve in a grilled brioche bun, with a little smattering of mango chutney, coriander and lime raita (see cook's note, page 27) and pink pickled onions (page 55).

I'm using bhaji here in the way many Bangladeshis will understand it: a stir-fried vegetable curry often served as a side dish. My version showcases the courgette, which continuing with the allotment theme is one of the easiest vegetables to grow. The flowers are not only very pretty, but you can eat them too – stuff them with a yummy filling, coat in a light rice flour-based batter and make tasty bhaja for your very own 'pitha party'.

ALLOTMENT COURGETTE BHAJI

SERVES 4 AS A SIDE

4 courgettes (about 450–500g prepped weight)
vegetable oil, for cooking

1 level teaspoon cumin seeds
½ teaspoon black mustard seeds
½ teaspoon nigella seeds
1 large brown onion, finely sliced into half-moons

2–3 green finger chillies, slit in half lengthways
5g garlic, grated
5g ginger, grated
½ teaspoon ground turmeric
1 teaspoon garam masala

1 teaspoon sea salt
approx. 150g baby plum tomatoes, cut in half (you can de-skin them if you like, see cook's note, page 123)
50ml water
chopped fresh coriander, to garnish

1. Cut the courgettes in half lengthways, then slice into ½cm thick pieces. Set aside.
2. Heat about 4 tablespoons of vegetable oil in a large saucepan on a medium to high heat, then add the whole spices to the hot oil: cumin seeds, mustard seeds and nigella seeds. When they start to release their aromas, tip in the onions and chillies, reduce the heat to medium, and allow the onions to soften and lightly caramelize – this will take 10 minutes or so.
3. Add the grated garlic and ginger, let them cook out for a couple of minutes, then add the ground spices – turmeric and garam masala – and the salt, toast them for 30 seconds.
4. Add the tomatoes and the water. Give everything a good stir, bring to the boil, pop the lid on to trap the steam, and reduce the heat to a simmer. Cook for 5 minutes or so.
5. Now use the bottom of your wooden spoon to smush the tomatoes down – yes, that's a technical term . . . Taste, and adjust the seasoning.
6. Mix in the sliced courgettes, add a splash more water, bring to the boil, and pop the lid on again. Reduce the heat to medium and simmer until the courgettes are cooked, which will take 12–15 minutes or so.
7. Garnish with chopped coriander. I like to eat this with parathas!

I don't think I've ever met a person from Manchester or the surrounding area who doesn't love pie! A galette is much like an open pie, and super easy to make. My grandparents used to love growing their own fruit and veg, and I have fond memories of 'scrumping' as a child – why is it that your neighbour's apples always look more enticing! (I would suggest paying for your apples or asking for consent from your neighbours now, I hasten to caveat.) I've used apples in this recipe, but you could use rhubarb, strawberries, pears or plums (all of which the grandpeople also grew) – any fruit really. You could also add a thin layer of frangipane at the bottom for a fancy touch. Simply switch up the spices to match your fruit.

'SCRUMPY' APPLE GALETTE

SERVES 4–6

Dough
190g plain flour
2 generous pinches of salt
1 tablespoon caster/ golden caster sugar

120g fridge-cold unsalted butter
90ml ice-cold water

Filling
1 tablespoon soft light brown sugar
1 heaped tablespoon cornflour

1 level teaspoon ground cinnamon
a little grated nutmeg (optional)
3–4 Royal Gala apples (approx. 350g prepped weight)
30g sultanas
a squeeze of lemon juice

Egg wash
1 small to medium egg, beaten with 1 tablespoon water or milk
demerara sugar, to sprinkle
5g unsalted butter
a drizzle of runny honey (optional)

1. First make the dough. Sift the flour into a large mixing bowl, then mix in the salt and sugar using a whisk. If you have a pastry cutter, cube the butter beforehand and use the pastry cutter to coarsely combine it with the flour – it's these coarse bits of butter that will create layers and flakes when baked. If you don't have a pastry cutter, use the coarse side of a box grater to grate the cold butter in, then incorporate using a spatula.

2. Add the cold water a little at a time – you may not need all of it or you may use slightly more, depending on the flour absorption. As soon as the dough starts to clump and ball, stop adding water. You don't want to add too much water, or overwork the dough. Using your hands, form the dough into a flat disc, then wrap in cling film and refrigerate for a minimum of 2 hours, or better still overnight.

3. When you are ready to make your galette, heat the oven to 190°C fan and line a large baking sheet with baking paper.

4. To make the filling, mix the sugar, cornflour, cinnamon and nutmeg (if using) in a small bowl and set aside. Peel, core and thinly slice your apples, then place them in a large mixing bowl with the sultanas. Coat evenly with the sugar mixture and a squeeze of lemon. Set aside.

→

5. Lightly dust your work surface with a little flour, and unwrap your dough. You can even up any frayed edges by patting them with the flat side of a dough scraper, or just revel in the rustic look. Roll out a circle to a ruler's length in diameter (30cm), rotating the dough as you do so. Then transfer to the lined baking sheet.
6. Arrange the apple mixture in the centre of the dough, keeping it flat and leaving a 5cm perimeter, discarding any apple liquid/juices. Gently fold up the edges, overlapping them as you do so to encase the fruit. Brush the top of the dough with the egg wash and sprinkle the galette generously with demerara sugar. Dot the exposed fruit with the butter, and you may wish to bury any visible sultanas so that they don't burn. Bake for 45 minutes, or until cooked through. You can check after 35 minutes as ovens vary.
7. Remove from the oven and drizzle the exposed fruit with a little honey for a nice glaze. Let the galette rest for 5 minutes before serving.
8. Serve with custard, ice cream or clotted cream – whatever you find yourself partial to!

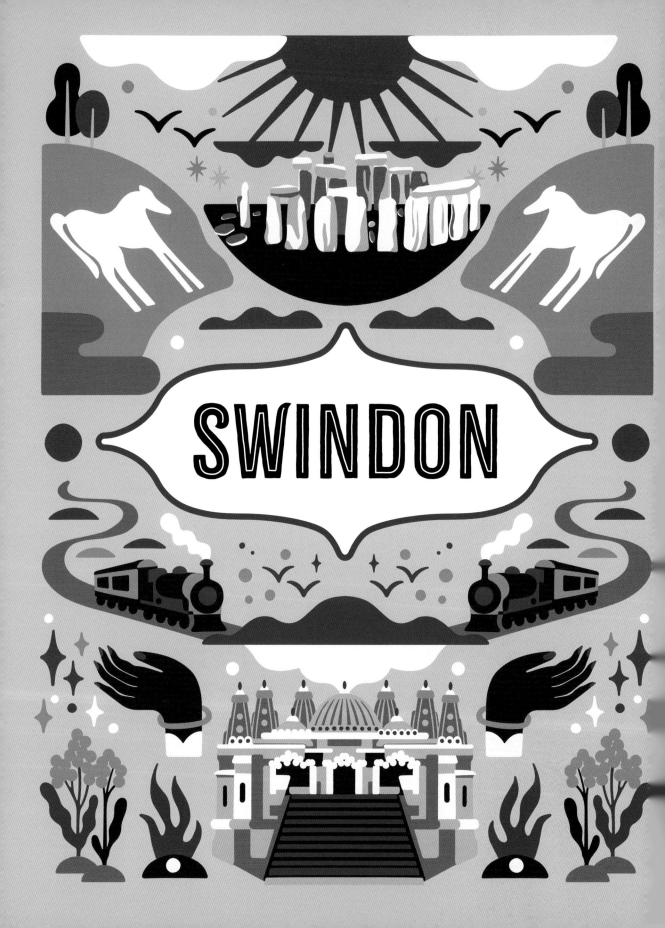

GOAN COMMUNITY

Goan food culture is quite unique, and is influenced heavily by Goa's Portuguese colonial history. Portuguese rule lasted for over 400 years, beginning in the sixteenth century and ending in 1961. Swindon has a significant Goan diaspora population, many of whom arrived in the early 2000s via Portuguese passports. Goan food has an essence of East meets West, a blend of vibrant southern Indian influences and European preservation techniques, and baking; 'pao' is the Portuguese word for bread, and in India it's the name for a soft dinner roll, which is also referred to as 'pav'. Goan food is naturally heavily seafood-based because of being coastal.

The majority of Goans practise the Hindu faith (about 60 per cent), and the second largest religious group is Christian or Catholic (about 25 per cent); Catholic missionaries arrived shortly after Portuguese rule was established. The Portuguese culinary influence is mostly evident in Christian and Catholic cuisine, which features a lot of meat – including pork and beef – and the use of vinegar and stock. Goan Hindu dishes are mainly vegetarian or pescatarian, and common features are tamarind or kokum for souring, asafoetida, urid dhal, black mustard seeds and curry leaves. It is also vital to note that it was the Portuguese who introduced chillies to India, originating from their territories in South America. Can you imagine Indian food without chillies? I certainly can't. Prior to chillies, the heat would have come from spices such as black peppercorns – just not the same.

The Portuguese also introduced tomatoes, potatoes – or 'batata' as they would have been called – pumpkins, cashew nuts, and much more; ingredients that are intrinsic to so many iconic Indian dishes.

NATASHA VAS (AGED 40)

Distribution centre manager

Natasha came to the UK as an adult in 2004, at the age of 21. She was born and raised in northern Goa, where she studied for a degree in accounting and commerce. After graduating she took up a position as a teacher at a local secondary school, where she taught for two years before joining her parents in the UK; there was a cultural expectation for her to do so. Her father had taken the decision to emigrate at the age of 57 – not really an age when you would want to settle in another part of the world, leaving a certain comfort level behind. He wanted to give his children a better life, Natasha tells me. Her father worked in a sandwich factory and bakery until forced retirement at 67. As a former Portuguese colony, Goans born prior to 1961 were given the right to apply for Portuguese citizenship under legislation passed in 1975, which can also be extended to their children and grandchildren. With Portugal being a member of the EU, and the free movement of people within this union, many Portuguese Goans came to the UK via this route. Swindon has become a hub, and the Honda factory was a big employer. It's estimated there are about 20,000 Goans in Swindon. When Natasha arrived she found work immediately, starting out as a stock handler working at the distribution centre where she is still employed, and working her way up.

The numbers and attendance at Swindon's Catholic churches have also swelled. Natasha attends St Mary's, under the stewardship of Father Michael McAndrew, and plays an active role within both the congregation and the wider community in Rodbourne Cheney. The greater level of diversity in Swindon's population hasn't been without challenge. Within St Mary's itself there is of course a large Goan contingent, also Nigerian and Irish. Language has been a barrier in some cases, and Natasha has organized many programmes for the young and older fellowship alike; Father Michael has rather cannily put her teaching skills to good use. Many children born in the UK to Goan parents (including her own daughter) have no connection with their Goan heritage and culture, so she teaches religious hymns sung in the Goan language – the choir has attracted a lot of engagement. Likewise Eucharist events and celebrations are translated, helping elders who don't fully understand English. For the wider community there are monthly dinners and dances. These cultural services and events have proven to be very successful in bringing people together.

The Feasts of the Saints are a massive celebration back in Goa, and they are something that has crossed over very successfully to the congregation – they take place each month and involve a huge buffet for all communities to attend. There is a special connection with the Saints, different Saints being celebrated throughout the year. In Goa there are festivities and processions in the streets, churches are dedicated to them, and indeed children are named after them too. Natasha advises me that there are two feasts that are of particular importance: the Feast of St Francis Xavier and the Feast of Our Lady of Fatima.

St Francis Xavier was a Spanish missionary in the 1500s, one of the first members of the Jesuit Order and patron saint of Roman Catholic missions. He travelled throughout Southeast Asia, spending a lot of time in India. Though he died in China and was buried there for a short period, his body was moved, and Goa is his final resting place. Miraculously his body has not decomposed and is kept in a glass casket. After Christmas and Easter his feast is the biggest celebration, on 3 December. Our Lady of Fatima is one of the Catholic titles for the Virgin Mary, whose feast is celebrated on 13 May, and is also an important one. Unsurprisingly Father Michael has complained about weight gain. The feasting food takes on a real significance on these occasions, and with Indians being intrinsically generous when it comes to food and hospitality there is never a shortage for all-comers; each family brings along dishes with them for everybody to share. We talk about rich stews like beef xacuti, pork sorpotel enriched with offal, vegetable caldine, prawn pulao and bebinka layer cake. Goan food is hearty to its core, and much like the people who work hard to integrate with the local community, adds to the flourishing food scene. I get the impression that integration is still very much a work in progress, and Natasha works closely under Father Michael's guidance to deliver and support as much as she can. As with all groups and communities there needs to be an emphasis on what unites different people, what they have in common, to bring them together.

Vindaloo has to be one of the most iconic 'curry house' dishes – often for the wrong reasons – and I wanted to include it here to dispel the preconceived stigma. It doesn't have to be fiery and doused with ten pints of lager! No, you want to taste the layers of flavour, including the tang from the vinegar – it's moreish, delicious, and the slow-cooked tender meat should melt in your mouth. If you'd like an authentic vindaloo, well, here's how to make it, and it will soon become one of your favourites.

PORK SHOULDER VINDALOO } WITH CRACKLING

SERVES 8

1 x 1.75kg boneless pork shoulder roasting joint

Onion purée
4 medium brown onions
vegetable oil

Masala marinade
40g garlic
2 tablespoons Kashmiri chilli powder
½ tablespoon hot paprika
2 teaspoons ground black peppercorns
1½ teaspoons ground cumin
1½ teaspoons ground coriander
125ml white wine vinegar

Masala gravy
vegetable oil, for cooking
2 star anise
5cm cassia bark
2 black cardamom pods
3–4 bay leaves
1½ teaspoons black mustard seeds
4 whole cloves
15g ginger, grated
15g garlic, grated

1 teaspoon minced bird's-eye chillies, or to taste
1 teaspoon ground turmeric
2 teaspoons sea salt, or to taste
500ml passata
1 tablespoon soft light brown sugar or jaggery
1 tablespoon yoghurt

Garnish
1–2 limes
fresh coriander

1. First the onion purée, which you should make ahead. Heat your oven to 200°C fan, and line a baking tray with greaseproof paper. Massage the unpeeled onions with a scant amount of vegetable oil, and place them on the lined baking tray. Roast for 45 minutes to an hour – the onions should be very soft to the touch and the outer skin should be caramelized. Cool, then squeeze out the 'flesh' from the skins, which should be discarded. Pulse in a blender until puréed, and set aside. (You can easily scale this purée up, batch-make, and freeze for using in your tarkas.)

2. Remove the skin from the pork joint (or ask your butcher to do it). Use this to make crackling (see separate recipe overleaf). Cut the pork into generous bite-sized pieces and remove any excess fat.

3. For the marinade, bash the garlic cloves into a purée in a pestle and mortar, then mix in the ground spices – chilli powder, paprika, peppercorns, cumin and coriander – and vinegar to make a paste. Coat your pork pieces with the paste and put into the fridge to marinate

→

for 3–4 hours. Note: The meat doesn't need any longer than that – overnight marination can result in tough meat, as the acidic vinegar will start to cook the meat.

4. When you are ready to make the masala or gravy, heat about 4–5 tablespoons of oil in a large lidded saucepan on a medium to high heat. Add the whole spices to the hot oil: star anise, cassia, black cardamom, bay leaves, mustard seeds and cloves. When they start to release their aromas, tip in your ginger, garlic and chillies and let them cook out for a few minutes. Add the turmeric and salt and toast for 30 seconds, then fold in the puréed onions and give everything a good stir. Simmer for 2–3 minutes over a medium heat.

5. Next pour in the passata, bring to the boil, then simmer for 8–10 minutes, until you see the tell-tale separation of the oil on the surface of the masala. Taste and adjust the seasoning as necessary.

6. Put the marinated meat into the sauce and mix well, then crank up the heat, to seal the meat. Then reduce the heat to medium and simmer for 30 minutes or so with the lid on.

7. Taste the sauce – you need to balance the vinegar and spice with sweetness. Stir in the brown sugar or jaggery, along with the yoghurt, which will also help to mellow things out.

8. You will need to add some water – maybe start off with 250ml, and keep a close eye so the pan doesn't dry out; you can add more water as required/to taste. Bring the pot to a simmer again.

9. Cook, covered, until the meat is tender, about another 45 minutes to an hour. While it's cooking, start on your crackling – see below.

10. Flavour and spice in a slow-cooked stew can become dull, so a spritz of citrus is needed to lift this and re-enliven it. Serve with a good squeeze of lime juice, lemon rice (page 273) or naan, crackling shards and kachumber salad (page 48).

TO MAKE THE CRACKLING

1. Once the skin/crackling is removed from the joint, pat it dry, score, and leave uncovered in the fridge to dry out (this will make the crackling really crispy).

2. Bring to room temperature before roasting.

3. Rub with vegetable oil and lots of sea salt. Place on a rack in a 220°C fan oven for 20–25 minutes, to allow the crackling to blister and colour. Then reduce to 175°C fan until crackling and ready.

I adore tenderstem broccoli, and stir-fried is my favourite way to eat it; here's a Goan twist. You could also use fine green beans in this recipe – just adjust the cooking time accordingly.

STIR-FRIED TENDERSTEM BROCCOLI

SERVES 4

1 tablespoon chana dhal

3 tablespoons unsweetened desiccated coconut

250g tenderstem broccoli

vegetable oil, for cooking

1 teaspoon mustard seeds

½ teaspoon cumin seeds

7–8 curry leaves

2 dried Kashmiri chillies, broken into pieces

1 tablespoon washed split urid dhal

½ teaspoon ground turmeric

½ teaspoon asafoetida (hing)

½ teaspoon sea salt, or to taste

lime juice

1. Soak the chana dhal in just-boiled water for 15 minutes, then drain.
2. Meanwhile toast the desiccated coconut in a dry frying pan, on a medium to high heat, until golden. Keep your eyes on the pan, you don't want the coconut to burn and it can turn quite quickly. Transfer to a small bowl and set aside.
3. Cut the broccoli stems into 3cm long pieces, and cut any thick stems in half lengthways.
4. Heat 3 or 4 tablespoons of vegetable oil in a kadhai, wok or large frying pan, on a medium to high heat, then add the whole spices and dhals: mustard seeds, cumin seeds, curry leaves, Kashmiri chillies, urid dhal and the drained chana dhal. You want your dhal to turn golden.
5. Add the ground spices: turmeric and asafoetida, and the salt, and toast for a few seconds.
6. Tip in the broccoli, and stir-fry for 5 minutes or until cooked al dente. Make sure the broccoli is coated in all the spices and add a splash of water – this will prevent the ground spices from burning and help the broccoli to steam cook. Cover with a lid to help trap the steam. A minute before the end of cooking, stir through the toasted coconut.
7. Serve as a side dish, with a little squeeze of lime juice.

Racheado is a classic spicy wet masala paste, with a vibrant red colour as a result of dried Kashmiri chillies being steeped in vinegar with various other ingredients before being blitzed. Goans love to smother and fill fish such as pomfret with this masala before shallow-frying. You need a robust fish to stand up to this gutsy masala, and it's mackerel that springs to mind. Now I'd run out of dried chillies when I came to make this masala, so I used ground Kashmiri chilli powder instead of steeping whole dried chillies. I have to say I liked the end result so much that I only make the masala this way now. I also love that cooking fish is so often the ultimate 'fast food'.

MACKEREL RACHEADO FRY

SERVES 2

2 butterflied mackerel fillets, tail on (400g combined weight)
vegetable oil, for cooking
lemon or lime wedges

Racheado paste
1 teaspoon cumin seeds
1 teaspoon black peppercorns
5 whole cloves
1 teaspoon sea salt, or to taste
3 teaspoons Kashmiri chilli powder

½ teaspoon ground turmeric
10g ginger, grated
10g garlic, grated
1 teaspoon tamarind paste
½ teaspoon caster sugar or jaggery
3 tablespoons white wine vinegar

1. Toast the cumin seeds, peppercorns and cloves in a dry frying pan, then transfer to a pestle and mortar and grind to a powder using the salt as an abrasive.
2. In a mixing bowl, combine the chilli powder, turmeric, ginger, garlic, tamarind, sugar and vinegar into a thick paste.
3. Generously smother each mackerel fillet with the paste, front and back. You won't need it all, so keep what is left over in an airtight container in the fridge.
4. Heat 3 or 4 tablespoons of vegetable oil in a large frying pan on a medium to high heat and fry the mackerel for about 3 minutes on each side, or until cooked through, being careful not to burn the spice paste.
5. Serve with lemon rice (page 273), tarka remoulade (page 267) – or stir-fried tenderstem broccoli (page 263) – and wedges of lime.

Deceptively, Goan cutlets are not necessarily meat, as we would usually think of cutlets – generally they come as patties or croquettes, a combination of mashed potatoes, vegetables with fish or meat and spices, coated in breadcrumbs or semolina and shallow-fried. This fishcake could be made with fresh salmon or tilapia, or shellfish. You can roast the fish in the oven and then flake the meat. If you use crab, bring the mixture together with breadcrumbs and mayonnaise rather than potato – see cook's notes. I thought I'd showcase tinned tuna to elevate the humble store cupboard stalwart. For a vegetarian alternative you could use beetroot; simply grate and sauté along with the onions.

FISH CUTLETS } WITH TARKA REMOULADE

SERVES 4 AS A STARTER

2–3 medium potatoes, peeled and cut into 3cm dice (approx. 525g peeled weight)

vegetable oil, for cooking

1 teaspoon cumin seeds

1 large brown onion, finely diced

15g garlic, grated

15g ginger, grated

1–2 green finger chillies, or to taste, finely chopped

1 teaspoon chaat masala

1 teaspoon garam masala

1–2 teaspoons sea salt, or to taste

1 teaspoon racheado masala paste (see page 264)

2 x 110g tins of tuna in spring water, drained

2 tablespoons chopped fresh coriander

lime wedges, to serve

Tarka remoulade

200g celeriac, peeled

1 small Granny Smith apple

3 tablespoons premium mayonnaise

vegetable oil, for cooking

½ teaspoon black mustard seeds

4 curry leaves

1 dried red chilli, broken into pieces

½ teaspoon ground turmeric

a pinch of sea salt

a pinch of asafoetida (hing)

1 tablespoon chopped fresh coriander

a squeeze of lemon or lime

Dredge

approx. 3 tablespoons plain flour

2 eggs, beaten

6–8 heaped tablespoons breadcrumbs

1. Boil the potatoes until soft and cooked through, then allow them to steam-dry.
2. Meanwhile heat about 4 tablespoons of oil in a large frying pan on a medium to high heat. Add the cumin seeds to the hot oil, and when they start to release their aroma, tip in the onions and cook out for a few minutes until soft and translucent.
3. Add the garlic, ginger and chillies, sauté for a couple of minutes, then tip in the ground spices: chaat masala, garam masala and salt. Toast for 30 seconds, then stir through the racheado masala paste, followed by the tuna. Remove from the heat.

→

4. Crush the potatoes, leaving a little texture, and mix them through the spiced tuna along with the chopped coriander. Taste and adjust the seasoning as required.
5. Once the mixture has cooled, divide into eight equal portions. Shape these into flat discs just over 5cm in diameter, then place them on a lined baking sheet and transfer to the fridge for 30 minutes to firm up.
6. Meanwhile make the remoulade. Using a mandolin or similar, cut the celeriac and apple into matchsticks, and place in a large mixing bowl. Stir through the mayonnaise.
7. Heat 2 teaspoons of vegetable oil in a small frying pan on a medium to high heat and add the mustard seeds – when they start to splutter, add the curry leaves and dried chilli, then remove from the heat and swirl in the turmeric, salt and asafoetida. Carefully transfer the contents of your sizzling pan to the dressed celeriac and apple. Stir, and take a moment to admire the golden hue as it marbles throughout the remoulade. Mix in the chopped coriander and season with a squeeze of lemon or lime juice. Cover and set aside in the fridge.
8. When you are ready to cook your fishcakes, place the flour, beaten eggs and breadcrumbs in separate wide and shallow bowls. Heat about 4 tablespoons of vegetable oil in a large frying pan.
9. Dip a fishcake first in flour, then in egg, then in breadcrumbs. Place in the frying pan and cook over a medium heat for 4–5 minutes on each side – you want a golden crust. Don't fry more than four fishcakes at a time – you can keep them warm in a low oven if need be.
10. Serve your fishcake tikkis with the tarka remoulade, a watercress salad and lime wedges.

> **COOK'S NOTE** I use a slightly different recipe for crab cake tikkis, using breadcrumbs rather than potatoes. It's a really easy one. Take a large mixing bowl, beat 1 egg with 1 heaped tablespoon of mayonnaise, 1 teaspoon of racheado masala paste, 1 tablespoon of chopped fresh coriander and a level teaspoon of salt. Then mix through 50g of panko breadcrumbs, followed by 200g of white crab meat. Divide into 6 equal portions, shape and refrigerate to firm up. Shallow-fry, and serve with lime wedges.

Chicken cafreal is also known as galinha cafreal – galinha is the Portuguese word for chicken. This dish has a vibrant green colour because of the coriander and green chilli marinade. It most commonly comes as a dry curry, and sometimes comes with a gravy. So it got me thinking about green curry and combining it with my love of laksa. Laksa is a Malaysian noodle soup, normally made with a jointed whole chicken, which is poached, with the cooking stock retained and used in the soup. My version here isn't entirely authentic! The cafreal masala would work with any kind of fish also.

CHICKEN CAFREAL 'LAKSA' } WITH CHILLI OIL

SERVES 4

800g boneless, skinless chicken thigh thighs, cut into bite-sized pieces

200g rice noodles (I use flat folded noodles, or you can use thin vermicelli)

vegetable oil, for cooking

1 x 400ml tin of full-fat coconut milk

400ml water or unsalted chicken stock

Cafreal masala/ marinade

1 tablespoon coriander seeds

1 heaped teaspoon cumin seeds

6 green cardamom pods

4 whole cloves

5cm cinnamon, broken into pieces

65–70g fresh coriander, including the stalks

25g garlic, peeled

25g ginger, peeled

2–3 green finger chillies, or to taste, split in half lengthways

4 spring onions, including the green parts, roughly chopped

1½ teaspoons sea salt

½ teaspoon ground turmeric

juice and zest of 1 lime

2 tablespoons white wine vinegar

50ml water

Garnish

2 spring onions, finely sliced, or a little finely sliced red onion

1 mild long red chilli, finely sliced

chilli oil

a scattering of bean sprouts

boiled eggs (optional)

crispy onions (optional)

fresh mint leaves

fresh coriander leaves

lime wedges

1. First you need to make the masala/marinade. Toast the whole spices – coriander seeds, cumin seeds, cardamom, cloves and cinnamon – in a dry frying pan over a medium heat, careful not to burn them. Remove from the heat and cool. Then blitz them to a powder in a coffee or spice grinder. Next place all the marinade ingredients into a blender and blend into a smooth paste.

2. Put the chicken pieces into a dish and smother them with half the marinade, then put into the fridge to marinate, covered, for a couple of hours or overnight. Place the rest of the marinade in an airtight container and refrigerate.

3. When you're ready to make the laksa, cook the noodles about three-quarters through (they will finish cooking in the hot laksa soup, so you

→

don't want to overcook them), then plunge them into a bowl of ice-cold water to halt the cooking process and set aside.

4. Heat about 4 tablespoons of oil in a large saucepan on a high heat, and sauté the marinated chicken pieces. You want to sear the meat on all sides. Then add the reserved half of the marinade. If you cook out from this point, it's a pretty authentic cafreal – you want to reduce the gravy until it's quite dry. However, we're going to add coconut milk and water (or unsalted stock) and bring to a simmer. Simmer, covered, on a medium heat for 20 minutes, or until the chicken is cooked and tender. Check your seasoning.

5. Drain the noodles and divide them equally among your serving bowls. Cover the noodles with the piping hot laksa soup.

6. Serve a platter of garnishes family style, so folks can load up to their own taste. I like a drizzle of chilli oil, which adds a pop of red colour.

COOK'S NOTE To me chicken cafreal very much represents a green peri-peri chicken: quintessential Portuguese cooking – marinated and grilled meat – with a Goan twist. Cafreal masala is a great marinade, and works well for barbecues. You can simply spatchcock a chicken, poussin or guinea fowl (see page 298), slash the meatier parts so the marinade can penetrate (overnight marination is best), then grill or oven roast. Serve with charred corn on the cob, dressed salad, spicy potato wedges and peri-peri sauce or mayonnaise.

This is a combination of two beef dishes: Goan roast beef and xacuti (pronounced: sha-kooti). The masala for the roast beef is rather more subtle, whereas the xacuti masala packs a real punch so I wanted to showcase it. It most commonly comes in the form of a curry and works well with mutton and lamb too. It's ideal for slow pot-roasting, and I think a Dutch oven or cast-iron casserole dish cooks the meat to perfection, yielding tender and juicy melt-in-mouth meat. You can put the leftovers in freshly baked bread, for a delicious sandwich, which is how Goans like to have their roast beef, with chips. This dish is ideal for a lazy Sunday afternoon. Marinate the beef the night before, and while your roast is slow-cooking in the oven, take a genteel country walk to build up an appetite.

POT ROAST BEEF BRISKET XACUTI

SERVES 4–6

1kg roasting beef or brisket
2 tablespoons coconut oil, plus extra (I use cold-pressed)
10–12 curry leaves (dried is fine if you can't get fresh)
6 banana shallots, peeled and cut in half
6 large carrots, peeled and cut into 5cm chunks
1 x 400ml tin of full-fat coconut milk
500ml beef stock
3–4 medium potatoes, cut into 3cm dice
salt, to taste (you won't need much if the stock is salted)
chopped fresh coriander, to garnish

Xacuti masala
8–10 dried Kashmiri chillies
1½ tablespoons coriander seeds
1 teaspoon cumin seeds
1 teaspoon fennel seeds
1 teaspoon black peppercorns
6 whole cloves
5cm cinnamon, broken up
1 star anise
1 black cardamom
6 green cardamoms
½ a blade of mace
25g ginger, peeled
25g garlic, peeled
1 red onion
40–50ml water

1. Start by making the dry masala. Put the spices into a dry frying pan over a medium heat, being careful not to let them burn: the dried chillies, coriander seeds, cumin, fennel, black peppercorns, cloves, cinnamon, star anise, both types of cardamom and the mace. You'll smell the fragrant aromas wafting up. Remove from the heat and allow to cool a little, then grind to a powder in a coffee grinder.
2. Roughly chop the ginger, garlic and red onion, place in a mini chopper or food processor along with the ground masala and water, and blitz to a paste. You can part-cook the ginger, garlic and onion in a little coconut oil beforehand, should you wish.
3. Pat your beef dry with kitchen towel, then smother all over with the marinade – you may want to wear disposable food-safe gloves for this to avoid any 'after-burn'. If you have a rolled piece of roasting beef, remove the string.

4. Place in an appropriate container, then cover and leave in the fridge to marinate overnight.
5. Take the meat out of the fridge at least 30 minutes before cooking to allow it to come to room temperature. Set your oven to 165°C fan.
6. Heat a little coconut oil in your Dutch oven pot/casserole dish on a medium to high temperature. Sear the beef on all sides without burning the spices, then remove to a plate and set aside. Add the curry leaves to the pot – you may need a little more oil – and when they release their fragrant aroma, add the shallots and carrots and sauté for a couple of minutes. Then add any remaining marinade and cook that out for a couple of minutes.
7. Tip in the coconut milk and beef stock, and bring to a simmer. Return the beef to the pot, ensuring it is almost submerged. You may need to add a touch more stock or water. Put the lid on and carefully transfer to the oven. Cook in the centre of the oven for 3 hours (you may need to remove a shelf).
8. After 2 hours add the potatoes, making sure these are mixed into the sauce. Put the lid back on and return the pot to the oven for another 45 minutes to 1 hour, or until the potatoes are cooked through.
9. Skim off any excess fat. Have a final taste – you will need to season with a little salt (the potatoes especially will need this) – and scatter with a garnish of chopped coriander. The meat will be fall-apart tender.
10. Serve with stir-fried tenderstem broccoli (page 263) and lemon rice (see below).

LEMON RICE

1. Cook the rice using the free-boiling method in a large saucepan. Place the rice in boiling water – ensuring it is well covered – then reduce the heat to medium, and simmer for 10–12 minutes. Drain thoroughly, cover and allow to stand for 3 minutes before forking through. (Or use leftover plain rice.)
2. Heat 3 or 4 tablespoons of oil in a separate large saucepan on a medium to high heat. Add the mustard seeds, lemon zest, urid dhal and curry leaves to the hot oil. Once toasted and golden, add the chillies, followed by the turmeric and salt – you may want to add a splash of water to prevent them from catching. Immediately remove from the heat.

3. Gently mix through the cooked rice, along with the lemon juice, using a fork and being careful not to break any long grains. You're ready to serve!

SERVES 4

300g basmati rice
vegetable oil, for cooking
1 teaspoon mustard seeds
2 large strips of lemon zest
1 teaspoon washed and split urid dhal

10–12 curry leaves (fresh is best but dried is OK)
2 green chillies, split in half lengthways
½ teaspoon ground turmeric
1 teaspoon sea salt
juice of 2 lemons
chopped fresh coriander (optional)

Dosas are not Goan as such but you would never go to South India without having a dosa, which is a delicious crispy crêpe made from a fermented rice and urid dhal batter. It's so popular it's found all over India. Indeed, I first tried one on a trip to the Punjab, which couldn't be further away in the outer northern regions! Traditionally dosas are a breakfast dish – not that I'd ever have them for breakfast – and are served with sambar, a thin spicy soup made of lentils and vegetables, and coconut chutney. For me, though, it's the masala dosa that is hands down the tastiest, with the masala potato filling. In South India dosa batter is also used to make idlis – these are steamed rice cakes, great for dunking in sauce and gravy – however, I would use a slightly different recipe for that, as these should be soft, and the addition of poha (cooked, beaten and flattened rice grains) is required. Dosas, on the other hand, should most definitely be crispy. I must note that Goans have their own variation of an idli, called a sanna, which can also have a sweet variety. Though we digress, it's all about the dosa and this recipe is too legit to quit!

MASALA DOSA

MAKES 12 DOSAS

Dosa batter
1½ cups idli rice
½ cup washed split urid dhal
1 tablespoon chana dhal

½ teaspoon fenugreek seeds
2–2½ cups water (reuse the soaking water)
1–1½ teaspoons sea salt

potato (aloo) masala (see page 276)
vegetable oil spray, for cooking

1. I'm using a batter that's 1:3 ratio dhal to rice. The chana adds a lovely flavour and the fenugreek seeds help with fermentation. Idli rice is the best rice to use, and you don't have to worry about using a combination of raw and par-cooked rice when using idli rice. It's easily available online or from Indian grocers.

2. Rinse the rice under cold water – it will need two or three washes. Place in a bowl, cover with water and soak for 4 hours. It will expand, so be generous with the amount of water. Place the urid dhal, chana dhal and fenugreek seeds in a bowl, and repeat the same process as with the rice. Do this during the day, at about lunchtime, so you can ferment it overnight while you are tucked up in bed.

3. After 4 hours drain the rice, but retain the liquid (using the water the rice has been soaking in will help with fermentation). Place the rice in a blender along with one cup of the liquid you retained, and blend into a smooth and creamy thick batter. It will still be slightly grainy but that's

OK. Place in a large mixing bowl and set aside. Next do the same with the dhals and seeds, again using one cup of the liquid you retained. Mix and combine the two batters with a whisk, adding the salt.

4. Transfer the combined batter to an airtight container. I reuse an empty 2.5 litre yoghurt tub – the volume won't increase by much. Ferment at room temperature (or somewhere fairly warm) for 12 hours or overnight.

5. After 12 hours check your batter. It will have increased in volume a little, and you may see little bubbles on the surface and condensation on the container lid. You'll certainly get a waft of sourness. If you plan on using the batter immediately, give it a good whisk so it's lovely and smooth. You may need to add a little more water – your batter should be a pourable consistency. If you are not using it immediately, you should re-cover it and refrigerate. Dosa batter can easily keep for 5 days. Note: If you accidentally add too much water you can bring the batter back with rice flour or fine semolina. Also if your batter goes sour after a couple of days – though some people like this flavour – you can add a little sugar.

6. Have your potato masala ready – it should be pre-cooked. I use a large non-stick 32cm frying pan. This needs to be hot, so use the biggest ring on your hob at the maximum temperature. It will need a couple of minutes to get to temperature.

7. Take a ladle full of batter and place it in the centre of the hot pan. Use the base of the ladle to spread the batter outwards, in a circular motion. You want a thin crêpe – you'll use approximately a quarter of a cup of batter at a time. The edges of the dosa will start to turn golden brown after a minute. Reduce the heat (a level equivalent to 7 out of 10). Spray some vegetable oil spray all over the dosa, especially the edges. (You could use 1–2 teaspoons of oil, but I feel the oil spray is better and healthier.)

8. You want a golden, crispy dosa, in no way anaemic or soft. It will take about 3 minutes to crisp up and dry out – the colour will change, and you'll see the tell-tale signs, golden rings emerging from the centre outwards following the motion of your ladle. It's then time to ease your dosa out. Take a flat spatula and gently tease the dosa from the pan, starting at the edges. You can either put your potato masala – which should be hot and on standby – directly on to the dosa in the pan, or transfer the dosa on to a serving plate first if you prefer. Place the potatoes in a long sausage shape across the middle of the dosa, and bring in both edges to form a cylinder.

9. Repeat for the next dosa. You must start on the highest heat setting, so the pan is at temperature. You can clean the pan each time with a splash of water – if it bubbles then you know you have the right temperature. Wipe down before adding the batter.

10. Serve and scoff immediately! You may want a little South Indian coconut chutney or even yoghurt raita on the side. Have whatever you fancy. These are just too good!

POTATO (ALOO) MASALA

This is delicious. The potato can be mashed, but I like to see the pieces. You get the gist, though, that the potatoes should be very soft.

· — · — · — · — · — · — · — · — · — · — · — · — ·

FILLING FOR 4–6 DOSAS

4–5 medium potatoes, peeled and cut into 3cm pieces (prepped weight 800g)

3 heaped tablespoons coconut oil (I use cold-pressed)

1 teaspoon black mustard seeds

4 green cardamom pods (bruise to release the seeds and pound some of these to a powder)

12–14 curry leaves (use fresh if you can get them but dried is OK)

1½ brown onions, finely sliced into half-moons

1–2 green chillies, to taste, sliced in half lengthways

1 teaspoon chilli powder

1 teaspoon ground cumin

1 teaspoon ground coriander

1 teaspoon ground turmeric

1 teaspoon fine sea salt, or to taste

1. Boil the potatoes until tender, then drain and allow to steam-dry.
2. Meanwhile melt and heat the coconut oil in a large frying or sauté pan on a medium to high heat, then add your whole spices – mustard seeds and all the cardamom. When they start to release their aromas, add the curry leaves, then the sliced onions and chillies.
3. Reduce the heat to medium, and cook the onions slow, allowing them to turn golden and caramelized – this will take about 15 minutes, so don't rush.
4. Add your ground spices – chilli powder, ground cumin, coriander and turmeric – and the salt and let them toast a little, then tip in the potatoes. Make sure the potatoes are well mixed and coated with the spices, oil and caramelized onion.
5. Sauté the potatoes a little, then taste and adjust the seasoning – bland potatoes need salt. Your potato masala is ready to be stuffed into crispy dosas.

> **COOK'S NOTE** I use the same recipe to make a Keralan cabbage thoran stir-fry, but I omit the chilli powder. Replace the potatoes with shredded white cabbage or seasonal greens. Spring greens are in season between April and June. Add a little toasted scraped coconut at the end as an option.

CHILLI CHEESE DOSA

Uh-huh, we're going there! So all you need is dosa batter, red chilli Szcechuan chutney (see page 278) and grated Cheddar (use half and half with a stretchy cheese like grated Gruyère if you want a 'cheese pull'). Prepare your dosa using the same approach as the Szechuan vegetable dosa (see below), except add a light sprinkling of grated cheese all over the dosa rather than filling with stir-fried vegetables. Also you don't roll these into a cylinder, you fold them into half-moons instead.

SZECHUAN VEGETABLE DOSA

See the red chilli Szechuan chutney recipe (page 278) – it's the chutney that makes this dosa, and Indo-Chinese dishes are hugely popular across India.

FILLING FOR 4 DOSAS

vegetable oil, for cooking
½ teaspoon grated garlic
½ teaspoon grated ginger
½ a red or green pepper, cut into julienne
1 small red onion, finely sliced into half-moons
1 large carrot, coarsely grated
½ a small Savoy cabbage, shredded (approx. 200g)
a dash of dark soy sauce
dosa batter (see page 274)
1 level teaspoon red chilli Szechuan chutney
vegetable oil spray

1. Heat 3 or 4 tablespoons of oil on a high heat in a wok, kadhai or large frying pan. First sauté the garlic and ginger, then toss in the pepper, onion, carrot and shredded cabbage in that order. Stir-fry for a few minutes until cooked. You may want to add a splash of water to help things along. Season with a dash of dark soy sauce. Set aside.

2. The first thing you need to do before making the dosa is to give your batter a good whisk, so it's lovely and smooth and lump-free. Pick up the method for making dosa from step 7. Before spraying with the vegetable oil, spread a teaspoon of Szechuan chilli chutney all over the dosa, using the back of the spoon in a circular motion, then spritz with the oil spray.

3. Allow your dosa to crisp up for 2–3 minutes as normal, then place the stir-fried filling in a line across the middle. Bring the edges in to form a cylinder and transfer to a plate.

4. Serve with coconut chutney (see page 278).

RED CHILLI SZECHUAN CHUTNEY

This is referred to as Szechuan chutney, even though it doesn't contain the pepper, because it has an Indo-Chinese vibe. It's fiery, so you only need to use it sparingly. (See the Szechuan vegetable dosa recipe, page 277.) It's also great for cheese on toast: put a thin layer on your toasted bread, the side that goes under the cheese, grill and try not to get addicted.

**MAKES ENOUGH
FOR 12 DOSAS**

30g dried Kashmiri chillies
approx. 200ml water
30g garlic, grated
30g ginger, grated
vegetable oil, for cooking
2 teaspoons white wine vinegar
1 teaspoon dark soy sauce
1½ teaspoons caster sugar
½ teaspoon salt

1. Soak the chillies in a little just-boiled water – about 150ml – to start the rehydration process. After 15 minutes transfer to a small pan, bring to the boil, then reduce the heat to medium and simmer for 5 minutes. The chillies will really swell up at this point and the liquid will reduce. Cool completely.
2. Grind the chillies into a paste in a small blender along with any remaining liquid.
3. Meanwhile, in a medium frying pan, sauté the garlic and ginger in a generous amount of vegetable oil on a medium heat for a few minutes, then stir in the chilli paste.
4. After a minute add about 50–60ml of water and cook out for another 5 minutes or so.
5. Season with the vinegar, soy sauce, sugar and salt. Taste – now beware, it is very spicy! Adjust accordingly. Remove from the heat, allow to cool completely and store in a sterilized airtight jar, in the fridge.

COCONUT CHUTNEY

1. Place the chana dhal in a small bowl and cover with boiling water for 15 minutes, to soften. Drain well, then toast until golden in a smidge of vegetable oil. Allow to cool.
2. Blend the coconut, ginger, chillies, toasted dhal, salt and water into a paste using a mini chopper or blender. Season with a squeeze of lemon juice. Transfer to a serving bowl.
3. We'll finish the chutney with a sizzling tarka. Heat a teaspoon of oil in a small frying pan, then add the mustard seeds, urid dhal, curry leaves and asafoetida. Once everything is crackling and your dhal has taken on a golden colour, pour it over your chutney.

**MAKES ENOUGH
FOR 12 DOSAS**

2 teaspoons chana dhal
vegetable oil, for cooking
90g unsweetened desiccated coconut (grated or scraped coconut would be better if you can get it)
8g fresh ginger
2 green chillies, roughly chopped
¼ teaspoon sea salt, or to taste
200–250ml water
a squeeze of lemon juice or 1 teaspoon tamarind paste

Tarka

1 teaspoon vegetable oil
¼ teaspoon mustard seeds
¼ teaspoon washed split urid dhal
7–8 curry leaves (dried is OK if you can't get fresh)
a generous pinch of asafoetida (hing)

Carob trees and pods are found all over Portugal. The seeds from the pods are dried and ground and made into a flour, which is used in baking – it's unique in flavour and utterly delicious! Carob flour and chips are widely used as a replacement for chocolate – yes, that's how delicious it is – and contain fewer calories and no caffeine. My first introduction to carob was in cookie form on holiday in the Algarve, and they were addictive! Your family and loved ones will do anything for these. Question is can you eat a whole one without licking your lips?

CAROB CHURROS } WITH NUTELLA DIPPING SAUCE

**SERVES 4
(4 LONG CHURROS EACH)**

300g plain flour
50g carob flour/ powder (you can replace with cocoa powder and make chocolate churros instead)
a pinch of salt
500ml water
150g unsalted butter
5 eggs

vegetable oil, for deep-frying

Nutella sauce
200g Nutella spread
200ml double cream

Sugar dredge
12 tablespoons caster sugar
2 tablespoons ground cinnamon

> **COOK'S NOTE**
> You can freeze churros – if you don't use all the dough – and deep-fry them from frozen, just adjust the cooking time. Pipe the dough on to a lined baking sheet, freeze flat for a few hours, then transfer to a space-saving freezer bag.

1. Sift the flours and salt directly into a mixing bowl. Set aside. Place the water and butter in a medium to large pan and let the butter melt over a medium heat. Once melted, bring to the boil, then remove from the heat immediately and chute the sifted flour mix into the pan, beating vigorously with a wooden spoon until the dough comes away from the sides.
2. Allow to cool slightly – you'll end up with scrambled eggs otherwise – then gradually beat in 1 egg at a time until the dough is smooth and glossy. If you add the eggs all at once it will split. Spoon the dough into a piping bag fitted with a star-shaped nozzle and set aside.
3. Whisk the Nutella and cream together to a nice dipping consistency. Refrigerate until serving.
4. Heat the oil to 170°C in your kadhai, wok or deep fryer. Mix the sugar and ground cinnamon together and spread on a large flat tray, ready to roll the hot churros in.
5. Time to fry the churros. You need to be quite ambidextrous for this, and have some kitchen scissors at the ready. Carefully pipe the dough directly into the hot oil, and snip to whatever length churros you are happy with – I like them quite long (about 15cm). Don't overcrowd your fryer – they need plenty of space, so fry three or four at a time. They will take about 7–8 minutes.
6. Drain the churros on kitchen paper, then immediately roll them in the spiced sugar. Eat instantly, along with plenty of the Nutella sauce to dunk them into.

There are all kinds of things made with fermented batters in southern India, which to me, with North Indian heritage, is utterly fascinating. It could get a little confusing with the variety, so here's a little breakdown. Appams are like dosas with a slightly thick centre and paper-thin crisp edges, like the Sri Lankan hoppers, which are also appams. Again you have them with sambar and chutneys. **Uttapam** are thicker pancakes, traditionally made with leftover dosa or idli batter when after a few days of dosa making the batter has a slightly sour taste, and they often have vegetables cooked into them. So we've gone one step further here and combined them with another breakfast item, the humble waffle. If you don't have a waffle machine, just use a frying pan and make a flat pancake, flipping to cook on both sides – aim for a Korean vegetable pancake vibe. I like to have mine with a honey chilli dipping sauce, and for meat lovers, load it up with some funky fried chicken too.

DOSA WAFFLES } WITH HONEY CHILLI DIPPING SAUCE

leftover dosa batter
(see page 274)

Filling
red onion, finely diced
red, yellow or green
   pepper, finely diced
white cabbage, finely
   shredded

carrot, grated
sweetcorn
green finger chillies,
   finely sliced
chopped fresh
   coriander
vegetable oil spray

**Honey chilli dipping
sauce**
5 tablespoons honey
1 teaspoon dried red
   chilli flakes
juice of 1 lime
a pinch of salt and
   pepper, to taste
1 level teaspoon
   white wine vinegar

COOK'S NOTE You could also make uttapam or waffles with sliced cooked sausage and bacon loaded into them, along with shredded cabbage and onion. Serve with fried or poached eggs and a squeeze of tamarind ketchup.

1. I haven't specified the amounts because it depends on how much leftover batter you have. Mix the prepped veg into the batter – equal parts red onion, diced pepper, cabbage, carrot and sweetcorn – then add chillies and a sprinkle of chopped coriander, to taste.
2. The waffle machine will take a few minutes to come to temperature – most of them have a light indicator. Spray the upper and lower plates with vegetable oil. Pour 2–3 tablespoons of batter carefully on to the lower plate – you don't want to overdo it and overspill. I quite like the non-uniform shape in any case.
3. Bake until ready – it will take between 5 and 8 minutes, depending on your machine. Obviously always follow the manufacturer's instructions.
4. If you'd like an extra crispy waffle you can place them under the grill.
5. To make the honey chilli dipping sauce, place all the ingredients (apart from the vinegar) in a small saucepan and heat through for a couple of minutes on a low heat, stirring constantly.
6. Remove from the heat, and stir in the vinegar.

BENGALI COMMUNITY

After partition in 1947, Bengal was split: East Bengal became part of Pakistan and eventually went on to become Bangladesh, and West Bengal remained part of India. Bengal was divided along religious lines, and it's estimated that around 75 per cent of the West Bengal population at that time practised the Hindu faith. Kolkata (previously Calcutta) is the capital of the state and was formerly the capital of the British Raj. The port of Kolkata – the oldest operating port in India – was constructed by the British East India Company. Kolkata remained the powerbase of the company's operations until rule transferred to the British Crown in 1858 under the Government of India Act (it wasn't until 1911 that the capital shifted to Delhi).

Bengal has been subject to many conquests over the centuries, given its strategic trading location, which has heavily influenced its food culture. Naturally there are many crossovers with neighbouring Bangladesh. Bengali food is typified by staples such as fish, rice, eggs and vegetarian dishes; and again regional cooking varies greatly, with distinct differences. There is prominent use of panch phoron, a blend made up of five spices: mustard, cumin, fennel, fenugreek and nigella seeds. It seems a fitting synergy to look at the Bengali community in the Welsh port city of Cardiff, itself ethnically diverse owing to the booming coal industry. Migrants came here from the 1800s onwards, as Welsh coal was transported all over the world. Cardiff is one of the oldest multicultural communities in the UK and is steeped in a rich history. I'm looking forward to celebrating wonderful Welsh seafood in this chapter – step aside Welsh lamb, as glorious as you are. Both Cardiff and Kolkata are port cities, surrounded by a coastline and possessing inland rivers rich in varied fish stocks.

TAMASREE MUKHOPADHYAY (AGED 49)

CEO and founder of the KIRAN Cymru charity

Tamasree came to Cardiff in 2001. Her husband had got a scholarship to do an MBA at the university, and she came with him; he studied for a PhD after that. Herself a qualified advocate, graduating from the University of Kolkata, she practised there before emigrating. Tamasree quickly settled and adapted to life in Britain: she took up a managerial post at Oxfam shortly after arriving, and has worked for international charities ever since then, founding her own community focused charity. The intention had always been to go back to Kolkata, but by the time her husband had finished his studies, the couple's son – born in Cardiff in 2002 – had just started school, so they decided to put down roots. They considered the idea of relocation to London but couldn't bring themselves to leave Cardiff, which they consider to be their second home. 'Honestly speaking, the Welsh people are the best I have ever met in my life . . . we had a very friendly welcome from the start.' She tells me that although leaving India was a wrench, integration in the UK was quite painless; they spoke English fluently, which helped to make the cultural adaptations.

KIRAN Cymru is a charity Tamasree founded in 2018. It was self-funded initially, with the unwavering support of her husband Anirban, who she describes as its 'backbone', and later gained National Lottery funding. KIRAN stands for Knowledge-based Intercommunity Relationship and Awareness Network. 'It's all about the community: engagement, education and empowerment. That's the basic tag line. We started our journey in 2018 and the aim is to promote well-being for BAME people in Wales – in particular mental well-being. Playing an active role in the community is very important for each of us.'

KIRAN runs a number of different projects and events. One such project, linked specifically with the Bengali community, is to engage the older generation. Loneliness and isolation were particularly acute during lockdown. 'Work has focused on the elderly in the Bengali community – the people who came here in the 40s, 50s, 60s. For some of them language is still a barrier; they can't express themselves. It's important to engage with them, to understand history. One of the biggest factors in dementia and Alzheimer's is loneliness. We organized events to bring people together; we maintained this through regular phone calls during lockdown. In Indian culture the elderly are very important. They understand the history of India and the history of Britain . . . I also got some great authentic recipes from them! Food is an important part of our culture, it bonds us.'

There are a number of diversity festivals, and events to celebrate Bengali culture, heritage and arts, and inevitably there's always a link to food. Food, culture, history, identity are all intertwined. Likewise there is an emphasis on the young. Tamasree tells me of a recent project in Tiger Bay that was designed to teach youngsters about the history of Cardiff: the phrase 'lest we forget we do not inherit the earth from our ancestors, we borrow it from our children' is very much at the heart of the project. Ultimately we don't have diverse and multicultural cities in the UK by accident. There is a history behind it – a story connected to it – our shared history, and it's so important to have custodians to safeguard and celebrate this from all generations.

I ask Tamasree about these recipes she has elicited. Undoubtedly it always comes down to the seafood for Bengalis. 'Bengali food is about fish and rice, always. It's the staple food of Bengal. The Ganges is there and all the seafood, fresh water prawns, the rivers. Our comfort food is machar jhol [fish curry] and bhat [rice]. Ilsa is our national fish, we have rohu . . . typical cooking involves mustard. I use Dijon mustard and mustard oil.' Back to mustard oil again! I tell her I'm not a fan; neither is her son. But she's promised to make me ilsa with mustard oil, in her special way. I take her up on the challenge, though even when the oil is 'burnt' I still don't like it, so it will take some convincing. I'll keep an open mind, as she's such a nice lady. There are many Bengali dishes that we have a shared love of, however: chingri malai (prawns cooked in a creamy coconut sauce), kosha mangsho (mutton/lamb curry), kathi rolls (a famous Kolkata street food). Tamasree tells me how she loves to eat mackerel, and sardines, which she feels have the taste of typical Indian fish.

There will always be a natural fusion when it comes to immigrant food. Food is a unique part of our culture and heritage: we can both preserve and evolve. It is an expression of identity, and for a second-generation British Indian like me, there will always be a balancing act between two very different cultures, which is the essence of desi food.

If Captain Birdseye was Bengali he'd be putting a bit of panch phoron in his fish finger crumb, I'm sure! You could use any firm white fish in this recipe, just check it's from a sustainable source: whiting, coley – which is also known as coalfish – and cod are all caught off the Welsh coast. The sides are standouts in their own right and can be paired with other mains and dishes. The pea and leek combination is always a winner for me. A lovely twist on 'Fish Friday' but without any frying! Catch of the day.

PANCH PHORON FISH FINGERS } WITH GUNPOWDER POTATOES AND HERO PEAS

SERVES 4

Fish fingers
400–500g skinless and boneless coley (aka coalfish) or sustainable cod
4 tablespoons rice flour or cornflour
1–2 teaspoons panch phoron (see overleaf)
½ teaspoon ground turmeric
½ teaspoon mild Kashmiri chilli powder
½ teaspoon sea salt
½ teaspoon garlic granules

1 egg
approx. 200g panko breadcrumbs (you can use golden breadcrumbs if you want to channel the Captain)
vegetable oil spray

Gunpowder potatoes
750g baby or new potatoes
4 tablespoons vegetable oil
1–2 teaspoons mild Kashmiri chilli powder
1 teaspoon Kasuri methi (dried fenugreek leaves)

1½ teaspoons cumin seeds
1 teaspoon fennel seeds
1 teaspoon dried red chilli flakes
1 teaspoon sea salt, or to taste

Hero peas
½ a leek, finely sliced into half-moons (about 65g)
2 tablespoons vegetable oil
½ a small clove of garlic, grated

1 red chilli, finely diced, or to taste
¼ teaspoon ground turmeric
½ teaspoon garam masala
½ teaspoon sea salt
250g garden peas (I use frozen)
100ml full-fat coconut milk
a pinch of chopped fresh mint or coriander (optional)

Garnish
lemon wedges

1. Cut the fish into 'finger' strips and pat dry. Mix the rice flour or cornflour, panch phoron, turmeric, chilli powder, salt and garlic granules in a mixing bowl. Beat the egg in a separate bowl, and place the panko on a flat plate.
2. Place each fish finger first in the seasoned dry dredge, then in the beaten egg, then in the panko. Place on a lined baking tray and pop into the fridge until you are ready to bake.
3. Set the oven to 200°C fan. Cut the potatoes in half lengthways, into bite-sized pieces – they should be roughly the same size so they cook evenly. Cut larger potatoes into three as necessary. Toss the potatoes with the oil and spices, then transfer them to a lined baking sheet and bake for 30–40 minutes, or until cooked and crispy. Turn and shuffle them at the halfway point.

→

4. Bake the fish fingers for about the last 10–12 minutes before the spuds finish cooking, squirting them with a little spray of oil before popping into the oven. Cooking time will vary according to how thick you cut the fingers.

5. Cut the leek in half lengthways. Rinse under running water, pointing the leek downwards so that any grit or dirt can wash away down the sink. Finely slice the leek, both the green and white parts, discarding the root.

6. Heat a couple of tablespoons of vegetable oil in a large frying pan, then add the leeks and sweat them for 5 minutes on a medium heat. Add the garlic and chillies and sauté for a couple of minutes, then tip in the ground spices: turmeric and garam masala, and the salt. Toast these for 60 seconds, then stir in the peas and mix together. Pour in the coconut milk and simmer for a couple of minutes, until the peas are cooked through. Taste and adjust the seasoning. Mash and crush the peas using a potato masher, then stir – this gives a nice texture. Remove from the heat. You can sprinkle over a little chopped mint or coriander if you like.

7. Serve the piping hot fish fingers, potatoes and peas with a wedge of lemon, and tuck in!

> **COOK'S NOTE** You can prep ahead and freeze the fish fingers, then bake them from frozen. You'll just need to extend the cooking time – it will take more like 18–20 minutes to cook them through.

PANCH PHORON SPICE BLEND

This is Bengali five-spice. You can scale this up or down. I use an equal amount of each spice except the fenugreek seeds, as these have a bitter taste. I also grind the fenugreek to a powder as it's bigger than the other seeds.

1. Toast the fenugreek seeds in a dry frying pan. Let them cool, then grind to a powder using a pestle and mortar.

2. Mix all the spices together in a mixing bowl, then transfer to a sterilized airtight container. Done – use as required.

½ tablespoon fenugreek seeds

1 tablespoon cumin seeds

1 tablespoon nigella seeds

1 tablespoon black mustard seeds

1 tablespoon fennel seeds

This is a recipe from my chef's training at Ashburton Academy, which I've adapted. Worcestershire sauce – and it's not proper rarebit without it, I feel – originated in India and indeed had links to a former Governor of Bengal. I've used non-alcoholic beer, as you still get a 'beery' taste that's not too overpowering and it also allows the fruity notes to come through in the chilli. The curry oil lifts this Welsh classic to another level, and you can use it to add a pop of flavour to all kinds of dishes.

WELSH CHILLI RAREBIT } WITH CURRY OIL AND CRISPY SHALLOTS

SERVES 4

Curry oil
2–3 banana shallots, finely diced (65–70g prepped weight)
10g garlic, finely sliced
vegetable oil, for cooking
sea salt, to taste
9 teaspoons mild curry powder

300ml corn or vegetable oil
lemon juice

Rarebit
175ml non-alcoholic beer
25g unsalted butter
25g plain flour
100g strong Cheddar, grated (perhaps a Welsh Tintern)

½–1 red chilli, finely diced
½ teaspoon Dijon mustard
1 teaspoon Worcestershire sauce
sea salt and black pepper, to taste
1 egg yolk
4 thick slices of bread of your choice

Crispy shallots
vegetable oil, for frying
2 small banana shallots, peeled and cut into rings
approx. 1 tablespoon plain flour
sea salt

1. Make the curry oil ahead – it will keep for a long while. Sweat the shallots and garlic in about 4 tablespoons of oil, plus 2–3 pinches of salt, which will stop them colouring. It will take about 5 minutes. Add the curry powder and toast for 10–15 seconds, being very careful not to burn the spices – you want a low heat.

2. Add the 300ml of oil, and gently warm to infuse the flavours of the curry powder. Remove from the heat and leave to stand for 30 minutes to an hour. Add salt to taste, a little squeeze of lemon juice, then strain through a muslin cloth. Use the back of a spoon to eke out every last bit of flavour. Place in a squeezy bottle until needed.

3. Warm the beer to 60°C in a small saucepan. In a separate medium saucepan melt the butter, then beat in the flour with a wooden spoon and cook out on a moderate heat – it will take 3–5 minutes. Carefully whisk in the beer a little at a time until you achieve a smooth, thick sauce. Add the Cheddar, chillies, mustard and Worcestershire sauce, whisking continually until you have a smooth sauce. Remove from the heat, season with salt and pepper and allow to cool, then mix in the egg yolk. You can refrigerate at this point if making ahead (see cook's note below).

→

4. For the crispy shallots, place enough oil in a frying pan to deep-fry the shallots and heat to about 170°C. While it's heating, separate the shallot rings and lightly coat them in the flour. Place in the hot oil and fry until golden. Remove from the oil and drain on kitchen paper. Season with salt. The shallots will become crisper as they cool down.

5. To make the rarebit, fully toast the bread on one side and lightly toast the other. Spread a generous layer of the cheese mixture on the lightly toasted side and cook under a hot grill for a few minutes, until browned and bubbling. You want a nice glaze.

6. I'd serve this with wilted spinach cooked in butter and a hint of nutmeg, a perfectly poached or fried egg, crispy shallots, and of course the curry oil – divine!

> **COOK'S NOTE** See how to poach an egg in the desi eggs Florentine recipe (page 174). You can poach it ahead and reheat it prior to serving. The rarebit mixture can also be made ahead and refrigerated. Lay a piece of cling film over the top, touching the surface of the mixture, so a skin can't form. It will keep for several days.

Kedgeree is one of the most iconic Anglo-Indian dishes, and unsurprisingly with the Bengali influence it includes fish and rice. Kedgeree was an evolution of a rice and lentil dish known as 'khichari' or 'khichdi' in other parts of India, typically made with mung beans. Everybody has their own kedgeree recipe – it's a great family-style meal that appeals to everybody and you don't have to restrict it to brunch. Traditionally you'd use haddock and salmon, but you can use any fish, or combination of fish. I've opted for Welsh trout and cod here; the soft-boiled eggs bring that decadence. Add poppadums and a chutney or hot pickle for texture and an extra hit of flavour – mango chutney or lime and chilli pickle is my choice.

KEDGEREE

· ▬ ▬ · ▬ · ▬ · ▬ · ▬ · ▬ ·

SERVES 4

Milk infusion
2 skin-on, boneless trout fillets (approx. 250g – you can use salmon if you prefer)
2 skin-on, boneless cod fillets (approx. 250g)
approx. 500ml milk
1 bay leaf
15g garlic, bashed and skin on

15g ginger, roughly sliced
3–4 sprigs of fresh coriander, with stalks
3 green cardamom pods (bruise to release the seeds)
6–8 whole black peppercorns

Kedgeree
vegetable oil, for cooking

1½ teaspoons cumin seeds
1 large brown onion, finely diced
1 cup basmati rice
1 star anise
5g garlic, grated
5g ginger, grated
2 teaspoons mild curry powder
½ teaspoon ground turmeric

1 teaspoon garam masala
225ml chicken/ vegetable stock (if using unsalted stock you will need to add extra salt)
salt, to taste
4 eggs
chopped fresh coriander
lemon wedges, to serve

1. Place the fish skin side down in a large saucepan. Pour over the milk, enough to cover the fish. Add the aromatics: bay leaf, garlic, ginger, coriander stalks, cardamom and peppercorns. Bring to the boil, then pop the lid on to trap the steam and immediately reduce the heat to medium. Simmer and poach until cooked – it will take 6–8 minutes, depending on the thickness of your fish.

2. Strain the milk and set aside in a small pan. Flake the fish into large chunks, check for any bones and discard the skin, then set aside on a plate. Cover the fish with foil so it doesn't dry out.

3. Heat 3 or 4 tablespoons of vegetable oil in a large frying pan on a medium to high heat, then add the cumin seeds. When they start to release their aromas, tip in the onions and reduce the heat to medium. Cook until the onions have softened – this will take about 5 minutes.

4. Meanwhile cook the rice according to the packet instructions, in a large pan of boiling water, seasoned with salt. Pop a star anise into the pot before adding the boiling water, and use a medium to large saucepan with plenty of water so the grains have enough room to move. Cook on a medium heat until about 90–95 per cent cooked. This will be about 9 minutes: set a timer.

5. Add the grated garlic and ginger to the onions and allow to cook out, then add the curry powder, turmeric and garam masala, stirring constantly to prevent the spices from catching. Pour in the hot stock and allow to reduce by at least half, on a medium to high heat.

6. Get the boiled eggs on. Use boiling water from the kettle – it will take 5 minutes for a soft boil. Set a timer.

7. Try a rice grain – it should taste cooked, and not chalky or raw. Drain the rice thoroughly through a sieve, then put back into the pan, cover with the lid and set aside.

8. When the onion mixture has reduced, stir in the cooked rice, forking it through to keep the grains long and unbroken. You can discard the star anise. Add enough of the strained infused milk to give it a nice creamy consistency. Taste – it will need a touch of salt. Gently fold in the flaked poached fish to warm through.

9. Plunge the eggs into cold water after the 5 minutes to halt cooking – this also makes them easier to peel. Once peeled, cut in half and season with salt.

10. Adorn the kedgeree with the soft-boiled eggs. Sprinkle with chopped coriander and serve with lemon wedges, poppadums and chutney or pickles.

TARKA HOUMOUS

Now this is a great little cheat, as I'm taking shop-bought plain houmous but giving it an Indian accent. A tarka (aka tadka) is the process by which spices are cooked in oil, and often other aromatics, either at the start of cooking to build layers of flavour or at the end, when sizzling oil is poured over whatever you are making. It's the method used across India that adds the injection of flavour. This houmous is a lovely make-ahead sharing starter or something to have simply with drinks and nibbles. You can whip up some flatbreads just before serving, and serve it with lamb kebabs or perhaps grilled halloumi and salad for a lovely main.

1. Decant the houmous into a small heatproof bowl. Set aside.
2. Heat 3 or 4 tablespoons of vegetable oil in a small frying pan on a medium to high heat. Then add the mustard seeds, cumin seeds and curry leaves. After 5 seconds tip in the chopped chilli.
3. Once the tarka starts to splutter and the mustard seeds are cackling, remove from the heat – will be another 5-10 seconds. Sprinkle the asafoetida immediately into the pan and swirl into the oil.
4. Carefully tip the hot tarka on to the houmous – listen to that glorious sizzle – stir and mix.

• ▬ • ▬ • ▬ • ▬ • ▬ • ▬ • ▬ • ▬ • ▬ • ▬ •

SERVES 4

200g pot plain houmous
vegetable oil, for cooking
1 teaspoon black mustard seeds
½ teaspoon cumin seeds
6-8 curry leaves
1 green finger chilli, finely sliced
a generous pinch of asafoetida

COOK'S NOTE See page 72 in the Kashmiri chapter for a lamb seekh kebab recipe – you can replace the basar masala with garam masala but you must use Welsh lamb!

Glamorgan sausages are famous for not actually containing any pork, or any meat for that matter – they are in fact made with leeks and Caerphilly cheese. These meatless kebabs are a little riff on that. You can use a strong Cheddar if you can't get your hands on Caerphilly, or even a mix of Cheddar and grated halloumi. Make the recipe your own. Usually a Glamorgan sausage would be coated in breadcrumbs; I prefer not to with the kebab, but feel free to go your own way.

GLAMORGAN STYLE 'KEBABS'

MAKES 4 LARGE KEBABS

1 small leek, finely sliced into half-moons (125g prepped weight)
vegetable oil, for frying
1 x 400g tin of kidney beans, drained and rinsed

5g garlic, grated
1 green finger chilli, finely sliced
100g breadcrumbs
140g Caerphilly cheese or mature Cheddar, grated

1 teaspoon sea salt
1 teaspoon chilli powder
1 tablespoon chopped fresh coriander
1 teaspoon garam masala

1. Cut the leek in half lengthways. Rinse under running water, pointing the leek downwards so any grit or dirt can wash away down the sink. Finely slice the leek, both the green and the white parts, discarding the root. Heat a couple of tablespoons of vegetable oil in a frying pan and sauté the sliced leeks until lightly golden. Remove from the heat and allow to cool.

2. Place the kidney beans in a large mixing bowl and coarsely mash with a potato masher. Mix with the leeks and the rest of the ingredients, apart from the frying oil, smushing them together – you'll find the mixture easily binds. Make up a little test patty and fry on both sides in a scant amount of oil until golden and hot through to the centre. Taste. You can make any adjustments at this point.

3. Divide the mixture into four equal portions. Take a portion and shape it into a kebab, say 18cm in length. Place on a lined tray, cover with cling film and refrigerate for around 30 minutes, to firm up.

4. When you are ready, heat a couple of tablespoons of vegetable oil in a large frying pan on a medium to high heat. Gently fry the kebabs until golden on all sides and hot through to the centre.

5. Serve with a kachumber salad (page 48), flatbreads (page 146) and mint chutney (page 27) or garlicky yoghurt, whatever takes your fancy.

'Dim' is the Bengali word for 'egg', and the 'dalna' element is the addition of potatoes. Bengalis love to put potatoes in their dishes, from opulent biryanis through to this recipe. Not only do potatoes make a dish more hearty, but they also thicken the 'gravy' in this case. Pretty much every region has its own variation of a whole egg curry; the point at which the yolk melts into the gravy is the magical moment for me. I'm adding the eggs at the end, though typically the boiled eggs would be fried separately in oil and spices as well. I'm also packing in the protein with black chickpeas.

DIMER DALNA } WITH BLACK CHICKPEAS

SERVES 4

4 eggs
vegetable oil, for cooking
1 teaspoon cumin seeds
1 black cardamom
2.5cm cassia bark or cinnamon

2 whole dried red chillies
2 whole cloves
1 large brown onion, finely diced
10g ginger, grated
10g garlic, grated
½ teaspoon ground turmeric
1 teaspoon garam masala

1 teaspoon chilli powder (hot or mild, to taste)
1 teaspoon sea salt
250ml passata
2 medium potatoes, peeled and cut into 3cm chunks (250–275g prepped weight)
250ml water

a generous pinch of Kasuri methi (dried fenugreek)
1 x 400g tin of cooked black chickpeas in water, drained (200g drained weight)
1 tablespoon chopped fresh coriander

1. First boil the eggs. Boil your kettle. Gently place the eggs in a medium saucepan on the largest hob. Submerge the eggs in just-boiled water from the kettle, then fire up your hob on maximum heat. Set your timer for 8 minutes for a hard boil. Remove the pan from the heat and carefully drain the water in the sink. Place the hot eggs under cold running water, then transfer to a bowl of cold water and set aside.

2. Heat 3 or 4 tablespoons of vegetable oil in a medium to large lidded saucepan on a medium to high heat, then add the whole spices to the hot oil: cumin, cardamom, cassia/cinnamon, whole dried chillies and cloves. When they start to release their aromas, tip in the onions, then reduce the heat to medium and sauté until lightly golden. This will take about 10 minutes.

3. Once the onions are on point, add the ginger and garlic and cook out for a few minutes. Add the ground spices – turmeric, garam masala and chilli powder – and the salt, and toast for 30 seconds, stirring continuously so they don't catch.

4. Pour in the passata and give everything a good stir, bring to the boil, then reduce to a simmer. When you can see the oil separate on the surface of the masala after a few minutes, taste and adjust the seasoning. Gently add the potatoes, stirring to coat all the pieces in the masala, then add the water and the methi, if using. Bring to the boil, put the lid tightly on the pan to trap in the steam, then reduce the heat to medium and simmer until the potatoes are just over halfway cooked, so 10 minutes.

5. Now add the black chickpeas. These are already cooked, which is why you hold them back until now. Simmer for a further 5–10 minutes, or until the potatoes are cooked and the chickpeas are heated through. Taste, and season accordingly.

6. Peel your eggs. I like to slice them in half, but you can leave them whole if you like. Put them into the pot, gently swirling rather than stirring them through the sauce, so they don't break – you want to warm them through.

7. Scatter over the chopped coriander and serve with rice or hot parathas.

> **COOK'S NOTE** Black chickpeas are utterly delicious! Try making this with a 'dry' masala, namely don't add the water and reduce the passata to 150–200ml, then stir-fry through some crumbled paneer or even halloumi at the end! Yummy! You can buy dried black chickpeas, aka kala chana, in which case soak them overnight, then boil them in water according to the packet instructions.

Jalfrezi is a very popular dish that hails from Bengal. Normally your chicken (or lamb, paneer, vegetables, etc.) would be stir-fried, in a thick and spicy sauce with peppers. We are going to let the oven do the heavy lifting here, however, with this one-tray wonder, made with a whole spatchcocked chicken. This technique halves the cooking time for a whole roast chicken, and with the addition of potatoes is a complete meal. You could also use chicken thighs in this recipe – simply adjust the cooking time – and shred any leftover chicken to make fajitas (see flatbread recipe, page 146).

SPATCHCOCK 'JALFREZI' CHICKEN TRAY BAKE

SERVES 4

1 chicken (approx. 1.6kg)

Marinade
100ml vegetable oil
30–40g ginger, roughly chopped
30–40g garlic, roughly chopped
30g fresh coriander, including the stalks
3–4 green finger chillies, slit in half lengthways

1 tablespoon mild Kashmiri chilli powder
1 teaspoon garam masala
1 teaspoon ground turmeric
1 teaspoon sea salt
1 teaspoon dried red chilli flakes
½ teaspoon ground cumin
½ teaspoon ground coriander

Sauce
2 x 400g tins of chopped tomatoes
⅓ of the marinade
2 large red onions, cut into chunky dice
3 peppers (2 red, 1 yellow), cut into chunky dice
750g baby potatoes (optional)
½–1 teaspoon salt, or to taste

1. Make the marinade by blitzing the oil, ginger, garlic, coriander and chillies to a paste in a blender. Decant to a mixing bowl and stir in the rest of the marinade ingredients: chilli powder, garam masala, turmeric, salt and chilli flakes, cumin and coriander. Taste, and add more salt or chilli to your liking.

2. It's really easy to spatchcock a chicken – all you need is a good set of kitchen scissors. Place the chicken breast side down on a chopping board. Using the 'parson's nose' (the pointy bit) as a guide, cut along the backbone on either side (don't discard this, as you can use it for stock). Having removed the backbone, flip the chicken over and open it out, gently using your body weight to flatten it down. Snip off any excess skin at both ends – this will allow you to get under the skin later on.

3. Smother the chicken all over with two-thirds of the marinade. Get into all the nooks and under the skin, especially under the breast. You may want to use disposable kitchen gloves. Pop the chicken into a suitable container,

→

and ideally marinate it refrigerated overnight, though you can get away with a few hours. Allow to come to room temperature an hour before roasting.

4. Heat your oven to 200°C fan. Take a large deep roasting tray and tip in the tomatoes, the rest of the marinade, the onions, peppers and potatoes, if using (cut larger ones in half). Season with salt to taste – remember, potatoes are bland! Give everything a good stir. Place the chicken on top of the veggies, ensuring the potatoes are positioned at the edges of the tray so they can crisp up. Roast in the middle of the oven for about 45 minutes to 1 hour, or until cooked through and the juices run clear.

5. Lift the chicken off the roasting tray and on to a separate tray. Cover loosely with foil and leave to rest for 15 minutes or so.

6. Meanwhile return the veggies to the oven so they can all crisp up a little more. This will take around 15 minutes.

7. Serve with a green salad. I can't resist a little crusty bread to dunk into the sauce, though Bengalis would definitely have this with plain rice.

OK, this dish isn't exactly Bengali but we are using the flavours. It's a bit 'cheffy' but it's very simple, intended to impress your dinner party guests with a refined little starter. I've adapted a surf and turf recipe I learned at chefs' school, which I am going to use to put a spotlight on fantastic Welsh produce: hand-dived scallops and Carmarthen ham. The story goes that the Romans discovered this ham when they settled in Carmarthen, obviously loved it, took it back to Rome and called it Parma ham! I'm staying neutral on the matter apart from vouching for how delicious it is!

PAN-SEARED SCALLOPS } WITH COCONUT AND CAULIFLOWER PURÉE AND CARMARTHEN HAM

SERVES 4–6

4 thin slices of Carmarthen ham or Parma ham (70–80g)

8–12 king scallops, prepped and coral removed (hand-dived scallops shouldn't need washing)

salt

2 tablespoons vegetable oil, for cooking

a couple of knobs of butter

curry oil (see page 289, this needs to be made ahead)

micro coriander leaves or pea shoots, for garnish

Coconut and cauliflower purée

250g cauliflower florets

300ml full-fat coconut milk

150ml milk

salt, to taste

Roasted cauliflower

3 tablespoons vegetable oil

½ teaspoon ground turmeric

½ teaspoon salt

a pinch of black mustard seeds

½ teaspoon cumin seeds

12 small cauliflower florets, 3cm in length (you can cut larger florets in half or quarters, etc.)

1. First make the purée – you can make this ahead and reheat. Cut the cauliflower into florets with just a little stalk. Finely slice the florets, say 2mm thick. Place the coconut milk and milk in a medium saucepan, along with the cauliflower florets. Gently bring to a simmer – I started at a heat level of say, equivalent to 7 out of 10 to bring the milk to temperature, then reduced to a simmer. You must not burn or curdle the milk. Simmer until the cauliflower is soft and tender. It will take about 20 minutes – keep an eye on it.

2. Meanwhile heat your oven to 200°C fan, to make the roasted cauliflower. Mix the oil, turmeric, salt, mustard seeds and cumin seeds in a small mixing bowl, then toss the cauliflower in the flavoured oil. Transfer to a lined baking tray and roast for 8–10 minutes, or until cooked and lightly burnished.

3. Back to the purée. Once the cauliflower is soft and tender, strain it, using a sieve and retaining the milk. Blitz the cauliflower to a smooth purée in a blender or using a hand-held blender – you'll need to add 5–6 teaspoons of the reserved milk, a little at a time as you may need less

→

and you don't want the purée to be too wet. Season with salt to taste, adding a little at a time – about ⅛ of a teaspoon is about right. Cover with cling film to retain the heat, then set aside (in a warming drawer if you have one).

4. Check on your roasted cauliflower. Once cooked, remove from the oven and drain on kitchen paper. Set aside in a warm place.

5. Grill the ham on either side, under your oven grill on the highest setting for the crispiest results – it will take a minute. Set aside – the slices will get crispier as they cool.

6. Pat the scallops dry with kitchen paper, and season with salt. Heat the oil and butter in a large frying pan on the highest heat. When the butter has melted, place the scallops around the pan as you would the hands of a clock, starting at 12 noon. That way you know which to turn first, and of course which to remove from the heat first. Use a timer – the scallops only need a minute on each side. For the first minute I sear on maximum heat, then reduce the heat to a level equivalent to 7 out of 10. You want a nice crust and colour, not a horrible, insipid-looking scallop. One by one drain the cooked scallops on kitchen paper as they are cooked.

7. To plate (and do warm your plates), start with a purée base, using the back of your spoon to spread it out. Place your scallops on top, and position your crispy ham shards, with the roasted florets spread out and dotted at the edges of the purée. Finish with a little curry oil, not too much, and be sure to put a few flecks on the purée.

> **COOK'S NOTE** Scallops go great with the hero peas (page 286) – serve them in their shells for an extra fancy touch! The roasted cauliflower is a great salad ingredient too: try it with giant couscous, feta and chickpeas, with a chilli, garlic, coriander and lime dressing. The cauliflower purée is delicious with tandoori sea bass (page 146 for the spice blend).

Of course you can't talk about Welsh mussels without namechecking the Menai Straits in Anglesey on the opposite end of the country – 50 per cent of UK mussel production comes from there. Cardiff's 'Tiger Bay' is the name given to the docks and Butetown area, renowned for its multicultural diversity. Naturally then these mussels have got a little spice and heat to reflect that. The only question is whether to have this with frites or a fresh baguette to dunk into the sauce! Or perhaps both, don't deny yourself . . .

'TIGER BAY' MUSSELS

**SERVES 2 AS A MAIN,
4 AS A STARTER**

1kg mussels
3 tablespoons coconut oil (I use cold-pressed)
1 teaspoon black mustard seeds

1 teaspoon cumin seeds
1 star anise
8–10 curry leaves (optional)
1 small leek, finely sliced into half-moons
15g ginger, cut into fine matchsticks
15g garlic, finely sliced

1 red bird's-eye chilli, finely sliced
½ teaspoon ground turmeric
1 teaspoon garam masala
½ teaspoon sea salt
400ml full-fat coconut milk

Garnish
1 tablespoon chopped fresh coriander
finely sliced mild red chillies

1. First you need to clean and sift through the mussels – maybe bring in a helper. Tap each mussel, then place in a large bowl of cold water. If you have a mussel that is open, and does not close when tapped, you should discard it. Using a small knife, scrape off any barnacles from the mussels and remove the 'beard'. Rinse and place in a separate bowl of cold water. You must clean and rinse the mussels thoroughly to avoid any grit in the cooked dish. Set aside.

2. Heat the oil in a large lidded saucepan on a medium to high heat, then add the whole spices: mustard seeds, cumin seeds, star anise and curry leaves, if using. When they start to release their aromas, tip in the leeks, then reduce the heat to medium and sauté until lightly golden – this will take around 10 minutes.

3. Add the ginger, garlic and chillies and cook out for a few minutes – you want the garlic to turn slightly golden.

4. Add the ground spices – turmeric and garam masala – and the salt, and toast for 30 seconds, then pour in the coconut milk and gently bring to the boil on a high heat. Have a quick taste: you can add a touch more salt if so inclined. Meanwhile drain the mussels. Once the coconut milk is bubbling, add the mussels, stir, bring back to the boil, then slam on the lid to trap the steam.

5. Reduce the heat to a level equivalent to 7 out of 10, still relatively high. The mussels will take 4–5 minutes to cook; the shells will open when

cooked. I like to use a see-through lid so I can see when the mussels open.

6. Remove from the heat. Give the mussels a good stir and scatter over the chopped coriander and finely sliced chillies. Discard any mussels with shells that are broken or do not open; you don't eat these.

7. Taste one of your mussels – you can pop the lid on and give them another minute of steam if need be.

8. Serve and eat immediately.

This is my version of chorchori. Bengalis make this simply with potatoes or with a whole myriad of mixed veggies, including gourds, cauliflower and aubergine. You can use any combination but I'm using classic roast dinner veg: potatoes, carrots, cabbage and peas. It's a comfort dish often served with parathas or 'luchis', a deep-fried bread. During times of puja, or worship, asafoetida (hing) is used in lieu of onion and garlic. On holy days Bengali Hindus follow a sattvic diet, which is based around organic, seasonal and fresh plant-based ingredients. It's linked to Ayurveda and being nourished in harmony with nature.

'CHORCHORI' MIXED VEGETABLES

SERVES 4

vegetable oil, for cooking
1½ teaspoons panch phoron (see page 288)
1 large brown onion, finely diced
1–2 bird's-eye chillies, to taste, slit in half lengthways

15g garlic, grated
15g ginger, grated
¼ teaspoon asafoetida, if omitting garlic and onion
1 teaspoon ground turmeric
1 teaspoon garam masala
1½ teaspoons sea salt, or to taste

30–40g butter
3–4 medium potatoes, peeled and cut into 3cm chunks (approx. 400g prepped weight)
2–3 carrots, peeled and cut into discs, pound coin thickness, (approx. 150g prepped weight)

200ml water
275–300g white cabbage, roughly sliced
75g frozen garden peas
1 tablespoon chopped fresh coriander

1. Heat 3 or 4 tablespoons of vegetable oil in a large lidded saucepan on a medium to high heat, then add the panch phoron. When it starts to release its aromas, tip in the onions and chillies, then reduce the heat to medium and allow the onions to soften and go translucent. This will take a few minutes.
2. Add the garlic and ginger and cook out before adding the powdered spices: turmeric and garam masala, and the salt. Toast these for 30 seconds. If the pan is dry, add a splash of water so the spices don't burn.
3. Taste the onion mixture and adjust the seasoning as necessary. Pop in the butter and let it melt, then stir in the potatoes and carrots along with the water. Bring to the boil, cover, then reduce the heat to medium and simmer for 10–12 minutes, until the spuds are over halfway cooked.
4. Add the cabbage and mix it through. Cook for another 4–5 minutes with the lid on, then remove the lid to evaporate any liquid for another minute or so. You want your cabbage to cook al dente.
5. Finally add the peas and mix them through, then turn the heat off under the pan. Allow to stand for a couple of minutes; the residual heat in the pan will heat through and cook the peas.
6. Scatter over the chopped coriander. Serve with rice, parathas or hot chapattis, or even buttered toast!

Kolkata in West Bengal was the capital of the British Raj, and of course Queen Victoria was the Empress of India, so it seems only fitting that the pudding for this, the final chapter, is crowned with a Victoria sandwich, which is named after her. I do have a weakness for Welsh cakes – as with most British cakes and biscuits – but I don't know anybody who doesn't love this iconic sponge cake! I was taught this recipe at secondary school, back when learning how to cook was called home economics. Thanks, Mrs Hobson, the recipe has stood me in good stead. I've kept it classic with jam and vanilla buttercream, but you can have a jam and whipped cream filling too, with fresh strawberries, or flavour your cream or buttercream with something else – perhaps a little damson gin liqueur for the grown-ups, salted caramel for the sweet-toothed, espresso or a fruit curd.

VICTORIA SANDWICH CAKE

MAKES 6 SERVINGS

Sponge
200g caster sugar
200g Stork or softened unsalted butter, at room temperature, plus extra for greasing
4 eggs
200g self-raising flour

½ teaspoon baking powder
2–3 tablespoons milk

Buttercream
100g Stork or softened unsalted butter
150g icing sugar
1 teaspoon vanilla extract

To assemble
175g strawberry or raspberry jam
½ teaspoon icing sugar

1. Heat your oven to 160°C fan. Line the base of two 20cm sandwich tins with baking paper and grease the insides of the tins with Stork or butter.
2. My secret is to use the 'creaming' method rather than the all-in-one. That means you cream together the sugar and butter until it goes pale – it will take a few minutes. Use the beater attachment on your stand mixer or a hand mixer, speed level equivalent to 3 out of 10. Use a spatula to push down the butter at the edge so it's all combined.
3. Beat the eggs, pour these in and combine – it will look a bit curdled, but don't worry. Beat for another 5 minutes at the same speed; you're getting air into the mixture this way, which will result in a light and airy sponge, as it should be. (If you were to beat the eggs for more like 10–15 minutes, you wouldn't need any baking powder.)
4. Sift in the flour and baking powder, then mix by hand, adding the milk until just combined into a smooth batter. Don't overwork the flour; you want to mix this as little as possible really. Over-mixing will activate the gluten strands and result in a dense cake.
5. Divide the batter equally between the two tins, using a spatula to spread and smooth it out to the edges.

→

6. Bake for about 25 minutes, though check after 20 minutes. The cakes are ready when golden and they bounce back to the touch.

7. Remove the cakes from the oven. Allow to cool in the tins for a couple of minutes, then release from the tins and transfer them on to a rack to cool completely. Keep the prettiest cake for the presentational top layer. Turn the other cake out, upside down. This way when you come to apply the butter cream and jam filling the sponge will be perfectly flat.

8. To make the buttercream, beat all the ingredients together until smooth and combined.

9. Assemble your cake. Place the bottom layer on a cake stand or plate. Dot with the buttercream and smooth it out, using a palette knife. Next a layer of jam – loosen this if it's thick by stirring it with a spoon. Then put the second layer of cake on top, and sift over a little icing sugar for a pleasing finish.

COOK'S NOTE A whipped cream filling is lovely in summer, especially with fresh berries. You could even add shards of meringue for a best-of-both Eton mess vibe. The cake needs to be eaten on the day if it has a cream filling, as it can toughen if refrigerated. Buttercream will keep at room temperature, and the cake will stay airy and light.

THANKS

A book doesn't come into being without a small army of people to pull everything together, so I have many people to thank.

Firstly, the two most important people without whom *Desi Kitchen* wouldn't be possible. My brilliant agent, Jane, who has been a stellar source of support, guidance and wisdom throughout. And my wonderful commissioning editor, Ione Walder, who just got the vision from the very start, and has been my strongest advocate ever since. Thank you for always being there for me, even during maternity leave. I'm in awe of you!

Huge thanks, too, to the peerless Michael Joseph family. Dan Hurst and Aggie Russell for doing such an amazing job in seeing the *Desi* baby through to delivery and nurturing it through each stage. Sarah Fraser for bringing the book to life – I feel blessed to have worked with somebody with such majestic attention to design detail. To Emma Henderson and her team for taming a little beast into a streamlined and polished copy (and containing it to **320** pages!).

The look and feel are such important features of a book and I was lucky enough to work with some of the best in the industry. Thank you to Carmi Grau whose illustrations capture the essence of the book with such beauty and wit. Thank you also to the super-talented recipe testers, stylists and home economists Emma Lahaye, Valerie Berry and Hanna Miller. Massive thanks to Liz and Max Haarala Hamilton for such stunning photography.

Of course, this book isn't just mine; it represents the lived experiences, history, food and culture of brothers and sisters from different communities. Thank you to all of the contributors that feature in each chapter. I have learned so much – thank you for sharing your stories and voices.

Thank you to my family. Especially to my mum and dad for helping me with my research, for all of the phone calls, the questions and the support. Most of all thank you to my husband, Harvey. Your love, support and faith has been unwavering. Every time I've had a wobble you've been there, when I've needed to take time out you've understood. Thank you for encouraging me to follow my dreams; I don't think I could do it without you! To Austin, you'll always be my little boy, and now, young man, you can get cooking – I've written the recipes down for you.

Finally, thank you, dear reader. I hope you have enjoyed the recipes and stories as much as I have enjoyed sharing them. I am so grateful for your support.

RESEARCH & ACKNOWLEDGEMENTS

Ananna, Manchester Bangladeshi Women's Organization

Ashburton Chefs' Academy

BBC TV series *Recipes That Made Me*

British Council, Our Shared Cultural Heritage Project

Centre for Nepal Studies UK

'Daughters of a Curry Revolution' Afreena Islam

'English Indices of Deprivation 2019'
(Department of Communities & Local Government Report)

Forever Manchester Charity

GlaswegAsians Exhibition: Glasgow Museums & Colourful Heritage

Jamie Oliver, *Jamie's Great Britain*

KIRAN Cymru Charity

London School of Economics – Super Diverse Streets Project
(Economies and Spaces of Urban Migration in UK Cities)

Manchester Museum, South Asian Heritage Month Project 2021

Office for National Statistics, Census Data

Runnymede Trust – Cardiff Migration Stories, Making Histories

St Mary's Catholic Church, Swindon

The Zoroastrian Trust Funds of Europe, UK

Wikipedia

INDEX

PENGUIN MICHAEL JOSEPH

UK | USA | Canada | Ireland | Australia
India | New Zealand | South Africa

Penguin Michael Joseph is part of the Penguin
Random House group of companies
whose addresses can be found at
global.penguinrandomhouse.com

First published 2023
001

Set in Sofia Pro, Citrus Gothic and Thailandesa

Colour reproduction by Altaimage Ltd
Printed and bound in Italy by L.E.G.O. SpA.

The authorized representative in the EEA is Penguin Random House Ireland,
Morrison Chambers, 32 Nassau Street, Dublin D02 YH68

A CIP catalogue record for this book is
available from the British Library

ISBN: 978–0–241–53774–9

www.greenpenguin.co.uk

Penguin Random House is committed to a
sustainable future for our business, our readers
and our planet. This book is made from Forest
Stewardship Council® certified paper.